"A shortcut into this conversation for many who have not read or seen what Tom Sine has. It will be well worth the money!"

ANDREW JONES, TALL SKINNY KIWI (HTTP://TALLSKINNYKIWI.TYPEPAD.COM/)

"Emergent types are helping the whole Western church to hear what Tom Sine has been saying all along. In *The New Conspirators* he gives on-the-ground examples of new ways of being Christlike and resources to help people take the next steps. This book is needed and will be well received."

KURT FREDRICKSON, FULLER THEOLOGICAL SEMINARY

"Tom Sine lays bare the church's Inconvenient Truth. Taking a broad overview of the challenges that we have to address in the twenty-first century, Tom has sounded a wake-up call that beckons us to reassess the way we have sold out to the values of modernity. Laying out an alternative future, this book is a bold challenge to all who think that the kingdom of God can be built from the starting point of compromise and comfort."

ANDY HARRINGTON, EXECUTIVE DIRECTOR, YOUTH FOR CHRIST: VANCOUVER

"This book is vintage Tom Sine: Always grounding us in the biblical narratives and never allowing us to domesticate our reading of them. Always highlighting the holistic nature of the gospel, never allowing us to diminish and privatize its reach. Always keen to highlight the role of the small and local but never allowing us to lose the global perspective of the kingdom. Always reminding us of the fundamentally communal nature of the faith but never for a moment diminishing our individual role and responsibility in God's plan of redemption. A great book from a great teacher and genuinely wise guide."

ALAN HIRSCH, AUTHOR OF *THE FORGOTTEN WAYS* AND *THE SHAPING OF THINGS TO COME* (WITH MIKE FROST), AND FOUNDING DIRECTOR, FORGE MISSION TRAINING NETWORK

"Through the years, Tom Sine's writing has repeatedly knocked me out of my comfort zone and challenged me to see the good news of God in richer and deeper dimensions. He repeatedly inspires me with hope and encouragement, both through his writings and his friendship. His new book is rich with challenge and inspiration, and it's full of signs that the tide is turning, a warm spring sun is shining, and good things are afoot in the church and for the good of the world. If you've never read a Tom Sine book before, here's the one to read, and if you have enjoyed his previous works, you'll want to come back for a second helping."

BRIAN D. MCLAREN, AUTHOR/ACTIVIST (BRIANMCLAREN.NET)

"Perhaps you are like me and sometimes wish the world would stand still so we could catch our breath, figure out where we are going, develop a travel plan, and then enter back into the global community all fresh and ready to enter its busiest places. Tom Sine reminds us that the world is not slowing down but we can still map where it is headed. Some of the most imaginative, courageous Christians are already on the path into the emerging edge, and Tom Sine maps what folks are already doing. Let's join this veteran Christian futurist as he maps where these young Jesus-following conspirators are journeying."

SCOT MCKNIGHT, KARL A. OLSSON PROFESSOR IN RELIGIOUS STUDIES, NORTH PARK UNIVERSITY

"As I travel around the world I am noting that even the most insensitive are sensing that something is happening! The question is, what is happening? The thing that most people in the church and in the community are grappling with is, what sort of future can we help create? In *The New Conspirators* Tom Sine has gathered a collective of understandings and has woven them together to give an emerging image of what the future could look like. It is insightful and essential reading for anybody wanting to make a difference and live out the prayer that God's kingdom might come on earth as it is in heaven."

FUZZ KITTO, DIRECTOR, SPIRITED CONSULTING, SYDNEY, AUSTRALIA

"Be prepared to get engaged as you enter this conversation with Tom Sine. This is not a quick read for pleasure. While giving us helpful handles on the different streams of 'conspirators,' Tom draws you into inescapable decisions about what kind of follower of Jesus Christ and what kind of church you will be for the journey ahead. A theology of hope rooted in the reign and kingdom of Jesus Christ provides the foundation for a look into the uncertainties and opportunities for the future."

ALLEN LIKKEL, DIRECTOR OF MINISTRY TEAMS, CHRISTIAN REFORMED HOME MISSIONS

"Wise and wide-ranging, thoughtful and thorough, provocative and probing, practical and hopeful, Tom Sine's book ranks among the very best of the growing body of literature exploring the very real question: *Does the future have a church?*"

DWIGHT J. FRIESEN, ASSISTANT PROFESSOR OF PRACTICAL THEOLOGY, MARS HILL GRADUATE SCHOOL

"Laying out an alternative future, *The New Conspirators* is a bold challenge to all who think the kingdom of God can be built from the starting point of compromise and comfort."

Jonny Baker, coordinator of worship, Greenbelt Arts Festival

"*Con-spiritus* means 'to go with the Spirit,' to surf its movement. That is what a 'con-spiracy' is, and this aptly describes this mission futuring book by Tom Sine. I endorse this book and hope that it is widely read, as the task of reimagining church and exploring missional futures calls for the kind of pocket GPS that *The New Conspirators* provides."

Karen M. Ward, abbess/vicar, Church of the Apostles (apostleschurch.org)

"Tom Sine reveals to all of us who are trying to faithfully follow Jesus the critical importance of being lifelong learners. Many at his age and level of incredible life and ministry experiences would be prone to sit down and write their memoirs. Tom sets out on a journey of discovery and learning to find out the creative ways that God is carrying out his upside-down kingdom revolution through today's younger generation. In *The New Conspirators* he tells the stories of God's quietly faithful followers who are making a lot of kingdom change without making a lot of noise. From young and imaginative entrepreneurs who are doing transformational business for the kingdom to urban orders of young people who bring love and hope to the forgotten urban wastelands by being Jesus with skin on, Tom shares their remarkable stories with us and teaches us how to open up our minds and hearts to the Spirit winds of change, transformation and hope that each one of us was designed and called to be a part of!"

Tomas Yaccino, connector, Del Camino Connection, La Red del Camino Network for Integral Mission in Latin America and the Caribbean

"This is a must-read for pastors, church planters and ministry leaders. The principles, research and insights within this book will prepare us to have a kingdom impact in an increasingly multiethnic and multicultural world."

Efrem Smith, senior pastor, The Sanctuary Covenant Church, and author of *Raising Up Young Heroes* and (with Phil Jackson) *The Hip-Hop Church*

"In his latest offering, *The New Conspirators,* Tom Sine presents us with a helpful and hopeful overview of new faith expressions. By situating them in their historic and cultural streams Sine helps us grasp the interconnected work of the church and understand the challenges facing us today. He presents the sobering realities of crises facing our world today and yet retains a hopeful perspective on how we can reimagine better ways forward. I found the stories of those pursuing integrated lifestyles of hope, sustainability and justice inspiring and easily applicable to the average reader's life. *The New Conspirators* is a valuable and important book in charting the future of this movement called Christianity—a must-read for anyone seeking to understand where the church is heading in these turbulent times."

Julie Clawson, Via Christus Community Church, Yorkville, Illinois

"Tom Sine does here what he does best—distills information and stories from a very broad range of sources and makes it understandable and useful to anyone concerned about the future forms of church, mission and community in the kingdom of God. This is not a book of theories. Nor is it just a collection of stories.

The New Conspirators is an excellent survey of the contemporary global movements that are reshaping the church, in all its forms, out of a desire to reconnect with the subcultures surrounding it. Down-to-earth, firmly fixed in the realities of living in our current environments, yet giving insightful and helpful tools to enable us to not simply accept the status quo as the inevitable future but to transform it for the sake of the world and the kingdom.

Sine presents an inspiring challenge for leaders in every stream of church life, without berating or criticizing anyone. He draws us forward with hope rather than attempting to drive us from behind with a whip. A significant resource for the whole church."

Mark Pierson, Urban Seed

"Tom Sine has persistently challenged the Christian community to take seriously the creation mandate to be good gardeners of creation. *The New Conspirators* continues this important ministry with a comprehensive survey of what is, in fact, happening and how much more needs to be addressed. There is cause here both to celebrate and to reevaluate Christian witness in the global village."

Darrell Guder, dean of academic affairs and Henry Winters Luce
professor of missional and ecumenical theology, Princeton
Theological Seminary

"In this wide-ranging survey of challenges and opportunities facing the church in the early twenty-first century, Tom Sine calls us to courageous and imaginative action, convinced that 'mustard seed' initiatives really are transformative. Combining cultural analysis, biblical reflection and stories that earth the principles, this is an inspirational tour de force that invites us to celebrate the future into being."

STUART MURRAY, CHAIR OF THE UK ANABAPTIST NETWORK, CHURCH GROWTH CONSULTANT AND AUTHOR

"The world is changing, and traditional forms of Christian community are less compelling in our culture than ever before, as evidenced by the continual decline in participation. In this provocative and engaging book Tom Sine invites readers into the ideas and conversations of those who are seeking to address this situation through alternative forms of church that are shaped by a commitment to the gospel of Jesus Christ and the experience of contemporary culture. This is an important and hopeful book for all who are concerned about the future of the church."

JOHN R. FRANKE, PROFESSOR OF THEOLOGY, BIBLICAL SEMINARY

"Tom Sine is a journalist, theologian and futurist, spotting trends, making connections and drawing conclusions for the benefit of the rest of us. With *The New Conspirators,* he offers an insightful look into the rapidly changing face of the church in the twenty-first century."

JIM WALLIS, AUTHOR OF *GOD'S POLITICS,* AND PRESIDENT, SOJOURNERS

"In *The New Conspirators,* Tom Sine plants dozens of seeds that have the power to grow into vast new missional communities around the globe. If you want hope for the future of the world and the role the church can play in it, then get your hands on a copy of *The New Conspirators* today."

WILL AND LISA SAMSON, AUTHORS OF *JUSTICE IN THE BURBS*

"The rising generations want to make a difference in our world. They don't want to stand on the sidelines—and they don't want to just 'talk.' They are activists. Often they are activists with a vision but with limited ideas of what can be done. Tom Sine raises our eyes to look at the world more deeply, prods our imaginations to see the opportunities, and calls us to a deeper understanding of what kingdom living might entail. This is a book which I will surely use with my students as I challenge them to 'join the conspiracy.'"

STEVE HAYNER, PEACHTREE PROFESSOR OF EVANGELISM, COLUMBIA THEOLOGICAL SEMINARY

"From Tom Sine, networker par excellence, we've come to expect work that connects the dots of diverse people and ministries globally. If Sine had only provided a map of fresh, vibrant, kingdomlike activities throughout the world, this book would be a wonderful gift to the church. But with *The New Conspirators*, he goes much further. He offers a rubric by which to interpret twenty-first-century ministries. Full of never-before published stories from across the globe, Sine shows how these ministries emerged. His descriptions do not overburden the narratives with dry, clinical interpretation, however. Instead, through Sine's writing, we see God doing amazing things through his people. With each passing story I felt moved, inspired and called to action. In my classes at Fuller Seminary, my students clamor for living examples of Christlike activity in the world. Sine's *The New Conspirators* more than fills that need. Highly recommended."

RYAN K. BOLGER, ASSISTANT PROFESSOR OF CHURCH IN CONTEMPORARY
CULTURE, FULLER THEOLOGICAL SEMINARY

"The hope-quotient of churches in the West is low. In this book Tom Sine highlights some of the daunting challenges we face in both the world and the church. Yet instead of compounding the despair he reminds us of the biblical vision and inspires our hope in recounting stories of individuals, families and communities whose imagination has been liberated for compassionate and creative responses to the challenges in our world. In the words of Cesar Lopez, whose mustard seed story is included in *The New Conspirators*, 'This is about transformation. . . . It's about turning something bad into good. . . . It's about possibilities.' Read this book and free your imagination as you rejoice in hope!"

STANLEY W. GREEN, EXECUTIVE DIRECTOR, MENNONITE MISSION NETWORK

THE NEW
CONSPIRATORS

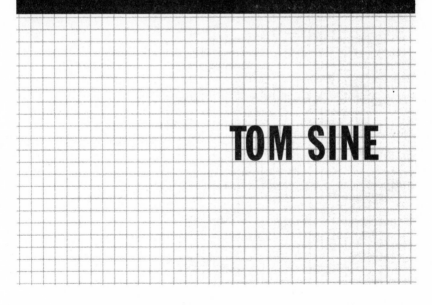

**CREATING THE FUTURE
ONE MUSTARD SEED AT A TIME**

TOM SINE

IVP Books

An imprint of InterVarsity Press
Downers Grove, Illinois

InterVarsity Press
P.O. Box 1400, Downers Grove, IL 60515-1426
World Wide Web: www.ivpress.com
E-mail: email@ivpress.com

InterVarsity Press® is the book-publishing division of InterVarsity Christian Fellowship/USA®, a student movement active on campus at hundreds of universities, colleges and schools of nursing in the United States of America, and a member movement of the International Fellowship of Evangelical Students. For information about local and regional activities, write Public Relations Dept., InterVarsity Christian Fellowship/USA, 6400 Schroeder Rd., P.O. Box 7895, Madison, WI 53707-7895, or visit the IVCF website at <www.intervarsity.org>.

Scripture quotations, unless otherwise noted, are from the New Revised Standard Version of the Bible, copyright 1989 by the Division of Christian Education of the National Council of the Churches of Christ in the USA. Used by permission. All rights reserved.

Broken Wheel, written by Bruce Cockburn, © 1981 Golden Mountain Music Corp. (SOCAN), and Santiago Dawn, written by Bruce Cockburn, © 1985 Golden Mountain Music Corp. (SOCAN), used by permission.

Design: Matt Smith
Images: group discussion: Janelle Rebel

ISBN 978-0-8308-3384-9

Printed in the United States of America ∞

Library of Congress Cataloging-in-Publication Data

Sine, Tom.
 The new conspirators: creating the future one mustard seed at a
 time / Tom Sine.
  p. cm.
 Includes bibliographical references and index.
 ISBN 978-0-8308-3384-9 (pbk.: alk. paper)
 1. Mission of the church. 2. Christianity—21st century. 3.
 Christianity and culture. 4. Christian life. 5. Civilization,
 Modern—1950- I. Title.
 BV601.8.S56 2008
 269.09'051—dc22

                                                            2007043215

| P | 19 | 18 | 17 | 16 | 15 | 14 | 13 | 12 | 11 | 10 | 9 | 8 | 7 | 6 | 5 | 4 | 3 | 2 | 1 |
| Y | 24 | 23 | 22 | 21 | 20 | 19 | 18 | 17 | 16 | 15 | 14 | 13 | 12 | 11 | 10 | 09 | 08 | | | |

In 1981 I dedicated my first book to Navie Sotr, who was ten years old when he died of virulent ear infection at Childrens Orthopedic Hospital here in Seattle. A small group from our church (including my son Clint who was seventeen years old at the time) had sponsored Navie and his parents; the Sotrs were refugees from Cambodia. We prayed with ardent prayers through several weeks of Navie's illness. His untimely death was hard on all of us, particularly Clint.

On May 20, 2006, we unexpectedly lost Clint at age forty-one to a prolonged illness. I am writing this on the one-year anniversary of his death. I deeply loved him and miss him so much. Clint was richly gifted by God. He was bright, creative, had a wicked sense of humor and always reached out to those in need, but he struggled with more than his fair share of demons.

Like Navie and so many others on our planet, Clint never had the opportunity to soar and fully realize the potential of the many gifts God had placed within him. The world is a poorer place without these and others we have lost. This book is dedicated to all those in our troubled world who are cut down before they can take wing and catch the rising thermals of hope and promise that are found in Christ.

CONTENTS

Foreword by Shane Claiborne 13

Acknowledgments 15

Traveling into Turbulent Times 17

CONVERSATION ONE:
Taking the New Conspirators Seriously

Emerging, Missional, Mosaic and Monastic 31

CONVERSATION TWO:
Taking the Culture Seriously

Coming Home to a Post-9/11 Global Neighborhood 59

Coming Home to the Good Life of the Global Mall 71

CONVERSATION THREE:
Taking the Future of God Seriously

Coming Home to the Good Life of God 95

Another World That Is Already Here 110

Coming Home to a Transformed Human Future 118

CONVERSATION FOUR:
Taking Turbulent Times Seriously

Taking the Future Seriously 129

Traveling Together on a Ship of Fools 135

Challenges Facing the Global Rich 144

Challenges Facing the Vulnerable Middle 154

Challenges Facing the Imperiled Poor 174

Challenges Facing the Western Poor 188

Challenges Facing an Endangered Church 203

CONVERSATION FIVE:
Taking Our Imaginations Seriously

Reimagining That World That Is Already Here 215

Reimagining Whole-Life Stewardship 243

Reimagining Whole-Life Community 253

Reimagining Whole-Life Mission 267

Joining the Entrepreneurial Edge 281

Afterword: Something Really, Really Small 299

Index of Organizations 302

FOREWORD

Tom Sine is the master of connecting the dots, those little places where God's conspiracy is alive in the shadows of empires. He is a dream-catcher, a hunter-gatherer of stories of divine mischief. This is his mosaic.

Tom's legacy will take decades to mature because he has spent his life as an unsung hero of the faith. He has not just tried to understand this generation like many of his peers, but Tom has tried to stand under it. He has been a learner and listener to a generation set on making its own mistakes and dreaming its own dreams for the church. He is a humble sower of mustard seeds, not the one who scrambles to devour the bountiful harvest.

This book runs the risk of making a few of us young tykes look too good, but that in itself is evidence of Tom's humility. His motivation for writing is to see a church that is *one* as God is one, a people that mirror the peculiar and countercultural politics of God's kingdom, a body that looks more like Jesus than the ole time religion of the past. It is that old, stale Christianity that threatens to inoculate us from the real thing. And it is books like this one that revive our imaginations to the things that are turning God on in the world. This book is a gift to the church, and to the world.

Shane Claiborne
author, activist, recovering sinner

ACKNOWLEDGMENTS

This book is the product of the help and prayers of many friends. I am particularly grateful to my wife, Christine, for the huge number of hours she invested and for her helpful counsel. I am also grateful for the prayers and support of those in The Mustard Seed House, particularly for Peter Geel's feedback. The creative input from my son Wes was invaluable. All the staff at Mustard Seed Associates have been very supportive, particularly our assistant Judy Naegeli, who spent hours editing my manuscript, and Eliacin Rosario who provided sensitive insights. Input from board members Jill Young and Paul Stevenson was invaluable, as were recommendations from International Circle members Mike Morris and Tom Balke. Steve Ruetschle's counsel and prayers were sincerely appreciated. I am very grateful for the professional guidance and thoughtful input that David Zimmerman at InterVarsity Press has provided and for his patience with my personal setbacks. Sincere thanks to Robin Parry at Paternoster as well.

Many people invested long hours reading and giving candid opinions about various sections of the manuscript; their contributions significantly improved the quality. Sincere thanks to Byron Borger, Scott Smith, Jonny Baker, Andrew Jones, Penny Caruthers, Richard Dahlstrom, Lisa Surdyk, Dwight Friesen, Tim Bednar, Jordon Cooper, Mark Scandrette, Gerard Kelly, Phil Wall, Eddies Gibbs, Kurt Frederickson, Luke Bretherton, Kerwin Kester, Ian Mobsby, Mathew Frost, Robin Parry, Andy Harrington, Efrem Smith, Tim Morey, Lucas Land, Steve Taylor, Shane Claiborne, Paula Harris, Brian Walsh, Brian McLaren, Tim Soerens, Karen Ward, Glen Stassen, Scot McKnight, Manny Ortiz, Norm Ewert, Kurt Frederickson, Phil Smith, Steve Hayner, Doug Downing, Charles Burgess, Alan Hirsch, Fuzz Kitto,

Jessica Stevens, Trevor Thomas, Dick Staub, Kim Porter, Michael Reeves, Mike Geertsen, Stan Thornburg, Trevor Thomas and Jeff Keuss.

I am particularly grateful for a sense of God's journeying with me and helping with my struggling efforts to make sense of how to live faithfully in changing times, and for the prayers of those that have gone before.

TRAVELING INTO TURBULENT TIMES

Our Jeep careened though the center of Hyderabad, India, during rush hour at forty-five miles an hour. It was an amazing achievement, since nothing else was moving more than fifteen miles an hour. Parents with kids and elderly folks spilled off the congested sidewalks into the gutters on both sides of the street. Bicycles, rickshaws and water buffalos competed with people for that gutter space. This barely left one solitary lane down the middle of the road for cars and trucks going in both directions.

Only an hour earlier, I had had a relaxed lunch with my four traveling companions. Over a wonderful dish of coconut chicken curry with fresh papaya and lime, they briefed me on small recycling businesses that poor families had started in Hyderabad. Now we found ourselves on a ride from hell.

We escaped multiple near-death experiences in that forty-minute race. We narrowly avoided colliding with a petrol truck, a crowded bus and three different rickshaws. Our young Muslim driver didn't speak English, and we couldn't find any way to communicate that we weren't in a hurry. While I tried to pray, I kept remembering what I had recently learned: more missionaries are killed in traffic accidents than from any other cause.

Suddenly our driver's reflexes weren't quick enough. He whipped the Jeep abruptly to the left and hooked the handle bar of a bike, dragging it and its rider thirty yards before skidding to a stop. The bike was mangled, but fortunately the rider wasn't injured. The two young Indians stood there yelling and waving their arms at each other until our driver abruptly jumped back in and took off as if nothing had happened. Thankfully, after the mishap our driver slowed down, my blood pressure returned to normal, and my prayers became less frantic.

TURBULENT TIMES, A CHANGING WORLD

Tsunamis, hurricanes, earthquakes, terrorist attacks, a storm brewing in the Middle East and volatility shaking our new global economy—doesn't it feel like our world has been on a harrowing ride, where no one is at the wheel, since we raced into this new millennium? I suspect this ride won't slow down anytime soon. We are rapidly becoming part of a global society in which the challenges are likely to escalate. Change and uncertainty are likely to become increasingly comparable to the reality that our poorest neighbors have always known—particularly economic uncertainty and crisis.

Some are working tirelessly to reduce the life-threatening uncertainty that the global poor have to contend with every day. These activists succeeded in persuading over 180 nations to commit themselves to the United Nation's Millennium Development Goals of cutting global poverty in half by 2015. As I write halfway to that target date, it is clear that nations that signed this pledge have failed to follow through with the promised investments. Recalling that 150,000 people lost their lives in a Southeast Asian tsunami at the beginning of the millennium, the passionate advocate for the poor and U2 lead singer Bono declared, "In Africa, 150,000 lives are lost every month. A tsunami every month. And it's a completely avoidable catastrophe."[1]

You can be sure that these chaotic events are keeping end-times prophecy buffs very busy, but my passion is for discovering what God is doing in these turbulent times, and how I can be much more a part of it. For followers of Jesus, times of challenge are always times of opportunity to give new creative expression to God's love for a people and a world. The character Gandalf in *The Lord of the Rings* reminds us that we can't choose the times in which we are born, but says, "We are responsible for the time that is given to us."

TURBULENT TIMES, A CHANGING CHURCH

Not only is the world experiencing a harrowing ride, the Western church is

---

[1]"Bono's Prayer Breakfast Speech," *Extracts: 54th Annual National Prayer Breakfast, Washington D.C.*, February 2006, accessed January 27, 2007, at <www.micah challenge.org.uk/uk/pages/content.asp?plid=122>.

as well. While the church in Africa, Latin America and parts of Asia is experiencing remarkable growth, this is not the experience of the church in the Northern Hemisphere. Not only mainline Protestant and Roman Catholic churches, but increasingly evangelical and charismatic churches in Britain, Australia, New Zealand, Canada and the United States are struggling with rapid change and declining participation.

Leaders in the emerging church in Britain argue that much of the focus, language and programs of traditional institutional churches no longer connect with a post-denominational, post-Christendom, post-Christian and postmodern culture.[2] Alan Roxburgh vividly describes our situation:

> We are all in the early stages of a massive transition. . . . We cannot return to the past like some nostalgic *That 70s Show*, nor can we jump over the present to go bravely where none have gone before, like some kind of *Star Trek* series. We are more like the strange, motley crew of creatures struggling to make sense of their situation on board the space station *Babylon Five*.[3]

In his book *The Forgotten Ways*, Alan Hirsch reports on a predominant concern of contemporary church leaders: "It is getting much harder for their communities to negotiate the increasing complexities in which they find themselves. As a result, the church is on a massive, long-trended decline in the West."[4] Declining levels of attendance, participation and giving are likely to have a major negative impact on the Western church's ability to sustain its present levels of support for local and global missions, much less develop innovative responses to the new challenges coming at us from tomorrow's world.

---

[2]Post-Christendom is a discussion comprised of those who are interested in connecting to the pre-Constantinian church, which saw itself as an exile movement within the dominant culture.

[3]Alan J. Roxburgh, *The Sky Is Falling: Leaders Lost in Transition* (Eagle, Idaho: ACI Publishing, 2005), p. 67.

[4]Alan Hirsch, *The Forgotten Ways: Reactivating the Missional Church* (Grand Rapids: Brazos Press, 2006), p. 16.

JOINING THE NEW CONSPIRATORS

In spite of these daunting challenges, God is stirring up some small renewing streams that are cascading over the dry roots of traditional churches, carrying the promise of new life. Though God works in all generations, as my wife Christine and I wander the world, we see the Spirit of God working largely through the vision, creativity and initiative of a new generation—through emerging, missional, multicultural and monastic streams—as well as in traditional churches that are hungry for a more authentic, vital, mission-centered faith. This book is written to invite you not only to support what God is doing through these renewing streams but also to join this conspiracy of compassion.

Brian McLaren, discussing the emerging church, observes a distinguishing perspective of young Christians in each of these renewing streams: "It's not about the church meeting your needs; it's about joining the mission of God's people to meet the world's needs."[5] Those involved in these streams almost always tend to be more outwardly focused, seeking to engage urgent needs in their communities and the larger world.

One of the other characteristics is an igniting of the imagination in ways I haven't seen before. Emerging church leaders, for example (I suspect because of their postmodern inclinations), are keenly involved in the arts, film and popular culture. A worship service Christine and I attended at Fremont Abbey in Seattle, led by Karen Ward, on the Sunday immediately after the 2005 tsunami, sensitively and artfully blended footage of the tragedy with ancient symbols and liturgy. We were drawn powerfully into both the pain of the event and the providential care of God.

These young leaders carefully read the cultural context of a particular community, then create a setting—a café or an art center, for example—to engage individuals in the surrounding community. A gathering place called Malt Cross Café-Bar in Nottingham city center, for example, offers hospitality and acceptance to young people out with their friends and neighbors.

---

[5]Brian McLaren, as quoted by Andy Crouch, "The Emergent Mystique," *Christianity Today*, November 2004, p. 39.

An outreach team helps those in the neighborhood who struggle with addiction issues, overdoses and other crises. The innovators who created this gathering place find their own nurture in a spiritual growth community called The Friary.[6]

I find this same kind of inspired imagination among those in the monastic stream. At Papa Fest, a gathering in Tennessee that brought together all kinds of U.S. Christian communities, the event planners created an innovative barter economy for the gathering. They also involved kids in the playful arts of clowning, juggling and improvised drama.

Russell Rook, a young officer in the Salvation Army in Britain, was part of the first wave of emerging church leaders in the early 90s. Out of the deep desire to see mission moved back to the center of the church, he was given permission to reimagine and reinvent the youth division of the Salvation Army in the U.K. as a mission preparation process.

Instead of running a standard youth program that focused inwardly on the needs of Christian young, Russell and his compatriots renamed the division ALOVE, focusing on God's love for the world. ALOVE now trains youth in an eleven-month program in a number of mission activities, including planting mission-centered churches. One of Russell's imaginative ideas is to persuade leading English chefs to share some of their best soup recipes. Young people from tough parts of Liverpool and London learn to make the soups as part of a job-training program. They then sell the soups back to local businesses to help fund new church plants.

JOINING THE CONSPIRACY OF THE INSIGNIFICANT

In spite of the fact that our world is changing at blinding speed and the church is going through some very tough times, God is still at work in ways that aren't always immediately apparent. For some reason, God seems to delight in conspiring through the small, insignificant and ordinary to renew the church and transform the world. Eugene Peterson wrote, "The met-

---

[6]Dave Ward, "Malt Cross Vision," *Stories*, October 2006, accessed January 27, 2007, at <http://emergingchurch.info/stories/maltcross/index.htm>.

aphors Jesus used for the life of ministry are frequently images of the single, the small and the quiet, which have effects far in excess of their appearance: salt, leaven and seed."[7]

Nearly thirty years ago I wrote a book called *The Mustard Seed Conspiracy* to explore an idea out of the teachings of Jesus:

> With what can we compare the kingdom of God, or what parable shall
> we use for it? It is like a grain of mustard seed, which when sown on
> the ground, . . . it grows up and becomes larger than all the garden
> plants, and puts out large branches, so that the birds of the air can
> make nests in its shade. (Mk 4:30-32)

I was taken aback by the hundreds of people who wrote in response to the book. Their letters described a host of creative ways in which they took the risk of discovering how God could use their mustard seeds to make a difference in the lives of others. Some started building homes for Habitat for Humanity or formed Mustard Seed groups on their university campuses to reach out to the poor in their communities. A few started larger ministries such as Christmas Cracker, a British organization that raised large amounts of money for the poor abroad. The Mustard Seed Foundation in the United States provides start-up grants for new ministries all over the planet.

Both the world and the church have changed enormously since 1981. But God's strategy hasn't changed. Jesus let us in on an astonishing secret: God has chosen to change the world through the lowly, ordinary and insignificant. This should give us all hope.

Changing the world through the conspiracy of the insignificant has always been God's strategy. God chose a ragtag group of Semite slaves to be the insurgents of a new order. God sent a vast army to flight with three hundred men carrying lamps and blowing horns. God chose a shepherd boy with a slingshot to lead his chosen people. And who would have dreamed that God would choose a baby in a cow stall to turn the world right side up?

---

[7]Eugene H. Peterson, *The Contemplative Pastor: Returning to the Art of Spiritual Direction* (Grand Rapids: Eerdmans, 1989), p. 25.

Paul reminds us that "God chose the foolish things of the world to shame the wise; God chose the weak things of the world to shame the strong. He choose the lowly things of this world and the despised things— and the things that are not—to nullify the things that are, so that no one may boast before him" (1 Cor 1:27-29).[8]

Shane Claiborne quotes British songwriter Martyn Joseph as he writes about the quiet revolution of Jesus:

> "What a strange way to start a revolution . . . and what a strange way to finish your world tour." We worship the seed that died. The revolution will not be televised. It will not be brought to you by Fox News with commercial interruptions. . . . It will not be sandwiched between ads to accelerate your life or be all you can be. There will be no reruns. The revolution will be live. The revolution will be in the streets. The revolution will be cleaning toilets and giving another blanket to Karen. The revolution will not be talking about poverty in hotel banquet rooms. It will be eating beans and rice with Ms. Sunshine and watching Back to the Future with our neighbor Mary. Get ready, friends . . . God is preparing us for something really, really—small.[9]

This book is an invitation to become a part of something "really, really small," a quiet conspiracy that is destined to change our lives and God's world. We will particularly focus on what God is doing through the emerging, missional, mosaic and monastic streams of the church. But we are all invited to join the creative edge by more fully discovering how God might use our mustard seeds to be a part of this conspiracy of compassion and hope.

The God who has always been a part of our stories invites us to become much more a part of God's story, and to see what will happen. If you are discontented with a "business as usual" faith that seems to have little impact on either your life or God's world, then this book is written with you in mind. If you are interested in what God is doing through the new con-

---

[8]Tom Sine, *The Mustard Seed Conspiracy* (Waco, Tex.: Word, 1981), pp. 11-12.
[9]Shane Claiborne, "The Marketable Revolution," *The Simple Way Online Newsletter,* March 2006, accessed at <www.thesimpleway.org/mailings/marchnewsletter.pdf>.

spirators, this book will put you in touch with those on the innovative edge. If you want to join followers of Jesus all over the planet who are creating new ways to give expression to the kingdom, then keep reading.

GLOBAL POSITIONING TOUR

We will rapidly cover a broad terrain in our journey together. I have the gift of disorientation and get lost a lot as I travel. But I really don't want to lose you. The major stops on our journey together are conversations that explore God's quiet conspiracy and how we can be much more a part of it.

Conversation I: Taking the new conspirators seriously. I want you to meet these young leaders who are creating imaginative new expressions of life, church and mission. I also want you to get acquainted with those of all generations who are fashioning new monastic communities where they devote their lives to relationships, prayer and working with the poor. And I want you to meet those who are giving new expression to their faith in art, advocacy and celebration. I suspect you will be as challenged as I am by these poets, monks, clowns, prophets and other conspirators.

I organized these creative conspirators into four major streams: emerging, missional, mosaic (multicultural churches reaching out to a new generation) and monastic. Throughout the book I will share creative examples of how God is at work through these four streams and grapple with the provocative questions they raise for all of us regarding what it means to be faithful disciples of Jesus in a rapidly changing world.

Conversation II: Taking the culture seriously. I will also be taking you on a tour of a post-9/11 world. We suddenly find ourselves in a new neighborhood, a one-world economic order raising a host of new opportunities and challenges for our lives, our churches and God's world. I will particularly examine how globalization is increasingly seeking to define what is important and of value for people everywhere. I will offer a robust critique of the ways in which I believe the new global economy magnifies the values of modern and postmodern culture, and promotes them all over the planet. I am particularly concerned that these values are increasingly replacing the values of ancient faiths and traditional cultures. In fact, I am convinced that the storytellers of the new global mall are trying to persuade us to make our home in the imaginary world they have fashioned in order to influence us to buy into their notions of what constitutes the good life and a better future.

Conversation III: Taking the future of God seriously. I believe that numbers of us have settled for a narrow, spiritualized eschatology that is divorced from both the urgent issues that fill our world and the important decisions of our daily lives. We will seek to offer an eschatological vision that not only more directly engages our world but also offers direction for our individual lives and communities of faith as well.

In this conversation, I will take you on a tour of some ancient/future images of hope that offer us a new way home. I will attempt to show that these images of hope offer an alternative view of the good life and better future from the one offered by the global mall. In other words, I will argue that we need a fresh grasp of God's new order as more than a kingdom theology we salute on Sunday; it's a reason to roll out of bed on Monday.

Shane Claiborne, of The Simple Way Community in Philadelphia, and a number of his friends conducted an impromptu demonstration regarding the new global economy and its impact on the poor. In front of a large crowd in a plaza on Wall Street in New York, he reimagined the focus of God's kingdom:

> Some of us have worked on Wall Street, and some of us have slept on Wall Street. We are a community of struggle. Some of us are rich people trying to escape our loneliness. Some of us are poor folks trying to escape the cold. Some of us are addicted to drugs and others are addicted to money. We are a broken people who need each other and God, for we have come to recognize the mess that we have created of our world and how deeply we suffer from the mess. Now we are working to give birth to a new society within the shell of the old. Another world is possible. Another world is necessary. *Another world is already here.*[10]

---

[10]Shane Claiborne, *The Irresistible Revolution: Living as an Ordinary Radical* (Grand Rapids: Zondervan, 2006), p. 188, emphasis added. The Simple Way is now the name of the nonprofit organization associated with The Potter Street Community (formerly The Simple Way Community).

That's it! That's the imagery that is at the very center of the future to which the creator God is giving birth—*"Another world is already here!"*

In their important study of the emerging church in Britain and the United States, Ryan Bolger and Eddie Gibbs report that this is also the vision of the emerging church movement. One emerging church leader said, "We try to live into that reality and hope. We don't dismiss the cross; it is still a central part. But the good news is not that he died but the kingdom has come."[11]

In the classic film *The Lion in Winter*, Eleanor of Aquitaine (played by Katharine Hepburn) declares, "Anything is possible in a world in which a Jewish carpenter is raised from the dead." Indeed, not only is anything possible, but by the power of the risen Christ, we can passionately affirm that a new world has indeed broken into this one. Another world is here! Jesus came announcing this very good news, and he invites us to be a part of it, not with the leftovers of our lives but with our entire lives.

Conversation IV: Taking the turbulent times seriously. It is essential that both those in traditional churches and those embracing new expressions learn to lead with foresight, so I will outline specific ways to both anticipate and creatively respond to new challenges before they fully arrive on our doorsteps.

Then we will examine in more detail how the global context and the church are likely to change in the next ten to fifteen years, and we'll consider innovative ways we might respond to those changes. I will particularly identify some of the new problems and perils that are likely to confront all of us—the wealthy, the middle class and the poor. I will also present new challenges facing the troubled church and will describe creative ways in which followers of Jesus are responding to these challenges as well.

Conversation V: Taking our imagination seriously. Finally, I will take you on a global tour of ordinary people who are finding a broad spectrum of new ways to imagine, create and live into that world that is already here. These

---

[11]Eddie Gibbs and Ryan K. Bolger, *Emerging Churches: Creating Christian Community in Postmodern Cultures* (Grand Rapids: Baker Academic, 2005), p. 54.

people are inviting God to ignite their imaginations to be much more a part of God's quiet conspiracy. A number of them inhabit one or more of the four streams, but others are simply followers of Jesus in conventional congregations.

I will share new models of whole-life faith, communities of celebration and subversion, ancient liturgies, transformational forms of missional church, new models of social entrepreneurship, and new ways to party the kingdom 24/7. Please understand that I am not simply calling people to be innovative for the sake of innovation. Rather I am encouraging you to invite the Spirit to ignite your imagination for two very specific reasons:

- to more fully and authentically give expression to the world that is already here in every area of life, community and mission
- to more effectively respond to the mounting challenges coming at us from a changing world and a changing church

This book is an invitation to be much more a part of something really, really small that is quietly changing our world. But it is also an invitation to revisit our images and understandings of the story to which we have given our lives.

REIMAGINING LIFE, FAITH, CHURCH AND MISSION

I find that many older evangelical Christians assume that all the important questions were answered decades ago and that we got all the answers right; now all we need to do is to simply improve our tactics and strategies. But as I look at the contemporary expressions of Christian life, church and mission, I am not convinced that we have gotten all the answers right. I am going to echo some of the tough questions I hear being raised by younger leaders on the conspiratorial edge. I am going to invite us to the challenging task of revisiting five important questions about life, faith and mission:

1. Did we get our eschatology wrong?

2. Did we get what it means to be a disciple wrong?

3. Did we get what it means to be a steward wrong?

4. Did we get what it means to be the church wrong?

5. Did we get what it means to do mission wrong?

NOT AN EASY RIDE

I am deeply grateful for what I am learning from a new generation. I realize my style is more modern than postmodern, and as an aging author I may not fully grasp all that God is doing through the young and the risk-taking. As a white author who has always been a part of a culture of privilege, I am certainly not the best one to write about multicultural expressions of the church. I have my share of broken places and blind spots. But I have attempted in this journey to candidly share both the growing problems and the new possibilities that are before us.

During this tour, you will confront some daunting challenges rushing at us from tomorrow's world. I don't expect you to agree with all my views or the views of the new conspirators. But I do hope to provoke a serious conversation about what it means to follow Jesus in a changing world and a changing church.

At the end of each section I will invite you to join the conversation. This book is designed to be used as a study or textbook. Questions are included at the end of each section, and a study guide is available on the Mustard Seed Associate website (www.thenewconspirators.com) for faculty and discussion leaders. I will invite you to think through new ways to give expression to what God is stirring up within you. I would also welcome hearing from you about your creative mustard seeds, your questions, critiques and humorous responses. You can contact us through our web address.

Welcome to a journey to discover how to become an active participant in something really, really small that is quietly changing our world!

TAKING THE NEW CONSPIRATORS SERIOUSLY

EMERGING, MISSIONAL, MOSAIC AND MONASTIC

How is God conspiring through those in the emerging, missional, mosaic and monastic streams of the church to give creative expression to that world that is already here?

We invite you to Dancing in the Streets with our homeless friends here in Tent City in Seattle," Nathan, a young emerging church planter, loudly announced at Trinity Methodist Church during our recent international gathering. At the final session of the conference, participants were invited to imagine and create ways to give expression to God's new order. Nathan's group came up with an imaginative way to serve the homeless.

"Dancing in the Streets will involve inviting middle-class neighbors to meet their homeless friends who are camped in the parking lot at Trinity Methodist Church. We plan to have a huge outdoor party including all kinds of ethnic food, piñatas for the kids, music from the tent city and the neighborhood, and dancing for everybody. We want to see the walls come down and everyone experience a bit of God's shalom."

Our gathering, "The Church Has Left the Building," sought to bring people together from different countries, across generations and from the four streams of renewal. While the gathering was comprised largely of twenty- and thirty-year-olds, people from across the age spectrum attended. We advertised, "All skateboards and walkers are welcome!"

PAYING ATTENTION TO THE LIVELY EDGE

For my entire adult life, I have tried to pay attention to the lively edge of

BEGINNINGS

"God is doing something new through ordinary radicals. Every day we are seeing ordinary people doing small things with great love," declared Shane Claiborne at the opening of our gathering. Shane is a part of the lively edge of what God is doing through the new monasticism movement. Shane is right! God is doing something new through new conspirators in all four streams—and through many of us in traditional churches as well.

In this conversation, I will take you on a brief tour of the four streams, offering a brief description and a bit of history, and introducing a few key players and resources. Please understand I am doing only some very rough sketching; this topic merits a more in-depth analysis than space allows.

---

what God is doing in our constantly changing society. Back in 1968, when I was in my thirties, recently converted hippies suddenly started appearing at the church I attended in Maui, Hawaii. It was clear to me from the beginning that God was working through the remarkable Jesus People movement. So when I moved to Seattle in 1970, I volunteered with Jesus People. Over the years, I have enjoyed working with my friends in the movement's last remaining remnant—Jesus People U.S.A. in Chicago. Their annual Cornerstone Festival still brings together Christians on the artistic edge.

In the late seventies and early eighties, I was involved in the Radical Christian Movement and the Christian community movement. With friends like Tony Campolo, Ron Sider, John Perkins, Jo Anne Lyon, Howard Snyder, Orlando Costas, John Alexander, Barbara Skinner, Tom Skinner, Manny Ortiz, Jim Wallis and a host of others, I witnessed thousands of people change their lifestyles to embrace a more radical form of discipleship: "to live more simply that others might simply live." Many fashioned a range of alternative Christian communities. I believe God's Spirit stirred thousands of people to join that movement and work for social change. It was during this season that I wrote *The Mustard Seed Conspiracy* and began experimenting with living in Christian community myself.

These days, God is working through a new generation of conspirators that won't be satisfied with anything less than an authentic faith that makes a real difference in the lives of others and in the care of God's good creation. I will briefly describe each of the four streams—emerging, missional, mosaic and monastic—though it is important to mention that the leaders in each stream don't agree on definitions that describe their movements, because the four streams are dynamic and fluid, and at points flow into one another.

Leaders in these streams are honest about their shortcomings. They freely admit they don't always get it right. But much of what they are doing is experimental and generally underfinanced, so we need to cut them a little slack.

EMERGING STREAM

Seattle is being swamped with young church planters. Last week I met two guys who had moved here from Pennsylvania. They said they came to Seattle because of the high numbers of unchurched people in this region. The more we talked, however, the more I sensed their move might have had more to do with the coffee and the microbreweries than with the unchurched. But then I am a little cynical. Let's go back to the early beginnings of all things emerging.

Many American Christians have never heard of the house church movement that swept through Britain in the late 1970s and early 1980s. Charismatic movements like Pioneer, Revelation and Ichthus Fellowship resulted in thousands of Brits coming to vital faith and hundreds of new churches being planted all over the U.K. Toward the end of the decade, however, this renewal movement began running out of gas.

In the late 1980s and early 1990s, I met a number of young Brits associated with groups like Revelation and the Anglican Church who began creating new expressions of church. These leaders included Peter and Samie Greig, Phil and Wendy Wall, Gerard and Chrissie Kelly, Andy and Helen Harrington, and Jonny and Jenny Baker. In a variety of ways, they took initiative to begin the world over again. Some described themselves as post-evangelical. Others were experimenting with alternative forms of worship.

They all seemed to share a postmodern critique of both culture and church. Those I met had a sincere passion to follow Christ and to seek first God's kingdom in a broken world. Gerard Kelly's *RetroFuture* reflects how thoughtfully these young leaders brought their faith to bear on understanding culture and faith.

I still remember how this first wave of young leaders in the U.K. prodded me to take a good hard look at my theological assumptions. As Scot McKnight observes, they believe that "God didn't reveal a systematic theology but a storied narrative, and no language is capable of capturing the Absolute Truth who alone is God."[1] Their arguments that some older Christians take a hyper-rational approach to the gospel were spot on—certainly for me. Jonny Baker wrote in a 1999 e-mail that "the old certainties of 'Modernity' and the 'Enlightenment Project' have been replaced with a huge level of uncertainty and questioning. 'Reality isn't what it used to be.'"[2]

He and others helped me to rediscover the gospel as narrative, filled with mystery and wonder. Yet in spite of all I learned from them, I was still having a difficult time getting my head around postmodernism. Graham Cray, who was also immersed in that first wave and is now Anglican bishop of Maidstone, U.K., was kind enough to sit me down and sort me out—a couple of times.

Church plants such as Moot, an Anglican church plant in London, and leaders such as Ian Mobsby, Matt Rees and Kester Brewin are connecting to ancient symbols and practices in their creative worship experiences. Ian Mobsby, speaking in Seattle during a United States tour, pointed out that the emerging church is not only inclined to draw from the ancient but actively searching for "the sacred in the profane" of popular culture as well.[3] Some of the most visible mentors to the emerging edge in the U.K. are Graham Cray and John and Olive Drane at St. Andrews College.

---

[1]Scot McKnight, "Five Streams of the Emerging Church," *Christianity Today*, January 19, 2007, accessed February 1, 2007, at <www.christianitytoday.com/ct/2007/february/11.35.html>.

[2]Jonny Baker, e-mail on postmodernity, November 18, 1999.

[3]Ian J. Mobsby, *Emerging and Fresh Expressions of Church: How Are They Authentically Church and Anglican?* (London: Moot Community, 2007).

In a fall 2000 *Leadership Journal* article, I described what I was learning from this new movement: "In the last 12 years, a new generation of leaders in Britain is engaging postmodern culture. They are relational, and experiential, involve the arts, are more into narrative than propositional theology. They are more tribal and local. . . . In the U.K. they tend to display more global awareness than their U.S. counterparts."[4]

The emerging church movement has not experienced the numerical growth of the house church movement; its influence is evident everywhere. To illustrate, in 2006 Christine and I spoke at Spring Harvest, a remarkable Christian worship/educational gathering created during the boom days of the house church movement. Spring Harvest hosts 50,000 Christians for four four-day sessions at two different locations. Every worship venue reflected the growing influence of the emerging church. Artists often visually interpreted the message. Off to the side were areas with candles and traditional symbols and places for private meditation. Worship venues for teens were a direct appropriation of the innovative edge of what is stirring in postmodern churches in the U.K.

The Church Mission Society maintains a website (www.emerging church.info) where many emerging leaders connect to one another. The best place to meet many of these young leaders is at the Greenbelt Arts Festival, which gathers every August at the Cheltenham Racecourse in the U.K.

In the early 1990s some young Christians in Nelson, New Zealand, created a sophisticated venue called the Led Zebra. This safari-themed center was drawing more teens than any secular venue in town. Meanwhile, in the red-light district of Auckland, New Zealand, Mark Pierson, Mike Riddell and some of their mates created Parallel Universe, a monthly alternative worship opportunity for twenty- and thirty-year-olds, most of whom made no profession of faith. They redesigned a night club, surrounding the space with three floor-to-ceiling screens, and artfully crafted film and music from pop-culture sources to create unique multimedia worship expressions. Some two hundred young adults would come out to this unique venue on

---

[4]Tom Sine, "Brave New Worldview," *Leadership Journal,* Fall 2000, p. 53.

Saturday nights to experience something of God's care for them. From those early beginnings, Mark Pierson went on to lead one of the most artistic churches in the emerging world—Cityside Baptist, also in Auckland.

In 2002 the Baptist church in Australia realized it needed to invest in something more than the standard Baptist model of church if it was to engage a new generation. They invested $1 million to train twenty church planters to create a range of new church models. Anne Wilkinson-Hayes, one of those church planters, reports that a tapestry of communities is beginning to spring up across Melbourne, including a group of artists that share prayer over paint and canvas, and exhibit their works to engage those in their community.

Steve Taylor, pastor of Opawa Baptist Church in Christchurch, New Zealand, is part of the latest generation of emerging church planters, authors and lecturers. His book *The Out of Bounds Church?* engages the postmodernity discussion and the need to create a post-Christendom church. Paul Fromont in Cambridge, New Zealand, along with Alan Hirsch, Michael Frost and their compatriots at The Forge in Melbourne, are also at the center of the emerging buzz Down Under.[5]

In the mid-1990s the emerging church movement made its way to North America. Funded by the Leadership Network, Doug Pagitt and a small circle of pastors started holding conferences around the country. Many young leaders at these conferences have subsequently planted new forms of church, such as Solomon's Porch in the Twin Cities, Minnesota, Ecclesia in Houston, Texas, and Mars Hill in Grandville, Michigan.

Since those first mustard seed experiments in the mid- to late 1990s, there has been an explosion of emerging church plants in North America, including Veritas in Southern California, which offers postmodern worship and the opportunity to make sandwiches for the homeless. At his church, Vintage Faith, in Santa Cruz, California, and in his writings, Dan Kimball (author of *They Like Jesus but Not the Church*) has significant influence on the

---

[5]The Forge in Melbourne is better-known as an example of the missional stream. As you will see, the missional and emerging streams often flow into one another.

emerging conversation. Rachelle Mee Chapman started the monastic flavored Monkfish Abbey and Mark Scandrette (author of *Soul Graffiti*) leads the Jesus Dojo in San Francisco. Sally Morgenthaler is one of the most creative leaders in the field of worship and use of sacred space in this movement. In Texas, Chris Seay is working with a group of artists to translate the Scripture in new ways that take both culture and the arts seriously. Andy Harrington, an immigrant from the U.K. who heads up Youth for Christ in Vancouver, British Columbia, has helped young Canadians plant new churches like Station X and Warehouse 180 to reach a new generation in British Columbia. There are a host of other emerging churches in North America that I regrettably don't have space to mention.

There is also a growing interest in all things emerging among younger leaders in mainline denominations in the United States. Check out Anglimergent (http://anglimergent.groups.vox.com), an online Anglican community focused on the relation between the emerging church, culture and mission. A number of young leaders in the Presbyterian Church (U.S.A.) have started an online forum called Presbymergent (http://presbymergent.org) to try to "find the balance" between a traditional denomination and the new emerging expressions. Dwight Friesen, from Mars Hill Graduate School, has been engaged in a yearlong conversation conducted by the National Council of Churches. He reported that those in attendance from the Orthodox Church were the most interested in joining the emerging conversation.

There is a wide array of understandings around the world of what constitutes an emerging church. Emerging leaders in Britain, Australia and New Zealand tend to be more involved in a conversation about postmodern culture and a post-Christendom church. Some younger leaders in all countries define emerging as the creation of post-denominational and post-congregational forms of church. There are some other young leaders in the United States for whom "pomo (postmodern) churches" seem to be simply another way to describe alternative worship. But much of what we are seeing is a spectrum of fresh expressions of what it means to be the church and do mission.

There are also a variety of definitions of what constitutes the emerging church. Eddie Gibbs and Ryan Bolger took a comprehensive look at this movement in Britain and the United States in their definitive book *Emerging Churches*. They offer a very succinct definition of this stream: "Emerging churches are communities that practice the way of Jesus within postmodern cultures."[6] Scott Bader-Saye observes that those in this stream often prefer to define the emerging church as a conversation instead of a movement—a conversation that "is still young, experimental and evolving."[7] Leonard Sweet sees it as "an ongoing conversation about how new times call for new churches, and that the mortar-happy church of the last half of the 20th century is ill-poised to face the promises and perils of the future."[8]

No matter how we may choose to define the emerging church, it really exists in the blogosphere as no other Christian movement has. In his provocatively titled "We Know More Than Our Pastors: Why Bloggers Are the Vanguard of the Participatory Church," Tim Bednar contends,

> Our network of blogs exceeds the reach of any single pastor. . . . Thousands of bloggers circumvent hierarchies and relate unmediated from one another. We are part of a participatory phenomena that is impacting mass media, technology, education, entertainment, politics, journalism and business.[9]

In North America the Emergent Village, led by Tony Jones, and TheOOZE, led by Spencer Burke, are the primary groups hosting young church planters and wannabes in gatherings and online venues. Youth Specialties is also a primary player in the United States. Up until now the emerging church movement has tended to be white and male. We are seeing more women

---

[6]Eddie Gibbs and Ryan K. Bolger, *Emerging Churches: Creating Christian Community in Postmodern Cultures* (Grand Rapids: Baker Academic, 2005), p. 44.

[7]Scott Bader-Saye, "Improvising Church: An Introduction to the Emerging Church Conversation," *International Journal for the Study of the Christian Church* 6, no. 1 (2006): 12.

[8]"God sent a person not a proposition . . ." a conversation with Len Sweet, interviewed by Tamara Cissna, *The George Fox University Online Journal*, <www.georgefox.edu/journalonline/archives/fall05/emerging.html>.

[9]Tim Bednar, "We Know More Than Our Pastors: Why Bloggers Are the Vanguard of the Participatory Church," <http://creativecommons.org/licenses/by-nd-nc/1.0>.

joining the movement, and it is beginning to go global. In fact, the Emergent Village has started reaching out to emerging leaders all over the planet. Brian McLaren has connected with leaders such as Claude Nikondeha in Africa; Sivin Kit in Asia; and Tomas Yaccino, volunteer facilitator for La Red del Camino.

There seem to be certain characteristics that are common to many different emerging expressions, though certainly not to all.

- Emerging leaders are much more into gospel as story, narrative and metaphor and have little interest in a propositional, dogmatic approach to theology common in many conservative churches.

- Unlike some megachurches that try to create programs that can be replicated all over the planet, emerging church leaders are committed to creating innovative ways to engage people in one specific cultural context.

- Emerging churches, informed by their postmodern instincts, tend to be highly experimental and artistic, often working compellingly with both image and word.

- Emerging churches tend to offer multilayered, experiential worship that draws on both ancient symbols and images from "profane" culture.

- Emerging leaders are committed to calling people to a more authentic, embodied, whole-life faith.

- Emerging churches, by their very nature, tend to be outwardly focused in mission, not only to engage a specific group, but with a desire to have an impact on the lives of people in their communities and the larger world.

- Emerging churches are relational, organic and communal with virtually no bureaucratic, hierarchical models of leadership, unlike many denominational and nondenominational churches.

- Emerging Christians tend to be concerned about a broad range of social issues, including social justice, reconciliation and creation care.

It is not clear to anyone where the emerging stream is headed in Britain, Down Under or in North America. *An Emergent Manifesto of Hope*, one of the newest books in this stream, features a host of thoughtful essays by younger authors, not all of whom are from the emerging stream. Meanwhile some leaders in the American church, such as theologian D. A. Carson, express serious reservations about the writings of Emergent leader Brian McLaren and all things emerging.

I think if critics took the time to get to know these leaders personally, they would discover, as I have, that most of them struggle to be true to both Scripture and the rich traditions of our faith. In fact, I find that a number of them actually take Scripture more seriously than some of their detractors in their call for "ortho-praxy"—not only intellectual assent to faith, but also a more authentic living out of a biblical faith in believers' entire lives.

Andrew Jones, something of a blogging apostle to the emerging movement, urges us to be more supportive of what God is doing through this movement, to "find what God is planting and . . . water it."[10] Many of us not only need to water and encourage what God is doing through these mustard seeds, but also to be open to learning from the commitment, risk-taking and imagination of these creative conspirators.

MISSIONAL STREAM

In 1996 I learned that my friend Phil Wall, an emerging church planter, was reading to Lesslie Newbigin because Dr. Newbigin's eyes were failing. I am deeply indebted to Newbigin for his many important books and particularly his *Gospel in a Pluralistic Society*, which I still use in a worldview course I teach for Fuller Seminary in Seattle. Phil was kind enough to arrange a meeting with Dr. Newbigin during a trip I took to the U.K.

I still remember that very leisurely afternoon with Lesslie Newbigin, discussing a broad range of topics over a pint of cider at his local pub. I recall the difficulty I had in keeping up with his keen intellect as he reflected on the writings of the early church fathers regarding the church and its mission. Dr. Newbigin expressed how impressed he is by the ways that Phil and other young emerging church planters reach out so decisively to do mission both locally and globally. He also expressed a longing to see traditional

[10]Gibbs and Bolger, *Emerging Churches*, p. 53.

churches place mission more at the center of their congregational life.

In fact, back in the 1980s the World Council of Churches, influenced by the incisive insights of Lesslie Newbigin, drafted a biblical statement that affirmed an integrated approach to word and deed mission and called churches everywhere to make mission central to congregational life. Inspired by his thoughtful writings on faith, culture and mission, a group of Christian scholars in the United States and Canada started The Gospel and Our Culture Network, publishing a book in 1998 titled *The Missional Church: A Vision for the Sending of the Church in North America*. There they called the church beyond itself in order to be a church for others. I am sure that when Darrell Guder and the other contributing authors wrote this book, they didn't have any idea it would stir a new stream of renewal. The book captured the attention of leaders in both established mainline and evangelical churches in Canada and the United States.

Whereas the emerging church movement was birthed by practioners reinventing the church for a postmodern context, the missional church movement was birthed out of the academy. Mature scholars challenged primarily traditional churches to focus more outwardly in mission and to rediscover their calling as "God's sent people." In 2004 the authors of *The Missional Church* addressed the question "What do missional congregations look like?" in *Treasures in Clay Jars: Patterns in Missional Faithfulness*. They sketched nine diverse congregations that have found an array of ways God could use their mustard seeds to focus outwardly in mission to their communities and the larger world.

One of the Network's newest books, *Storm Front: The Good News of God*, is particularly helpful in moving beyond scholarly concepts to a practical understanding of what a more mission-focused congregation looks like. This book makes clear that missional churches, at their best, shift their focus from creating programs that meet the needs of those within the building to equipping members to address the needs of those outside the building. This shift should be reflected in practical choices like the stewardship of time and money.

In 2006 I discovered a couple of important British books that echo some of these same themes. *Post-Christendom: Church and Mission in a Strange New*

World by Stuart Murray asks a provocative question about how we do mission in a post-Christendom world. David Smith's *Mission After Christendom* sees the churches in the majority world radically changing our understanding of faith and mission.

Australians Alan Hirsch and Michael Frost wrote *The Shaping of Things to Come*, one of the first popular books to reach out to those dissatisfied with the conventional church. Not surprisingly this book is also popular with the emerging church crowd and became one of the first bridges between the two streams.[11] In 2005 Hirsch and Frost led a conference called "Dangerous Stories" in Melbourne, Australia. Sponsored by The Forge, this high energy conference was the first I had been to that brought together people from the emerging and missional streams to explore innovative ways to become more a part of God's missional work.[12]

The missional movement deserves credit for raising important theological questions regarding what it means to be church and do the mission of the church. Several seminaries in the United States have responded: Fuller Theological Seminary, guided by Ryan Bolger, Eddie Gibbs and Kurt Fredrickson; Biblical Theological Seminary in Pennsylvania, with the leadership of John Franke; North Park University in Chicago, with the support of Scot McKnight; Duke Divinity School, guided by Steve Hayner; and Mars Hill Graduate School in Seattle, under the guidance of Dwight Friesen. George Fox Theological Seminary also offers an emphasis in this area that often includes Leonard Sweet. One of the most recent offerings is Missional Leadership, started by Alan Roxburgh.

Slowly, practioners have responded to this missional call. These conspirators tend to look like their emerging church counterparts except that they are often seminary-trained and more multiculturally focused. Many, though not

---

[11]I am sure Alan Hirsch's recent work *The Forgotten Ways* and Michael Frost's *The Exiles* will continue to feed the appetite of those in both traditional and emerging churches who are searching for new ways forward in a changing world.

[12]The Forge is a unique missional training center that enables students to actually create new missional church plants and mission ventures. Their training program emphasizes the need for both reflection and action. They maintain a network of innovators all over Australia <www.forge.org.au>.

all, are seeking to plant missional churches within traditional denominations. The Anglican Church in the U.K. has started sponsoring a host of new
missional experiments called Fresh Expressions. Andy Harrington reported
that the Evangelical Alliance of Canada has created a nationwide program
called Cadence to train younger Christians to become missional leaders.

In the United States, several major denominations have seen the hand-
writing on the wall regarding the serious decline of traditional congregations, and are making substantial investments in planting a broad range of
new, experimental, missional churches with hopes of reaching a younger
and more multicultural generation. Dave T. Olson, who directs church
planting for the Covenant Church, is planting new churches that seek to reflect missional assumptions almost exclusively. These include NewSong in
Irvine, California, and Life Covenant in Edmond, Oklahoma. Both the
Christian Reformed Church (CRC) and the Reformed Church in America
(RCA) are making major commitments to plant a broad spectrum of new
missional congregations to reach diverse populations. Tim Vink, who
heads the RCA initiative, says its goal is to involve existing congregations
in planting four hundred new churches by 2013. Allen Likkel is heading up
a similar effort for the Christian Reformed Church as well.

Today, Christians all over the world in both traditional and emerging
churches have embraced the word *missional*. Darrell Guder, editor of the
book *The Missional Church*, says the word has taken on a life of its own. In
the article "Missional Buzz: Will the Real Missional Church Please Stand
Up?" Tim Conder, pastor of Emmaus Way in Durham, North Carolina, con-
siders *missional* the new buzz word: "So many fellowships that once boldly
self-identified as cell churches, meta-churches, seeker-style or purpose-
driven now claim to be missional." Conder defines the term as "a corrective
to or an outright rejection of commodified and cultural Christianity,
steeped in institutionalism, individualism, and sentimentality" where "pro-
gramming and finances are directed outwardly."[13] I like his outward empha-

---

[13]Tim Conder, "Missional Buzz: Will the Real Missional Church Please Stand Up?"
Out of Ur, January 12, 2007, accessed January 28, 2007, at <http://blog.christianity
today.com/outofur/archives/2007/01/missional_buzz.html>.

sis, but in my research I find that description reflected in emerging churches more consistently than in many of the churches that identify with the missional label.

MOSAIC STREAM

Efrem Smith and Phil Jackson's book *The Hip-Hop Church* and Tommy Kyllonen's *Un.orthodox* offer compelling evidence that God is doing something new through young people from a spectrum of different cultures. Both books recognize hip-hop as not just an expression of urban African American culture but the language of a new generation all over the planet. In fact, as I write, a young friend from England is having back surgery as a result of break dancing with youth over several years in an urban ministry in Manchester, England.

Observing that most of the leadership in the mainstream church—and most of those he meets at emerging church conferences—are Caucasian, Kyllonen reminds us that the times are changing.

> The emerging church is also the young black male in the hood. It is the second generation Mexican in LA and the child of the Chinese immigrant in Houston. The emerging church is the Puerto Rican female on Wall Street.[14]

Though most of those in this stream have never heard the word *postmodernity*, many of the urban young that are a part of hip-hop culture share with the emerging young a suspicion of modernity, authority and pat answers.[15] Efrem Smith tells me that urban hip-hop culture isn't just postmodern but also post-institutional, post-soul and post–civil rights too.

Urban African American young are hungry for a spirituality they can relate to. There are reportedly some twenty hip-hop churches in the United States and their numbers are growing. Phil Jackson's multicultural congregation, Lawndale Community Church in Chicago, responds to this hunger

---

[14]Tommy Kyllonen, *Un.orthodox: Church, Hip-Hop, Culture* (Grand Rapids: Zondervan, 2007), p. 180.
[15]Ibid., pp. 126-27.

by offering hip-hop services on the first and second Saturdays of every month. The first service is called House Party and the second is called House Unplugged.

Hip-hop churches are only one expression of what God is doing through a growing number of multicultural churches. A number of second-generation Asian churches in Canada and the United States have chosen to become multicultural congregations. Some churches in California came together around interracial families that didn't feel completely at home in monocultural churches.

There are even a few monocultural churches that are beginning to question whether that model is fully biblical. Kingston United Reformed Church in Britain, comprised of Koreans, Russians, Nigerians, Chinese and English, has intentionally worked to become a multicultural congregation. Pastor Leslie Charlton believes diversity is essential to being church. "You cannot call yourself a church if you are all the same," she says. "It may be a nice group, but a church, like the kingdom of God, must have room for everybody."[16] Of course race and class diversity may not always be possible in monocultural communities, but Pastor Charlton certainly has Scripture to support her case.

There is another important reason to consider moving beyond a monocultural church experience. I have seen the future and, whether we recognize it or not, it looks like London, Los Angeles and Auckland. These cities reflect the wonderfully diverse cultures of our world. In fact by 2060 the United States will become the first non-European Western nation—a nation of Latinos, African Americans and Asians. Those of us from European roots will just be another group. Our churches need to help people prepare to not only live in this future, but to receive and celebrate the gifts from other cultures.

God is indeed raising up new conspirators who are determined to create churches that look like God's multicultural kingdom. A recent article in the

---

[16]"Council for World Mission: Welcoming Strangers," <www.cwmission.org.uk/features/default.cfm?FeatureID=1607>.

Christian Science Monitor reports that one of the major characteristics of the fastest growing churches in America is that they are multiracial.[17] Peter Brierley, who directs Christian Research in Britain, reports that the multicultural church in London is one of the few parts of the church in the U.K. that is growing, comprising 17 percent of churchgoers.

For those of us who are part of white culture to join what God is doing in this stream will involve first coming to terms with the history of slavery, racism and oppression that is a part of all Western societies. Inspired by the horror of slavery that is powerfully documented in the film *Amazing Grace*, David Pott started Lifeline Expeditions in Britain in 2000. He invites whites to walk in chains in former slave ports in Western countries, including the United States, as an act of contrition for their ancestors' enslavement of peoples of African ancestry. These demonstrations have had a powerful effect on both blacks and whites who have witnessed them.

In Australia, European and Aboriginal Christians gather at former massacre sites and pray for God's healing and reconciliation. (I would love to see European Americans and Native Americans in the United States follow this model and pray for healing and reconciliation at genocide sites on our continent.)

Eric Dyson declares, "Whiteness looks like the universal, therefore it never gets talked about in any particular fashion." Dyson recommends "white study programs" in universities for those of European heritage to learn about the issues of race, class and power.[18] Differences of race and class are painfully evident in a film like *Crash*. The film makes it clear that prejudice and racism are universal. However, while those of us who are white may deplore a past that has discriminated against and oppressed other people groups, we are still beneficiaries of that past. As we travel into the future, we all need to come to terms with the reality of white power and privilege. In addition, followers of Jesus from all racial and cultural groups need to create new ways of celebrating and receiving the varied gifts we share with one another as a foretaste of our coming home to God's great multicultural homecoming.

---

[17]G. Jeffrey MacDonald, "From US Churches That Are Growing, a Sound of Drums," *The Christian Science Monitor,* January 3, 2007, pp. 1, 10.
[18]Eric Dyson, *Debating Race with Eric Dyson* (New York: Basic Books, 2007), p. 117.

Doug Lee, pastor of the church plant Catalyst in Culver City, California, shared how his congregation is already enjoying some of the rich gifts of different cultures. "South Pacific Islanders bring a spirit of warmth, welcome and generosity to our community. Our African American friends have taught us much about really being fully present to God and highly invested in worship. Our Latino brothers and sisters remind us of the importance of family and hospitality. . . . Our Asian members bring the importance of service without the need for recognition. As a new family we are all richer because of the diverse gifts we bring."

I experience something of the rich gifts of tapestry of God's new community at the annual conference of the Christian Community Development Association, started by John Perkins. CCDA always has an urban choir that lifts our souls to the rafters. I also experience the rich gifts at Urbana Student Missions Conventions because those who lead us in worship represent the many parts of our world. We at Mustard Seed Associates hosted an evening with community activist Rudy Carrasco called "The Color of Love in the City." The event was designed to start a conversation about color in our communities. After Rudy shared his stories Eliacin Rosario, a member of our MSA team, led a discussion on race and culture. To my surprise people from a range of racial backgrounds shared openly about both their pain and their attempts to live faithfully in a multicultural society.

One of the most innovative U.S. congregations in the area of ethnic diversity is a church in Southern California called Mosaic. It is comprised of "people from all over the world who have settled in the Los Angeles, California area. Their audience is multi-cultural, postmodern, pluralistic and global culture seekers."[19] Like the emerging church, Mosaic gives a major place in its life and mission to the arts; its group Urban Poets includes artists, dramatists and social innovators.

Most of the pastors of these multicultural churches are not content to simply create interesting programs to meet the needs of people within the building. They are intent on involving their members in word and deed min-

---

[19]Text taken from the Mosaic website: <www.mosaic.org>.

istries that impact the lives of people in their communities. In this sense, many of these churches are close to the missional models we discussed earlier. For example, Eugene Cho's multicultural church plant in Seattle, called Quest, from its inception has been devoted to local and global mission. Quest's coffee shop, the Q Café, serves as a place to engage the surrounding community and provide a performance space to local artists. Members also work with the homeless and offer computer education classes for kids struggling in school, and contribute time and resources to global initiatives.

Church of the Redeemer, a three-year-old church plant in South Central Los Angeles pastored by Danny Martinez, was started by people strongly committed to social justice, working with the poor at home as well as mission abroad. Congregants serve their communities through activities such as working with the homeless, volunteering in a local convalescent hospital and serving in urban schools.

David T. Olson told me that over 50 percent of the new missional church plants in the Covenant Church in America are ethnically or culturally diverse. Covenant's Pacific West Coast Conference actually requires all church planters to take a "Journey to Mosaic," a three-day bus trip for forty-eight people that begins in Oakland, California, and ends in Los Angeles. Typically it begins with hearing the stories of those in an African American congregation in one of the toughest neighborhoods in Oakland. The next stop is in the farm region, where participants hear the stories of immigrant Hispanic farm workers. Then the bus heads south to Los Angeles, where time is spent with those who lived through the Japanese internment camps of World War II. After a visit with leaders in an ethnic church, the trip concludes by hanging with the homeless in East Los Angeles. Another Covenant Church Conference sponsors a bus tour, called Sankofa, that takes riders 3,500 miles along some of the historic sites of the civil rights movement: Sixteenth Street Baptist Church in Birmingham, Alabama, the Martin Luther King Memorial in Atlanta, Georgia, the Civil Rights Memorial in Montgomery, Alabama, and the historic slave market site in Mobile, Alabama.

As you can see from this brief overview, multicultural churches—along with the increasing number of immigrant churches—are going to be one aspect of the growing edge of the church in Western countries. This new mosaic stream is quite diverse, but what its adherents all seem to share (like those in emerging churches) is their desire to reach out to a new generation. Like the missional churches, they also focus their mission on the needs of those beyond their own congregations. As a consequence they are much more significantly involved in local and global mission. We need to pay much more attention to what God is doing through the mosaic stream as well as ethnic and immigrant churches and explore new forms of collaboration that enable the church to lead in celebrating the gifts that will be a part of our multicultural future.

MONASTIC STREAM

The final new stream of renewal I will be describing is the monastic stream. This stream is different in several ways from the other three. Most of the groups in the monastic stream have no interest in church planting. While large numbers of twenty- and thirty-year-olds are involved, it is comprised of a larger number of the over-forty crowd than the other three streams. It is also significantly more multicultural and multinational than the emerging and missional streams.

These conspirators perhaps raise more questions than any of the other streams regarding what it means to be disciples of Jesus, be the church and do the mission of the church. Though the people involved in new monastic experiments tend to come from evangelical backgrounds, they are being drawn into the richness of the Catholic, Orthodox, Celtic and Anglican monastic traditions.

Monasticism with the middle class. First, there are a few groups I will describe that are drawn principally to the spiritual aspects of the monastic life. The expectations for these followers of Jesus are to pursue more serious spiritual practices in the midst of their regular middle-class lives. These Protestant monastic streams draw most directly from monastic traditions like the Franciscans, Benedictines and Celts.

The lay monastic Third Order of Franciscan movement, which started at the beginning of the twentieth century, paved the way for this new stream. Today, over two million lay Christians all over the world develop and follow a rule of life under the oversight of Franciscan brothers, which enables them to live a life of prayer and service. Since this small beginning, a number of other lay monastic orders patterned themselves after the Third Order model. The Iona Community in Scotland, the Northumbria Community in England and the Order of Saint Aidan and Saint Hilda in England are primarily devoted to helping participants more fully enter into a life of spirituality. Though some may live in residential communities or work with the poor, the majority of people who participate in these orders do not.

A few years ago a group of Christians at St. Thomas Crookes Church in Sheffield, U.K., started a monastic order called The Order of Mission. This is now an official order within the Anglican Church in the U.K. and has roughly three hundred people following its rule of life. Like other lay orders, this order takes the life of prayer seriously. Adherents are also active in small groups called huddles and participate in a broad range of ministries, including working with the poor. But most of them don't live in residential communities.

Even more recently, Peter Greig, who started the global 24/7 Prayer Network and has been involved in the emerging church movement in the U.K., has founded yet another group called The Order of the Mustard Seed. This order also emphasizes a life of prayer and service. But adherents tend to be less structured than most of the other models described here.

There is a growing interest among a new generation of Western Protestant church leaders in exploring ancient monastic practices too. For example, Karen Sloan is a Presbyterian minister who has written her intriguing journey into Dominican spirituality in her book *Flirting with Monasticism: Finding God on Ancient Paths*. In fact, a number of those in the emerging and missional streams are drawn not only to ancient liturgies but to ancient spiritual practices as well.

Monasticism with the poor. The most radical expressions of the monastic stream are comprised of groups, inspired particularly by the Franciscans, who view following Christ as living in community, working and living incarnationally with the poor, and taking time for serious spiritual practices. In fact many of them choose to live at the economic level of the people around them. John Hayes, who leads the monastic movement InnerCHANGE, insists that "the world doesn't need more words, not even more 'right' words. The world needs more words made flesh. The world needs more people to live the good news incarnationally, in a way that can been seen heard and handled."[20]

A ministry of Christian Resources Ministry, InnerCHANGE is an expression of the leaders' discovery that God was calling them to a Franciscan lifestyle, living incarnationally with the poor and maintaining a strong commitment to prayer. Out of that small beginning, InnerCHANGE has birthed communities in Cambodia, Romania, Venezuela, Los Angeles, San Francisco and Minneapolis. Recently over dinner, John Hayes told Christine and me that he is headed to Britain to start a new community there. John reflects in his book, "We have found that incarnational ministry among the poor is worth the personal costs. To be told by our neighbors, 'you are one of us' is a sacred moment."[21] However, John makes clear that it takes time and a serious investment in the life of one's larger community to reach that moment.

During the radical Christian movement of the 1970s, a new Protestant monastic expression was birthed that focused on service to the poor. Viv Grigg, a Kiwi who had been ministering as a missionary in Asia, was astonished to find no missionaries living in the slums. So he decided to take initiative and move into the squatter settlement of Tanalon. In his book *Companions with the Poor*, he called other followers of Jesus to consider this radical new vocation. His initiative gave rise to two of the earliest new monastic orders: Servant Partners and Servant to Asia's Urban Poor. Servant Partners is involved in creating monastic communities in Bangkok, Northeast Africa, North Africa, Nairobi, India, the Middle East, Manila and Mexico City. Their community in Mexico City is building bridges between the rich and poor to support programs in holistic health care, small business

---

[20]John B. Hayes, *Sub-merge* (Ventura, Calif.: Regal, 2006), p. 113.
[21]Ibid., p. 140.

creation and children's ministry. Servant to Asia's Urban Poor works in the Philipines, Cambodia, India, Indonesia, Australia, Canada, New Zealand, Switzerland, the U.K. and the United States. Recently Servant Partners in Manila opened a two-room center for street children. Onesimo Kids hosts twenty children a day. They are also involved in a broad range of ministries with the poor in the other areas where they live and serve.

Urban Neighbours of Hope (UNOH) was started in 2001 as a "missional order among the poor" by the Churches of Christ in Australia with the help of InnerCHANGE. The vision is to be a missional order living out the gospel and seeking the transformation through Christ of urban neighborhoods facing poverty in the Asia-Pacific region. UNOH has teams living in Bangkok, Sydney and Melbourne. Participants feel God calling them to live in neighborhoods facing poverty, "inviting the homeless to live with us; limiting our work and income (partnership or outside work no more than 20 hours/wk and our income pegged to Henderson poverty line in Australia)."[22]

Word Made Flesh (WMF) started in 1991 to serve the poorest of the poor. In 1994 WMF started its first children's home in Madras, and today WMF communities can be found not only in South Asia but in Africa and South America as well, "in the sewers of Eastern Europe meeting with children living on the streets, with former child soldiers in the refugee camps of West Africa, among victims of sex trafficking and children with aids throughout Asia, and in the shanty-town and *favelas* of South Africa."[23] WMF strives to create a multicultural and multinational staff and also takes an ecumenical approach to life and faith.

One of the newest expressions is a group of young Christians, connected to the 24/7 Prayer Network and led by Ralf Neumann, moving to East Germany to start a monastic order. They want to be salt and light in an economically depressed region, where the people are struggling with depression and addiction.

---

[22]"UNOH Constitution 2004" <www.unoh.org>.
[23]Christopher L. Heuertz, "A Community of the Broken: A Young Organization Models What It Might Mean to Be the Church in a Suffering World," *Christianity Today*, February 9, 2007, <www.christianitytoday.com/ct/2007/february/36.90.html>.

In his book *The New Friars*, Scott Bessenecker (director of global projects for InterVarsity Christian Fellowship/USA) writes, "God's Spirit is moving through [these twenty-first century monks and nuns] . . . intent on pouring out their lives for people on the fringe."[24] Scott's summer program for college students, Global Urban Trek, is designed for students who want to discover whether God is calling them to live alongside the poor in cities from Cairo to Manila. Mission Year offers college grads a similar opportunity working with the poor in American cities. Recently Christine and I had the opportunity to work with the students from Mission Year. We were impressed at how many of these young people were deeply influenced by this experience to discover new ways in their lives and vocations that God might continue to use their mustard seeds to make a difference with those at the margins.

New monasticism with the poor and the middle class. One of the newest expressions of the monastic stream is called the "new monasticism movement." It was birthed at a 2005 gathering in Raleigh-Durham that was comprised of several hundred young people (plus a few of us who are older). I was impressed by the commitment of the young at this gathering, many of whom are already investing their lives in living and working with the poor in the United States. However, this gathering had much more the flavor of a modern academic classroom than some of the more free-form, postmodern gatherings I have attended with the emerging tribes. Out of the initial conference a book was published, *Schools for Conversion: Twelve Marks of the New Monasticism*. These adherents offer hospitality in their communities as well as educational opportunities in several locations known collectively as the Schools for Conversion.

Shane Claiborne, one of the founders of the new monasticism movement, recalls that the earliest monastic communities "found it necessary to go into the desert to find God. . . . Our desert is the inner cities and abandoned places of the empire."[25] Jason Byassee, writing in *The Christian Cen-*

---

[24]Scott Bessenecker, *The New Friars: The Emerging Movement Serving the World's Poor* (Downers Grove, Ill.: IVP Books, 2006), pp. 24-26.
[25]Shane Claiborne, *The Irresistible Revolution: Living as an Ordinary Radical* (Grand Rapids: Zondervan, 2006), p. 166.

tury magazine, describes the new monastics as "living in the corners of the
American empire . . . a harbinger of a new and radically different form of
Christian practice."[26] These conspirators not only make their homes in the
abandoned places of the empire with the poor; they reach out to those of
us in the middle class and invite us to become more a part of God's mustard
seed revolution.

New monastic communities include Rutba House in Durham, Camden
House in Camden, New Jersey, Communality in Lexington and The Simple
Way in Philadelphia. Their network also includes older communities from
the radical Christian era, like Sojourners Community and Reba Place. Many
of these communities are comprised of more mature believers and not all
are working directly with the poor, nor do they all identify with the monastic tradition.

Other monastic groups who work with the poor share with the new monastic participants a strong commitment to work for social justice, reconciliation and political advocacy for the poor. However, the new monastics
seem to have spent more time reflecting on the theological basis for their
movement than most of the other groups. They position their small initiative against the backdrop of the analysis in *After Virtue* by Alasdair Mac-
Intyre: the Enlightenment project is a failure and modern culture is a
threat to vital faith.[27] In *Living Faithfully in a Fragmented World*, Jonathan
Wilson argues that "the church is in grave danger of compromising its
faithfulness to the Gospel." He expresses concern that the church has become increasingly subverted by the values of the global culture of modernity and asks the important question, "What must the church do in order
to live and witness faithfully as a minority in a culture where we were once
the majority?"[28] In the final chapter he answers his own question, calling
for communities of faith to not withdraw from the world but rather to seek

[26]Jason Byassee, "The New Monastics," *The Christian Century*, October 18, 2005,
<www.christiancentury.org>.
[27]Alasdair MacIntyre, *After Virtue: A Study in Moral Theology*, 3rd ed. (Notre Dame,
Ind.: University of Notre Dame Press, 2007).
[28]Jonathan R. Wilson, *Living Faithfully in a Fragmented World: Lessons for the Church
from MacIntyre's "After Virtue"* (Harrisburg, Penn.: Trinity Press, 1997), pp. 1-19.

to more authentically embody the gospel as small living, breathing communities in the world.[29]

This analysis raises huge new issues for those of us in conventional churches and even for those in the other three streams. Many of us seem largely content with our own understanding of church as a place you go once a week for worship and fellowship. The monastic stream is calling us to fundamentally transform the church into a community in which we live seven days a week—in order to live more faithfully in our deeply fragmented world.

We need to not only celebrate and support what God is doing through those on the conspiratorial edge, we need to join them in order that we might fully discover how God can use each one of us to quietly change our world. To do that, we need to make sense of some of the forces creating turbulence and impacting our lives and values in ways we don't always recognize. Join me as we travel back to the year 2001 and try to make sense of how the global context is changing in a post-9/11 world, and also the ways in which the new global mall is seeking to influence our sense of what is important and what is of value.

JOIN THE CONVERSATION

- What examples from these four streams have particularly provoked your interest or stirred your imagination?
- What theological questions came to mind in this brief tour of those on the creative edge?
- Imagine one new possibility for your own life or church that was stimulated by reading about these experimental groups.

---

[29]Ibid., pp. 68-78.

TAKING THE CULTURE SERIOUSLY

COMING HOME TO A POST-9/11 GLOBAL NEIGHBORHOOD

To what extent is globalization playing a major role in defining the character and quality of our common future in a divided world?

We have just received a report that a small plane crashed into one of the Twin Towers in New York City," the reporter on National Public Radio announced in a matter-of-fact voice. I immediately sensed a major crisis was under way. What had just happened was not in any way matter-of-fact. I was one of millions of Americans who spent that entire day watching the tragic events unfold on television, and struggling to make sense of the horrific images we were viewing.

Of course, not only Americans but people from all over the world were killed in these and other attacks. Numbers of Australians lost their lives to a terrorist bombing in Bali on October 12, 2002. Innocents had their lives snuffed out in a Madrid train bombing on March 11, 2004. The British also suffered in the latest wave with attacks on London's mass transit system on July 7, 2005.[1] Terrorist attacks have occurred all over the world, from Indonesia to India.

The reality is that our world will never be the same again. We are now living in a world in which ongoing acts of terrorism make life more uncertain for all of us and the worst may still be ahead of us. As I viewed the chilling film *The Children of Men*, set in Britain in 2027, I was overwhelmed by scenes of urban anarchy and terrorism that are the daily experience of too many

---

[1]The British, due to "the troubles" in Northern Ireland, have suffered many such attacks over several decades.

today in countries like Iraq and Afghanistan. My prayer as we face these uncertain times is that we not retreat into survival mode but instead be God's
compassionate servants in the midst of crisis and chaos.

The United States and coalition forces responded to the attack on September 11, 2001, by invading Afghanistan to rout al-Qaeda. Then the White
House decided to invade Iraq, even though as we now know, there was no
direct connection between Iraq and the terrorist attacks in the United
States. I think history will demonstrate that the invasion of Iraq has done
more to spread terrorism than quell it, by catalyzing a terrorist training
ground for the disaffected. Thankfully, we are seeing a U.S. return to mul-
tilateral approaches to foreign policy.

This war has demonstrated the serious limits to the use of overwhelming
military force to resolve complex geopolitical issues. Secretary Ban Ki-moon
of the United Nations stated that the Iraq crisis is now "a problem of the
whole world" and that the UN is prepared to help the people and government of Iraq to seek to resolve this crisis.[2] There are many dire scenarios of
what could go wrong in the region if this chaos spills over into other countries. It is too early to tell if Islamic extremists or moderates are going to have
greater influence on the Arab streets or if the Sunni Shia conflict will spread.

What is clear is that those of us from the major faiths in the region—
Jews, Muslims and Christians—need to find ways to work together to build
bridges of understanding and reconciliation.[3] Ron Sider was spokesman for
a group of thirty evangelical leaders in the United States that called for the
creation of a Palestinian state and a recognition of the suffering of Palestinian people. The letter these evangelicals signed was not only sent to leaders
in the U.S. government but also to Muslim leaders in an effort to reach out
at this critical time.

One of the reasons this letter is so important is that it recognizes the suf-

---

[2]Zalmay Khalilzad, "Why the United Nations Belongs in Iraq," *The New York Times*,
July 20, 2007, p. a23.
[3]Tom Sine, "Divided by a Common Faith," *Sojourners*, October 2004. This article con-
trasts the view of the war in Iraq between U.S. evangelicals and those in Britain, Australia and New Zealand.

fering of Palestinian people who have lived under occupation for over thirty-five years. In fact, Muslim people throughout the region experience a sense of humiliation because of the plight of the Palestinians. This sense of humiliation has its roots in the Crusades, Western insensitivity to Muslim culture and faith, and the spread of Western values through growing influence of globalization. In light of this situation I join the authors of this letter in strongly supporting the creation of a Palestinian state that insures the security of Israel while bringing justice for the Palestinians. I believe such an initiative would not only dramatically reduce the incidence of terrorism but set the stage for building new ties between all the nations and cultures concerned for this volatile region. We need to pray daily for the peace of Jerusalem. But we also need to join with those in the Middle East and work for a lasting peace and justice for all those in the region.[4]

As followers of Jesus, it is important to recognize that our first loyalty is not only to God but to the transnational community of God's people. We are an alien community, in every nation, that seeks to reflect a different way of life than the culture around us. This includes Jesus' admonition that we love our enemies. Like the imagery of the mustard seed becoming a sheltering tree for all the nations, we need to be a source of God's peace and reconciliation among all peoples.

Back in the 1990s, a group of Christians from Europe reflected the reconciling way of Jesus by walking the old Crusader trail, asking for the forgiveness of Orthodox Christians, Jews and Muslims for the Crusades. Muslims, Jews and the Orthodox often responded by embracing these pilgrims with tears and asking them for forgiveness of the deep anger they have harbored toward Christians.

---

[4]Laurie Goodstein, "Coalition of Evangelicals Voices Support for Palestinian State," *The New York Times*, July 29, 2007, p. 15. There are several universities that deal with these issues in the United States: Eastern Mennonite University and George Fox University have peace studies programs and Duke University has a center for reconciliation. There are groups like Evangelicals for Middle East Understanding, Churches for Middle East Peace and a blog called Middle East Window (http://middleeastwindow.com) that offer vital insights on the journey to understanding. Finally there is a great bibliography on the issues at <www.elca.org/middleeast/bibliography.html>.

The last time I was in Israel, I met a Messianic Jew named Benjamin. He had recently sold his home in Israel to Thomas Kutab and his family. The Kutab family are Palestinian Christians who for years lived in a refugee camp on the West Bank. Like many other Palestinians, their home had been confiscated by the Israeli government, which paid them five cents on the dollar for what it was worth. Benjamin decided to plant a small seed by selling his home to the Kutabs for the same amount as they were paid by the government for theirs. The book *The Lemon Tree* by Sandy Tolan offers a very human understanding of the struggles of one Jew and one Palestinian to understand each other's story.

For years Mennonite mission agencies like the Mennonite Central Committee have been reaching out in the reconciling Spirit of Christ to those in need in Palestine, Pakistan, Iran and Jordan. As a result, recently they have been invited to sit down with top Islamic Clerics in the region to explore how people from different faiths can build bridges of reconciliation and hope.[5]

Join me on a trip to the Middle East just four months before the terrorist attacks on September 11, 2001. In my meetings there, we discussed a force beyond terrorism that has contributed to the turbulence we are experiencing: globalization within a new majority world.

WELCOME TO LIFE IN A NEW "MAJORITY WORLD"

Lebanon 2001. We arrived in Beirut, Lebanon, at 2:00 a.m. Christine and I had been invited by Arab Christian Media to speak at a conference on globalization and mission. As we emerged from the airport, we were engulfed in a swarm of some three hundred other passengers and those there to greet them. The people assigned to pick us up and drive us to the conference site weren't able to find us, even though we appeared to be the only Europeans in the airport. We were feeling displaced and anxious.

A local tour guide approached and asked several times in English if we

---

[5]James R. Krabill, David W. Shenk and Linford Stutzman, eds., *Anabaptists Meeting Muslims: A Calling for Presence in the Way of Christ* (Scottdale, Penn.: Herald Press, 2005).

wanted a taxi. We finally relented at 4:00 a.m. and followed the driver to a car with no indication that it was a taxi. As we headed south to Beirut, we suddenly realized how vulnerable we were. No one knew where we were or who was transporting us. Thankfully we were delivered safely to a comfortable motel and the conference coordinator picked us up the next day.

On reflection I realize I felt anxious not just because our driver didn't pick us up, but also because we were a very small minority in a part of the world that is often unhappy with those of us from the West, sometimes with good reason. We were really quite vulnerable to a situation over which we had little control.

Flash forward. This experience is representative of a new reality. We live in a new "majority world." Over 80 percent of the world's population now lives in the Middle East, Africa, Asia and Latin America. Beyond concerns about the growing Islaminization of Europe, Americans, Australians and Europeans are seriously struggling with the growing numbers of immigrants from the majority world who want to come to our shores. As I told the Europe 2020 conference in Spain, "Europeans didn't have enough children to continue running your factories and operating your stores. As you face rapidly graying societies in Europe, how can you possibly keep your economies going without the increasing participation of immigrants?" No one answered.

WELCOME TO LIFE IN A NEW GLOBAL NEIGHBORHOOD!

Lebanon 2001. In my opening address to the delegates at the 2001 Christian Arab Media conference in Lebanon, I noted that virtually overnight "all the earth's inhabitants have moved into a new neighborhood we have never lived in before, with a host of new opportunities and new challenges." We are now living in a global economic order in which distance is dying, borders are melting, and we are being permanently linked to one another in ways we never have been before, as I described in a book I had published shortly before my trip, *Mustard Seed Versus McWorld.*[6]

---

[6]See my in-depth discussion in *Mustard Seed Versus McWorld: Reinventing Life and Faith for the Future* (Grand Rapids: Baker Books, 1999).

64

THE NEW CONSPIRATORS

Globalization has brought a number of benefits to the middle class in all countries. Many make more money than ten years ago. This new economy produces more products than we can consume and new technologies that are almost out of date before we take them home. Through the Internet we can instantly communicate with people all over the world and secure huge amounts of information from a broad range of cultural and political perspectives.

But this new global economy has a number of downsides we also need to be aware of. National economies are rapidly being knit together into a single global economy that is not only extremely complex but highly volatile. I found that the Christian leaders gathered from Lebanon, Syria, Egypt and North Africa were keenly aware of the powerful potential of global satellites to evangelize their Muslim cousins. But they didn't seem aware or particularly concerned about the growing volatility of this global economy or the need to learn to prepare themselves and their ministries for an increasingly uncertain future.

Flash forward. Several years later I raised some of these same concerns about growing volatility of the global economy with the leadership of a U.S. mission organization. They pay salaries to their international staff in U.S. dollars. I suggested they consider diversifying their funds into other currencies since the U.S. dollar is in trouble and is likely to continue to decline against other currencies as a result of the enormous cost of the war in Iraq, growing U.S. debt and the growing balance of trade deficits.

In 2005 emerging economies, including China's, ran a combined current account surplus of $500 billion. A large chunk was invested in Treasury securities, in what Ken Rogoff of Harvard University calls "the biggest foreign aid programme in world history." Remarkably, the poor countries are actually subsidizing the world's wealthiest consumers.[7]

The leaders in this mission organization didn't heed my advice. Since I spoke to them the U.S. dollar has declined over 15 percent against other major currencies. I suspect the U.S. dollar is going to continue declining in

---

[7]"A Topsy-Turvy World," *Economist*, September 16, 2006, p. 25.

the immediate future; American mission organizations would be wise to look into diversifying. The declining dollar is also causing U.S. relief agencies to cut back the amount of food they are able to purchase to ship to those in need.

Since all national economies are increasingly linked together in this new single global economy, we are all more vulnerable to ripple effects of an economic recession in a country outside of our own. In other words, if the U.S. economy sneezes, there is a high risk that everyone could catch the cold. As I write, the American economy, due to declining economic growth, rising inflation, a rapidly declining housing market and record federal debt, could be vulnerable to a major recession. Christian organizations in the United States and all over the world need to develop specific contingency plans to buffer coming downturns and volatility that could undermine their ability to carry out their mission in turbulent times.

WELCOME TO A WORLD WITH A WIDENING GAP

Lebanon 2001. "The architects of this new global economy sincerely believe if global free enterprise and global free trade are allowed to operate without interference, then all the outcomes will be positive and all the world's people will share the bounty. But the reality is that not all the outcomes are positive and this new global economy doesn't work nearly as well for the global poor as it does for the global rich," I explained to my audience at the conference in Lebanon.

The power in this new global economic order is increasingly being centralized in the hands of a few at the expense of the many. Policies made by leaders in the World Trade Organization and International Monetary Fund fashion trade and economic policies that favor powerful nations and corporations, often at the expense of poorer countries. While these leaders in Lebanon understood my concerns, I am not sure I convinced them either of what I believe the inherent problems with how globalization works are or of our Christian responsibility to do something about it.

Flash forward. Thomas Friedman's book *The World Is Flat*, which was published shortly after my presentation in Lebanon, reflects a much more opti-

mistic view of globalization than my own. Friedman argues that globalization is actually flattening the economy and creating greater opportunity for
people everywhere. One can certainly find examples of increasing economic
opportunity, like those Friedman cites, but they are far from universal.

While some Asian countries have directly benefited from globalization,
many in Latin America and most in Africa and the Middle East are being left
behind. Joseph Stiglitz, in his book *Making Globalization Work*,[8] directly
counters Friedman's optimism. He insists that globalization doesn't work
at all for many of our poorest neighbors and won't unless we all become
much more actively involved working for just economic policies. The poor
need Christians to both lobby for a more just order and design ways
through economic empowerment to help them to more fully participate in
this new economy.

In fact this new global economy is creating not only global disparities
but increasingly glaring disparities within countries. Developers in Bangladesh, one of the most impoverished nations in Asia, have erected an enormous $80 million, eight-story super mall with two thousand stores that
would rival any mall in the West, complete with an amusement park, movie
complex and recreational center, located in Bashundara City. Remarkably,
over half of Bangladesh's 140 million people live in abject poverty and only
20 percent have any access to electricity. As a consequence, most of those
who live in the region where this super mall is located can't afford to shop
there. And yet, an economic researcher in Bangladesh, Mushfique Rahman,
when asked about the new mall, remarked, "The whole world is getting
Westernized. Why should we be left behind?"[9]

India, their next-door neighbor, is much further ahead in "getting Westernized" and globalized, but with troubling results. Childhood obesity and
diabetes are growing at concerning rates among the new middle-class
young who have recently discovered the joys of Western junk food. One
study among teens in Delhi saw the ranks of the obese jump sharply from

[8]Joseph E. Stiglitz, *Making Globalization Work* (New York: W. W. Norton, 2006).
[9]David Rohde, "A Lot of Cash in a Very Poor Nation: Welcome to the Mall," *The New
York Times*, July 19, 2005, p. 4.

16 percent to 29 percent in two years. At the same time, the study reports, in the state of Uttar Pradesh 47 percent of children under age three are clinically underweight and suffering from malnutrition. Among India's indigenous population the rate is a staggering 60 percent.[10] Clearly this new global economy is not always good news, even for those who catch the escalator of economic growth.

WELCOME TO LIFE IN THE NEW IMPERIAL MALL

Lebanon 2001. "We are not only becoming a part of a new global economy, but increasingly living our lives and raising our young in a new global mall. In fact the architects of this new global economy are intentionally seeking to influence all of us and our children to buy into the Western values of individualism, materialism and the pursuit of more," I stated in my presentation to Arab Christian leaders at the conference in Lebanon. "These values that are being promoted in this new global mall clearly undercut many of our most deeply held Christian values. Many of your Muslim neighbors are deeply concerned about the impact of the values of globalization, popular Western culture and consumerism on their faith, culture and particularly the values of their young. Those of us of Christian faith should be no less concerned."

As I chatted with participants after my presentation, it was clear that my remarks had not been a soaring success. My concerns about the impact globalization has on values clearly had not been convincing. Later in the conference when I shared some of the same concerns during a panel discussion, I was pulled aside by a Christian leader from Egypt who had worked with InterVarsity campus ministries in Canada. "I understand your deep concerns and share many of them," he explained. "But your efforts to raise concerns about the negative influences of globalization won't wash with this audience. For most Arab evangelical believers to be a Christian means to be Western and modern. It means that their children can buy Barbie dolls and they can drive Mercedes."

---

[10]Somini Sengupta, "India Prosperity Creates Paradox; Many Children Are Fat, Even More Are Famished," *The New York Times*, December 31, 2006, p. 8.

This was a stunning wake-up call for me. I suddenly realized that what my friend shared was likely true for many Christians that I worked with in Western countries as well. Many of us seem to easily accommodate to the values of modern culture and the global mall, while many of our Muslim neighbors are more concerned about the impact of globalization on values.

Flash forward. "When Jihad takes on McWorld today, it's not religion against commerce, it's religion against religion,"[11] asserts Benjamin Barber in his most recent book *Consumed.* Essentially Barber is arguing that globalization is not just about an increasingly globalized economy; it is taking on the character of religion.

I still run into a few economists who don't see any downsides to the global economy. Many of these economists insist that the global free market is "values free." But growing numbers of economists recognize that our new global economy not only reflects the hyper-individualistic, materialistic, self-interested values of modernity but also magnifies them. Robert Nelson, in his incisive critique of conservative economic theory in *Economics as Religion*, charges that economists are not merely promoting the values of modernity; their economic views take on a decidedly religious character.

> Economists think of themselves as scientists, but . . . they are more
> like theologians. . . . Another basic role for economists is to serve as
> the priesthood of a modern secular religion of economic progress
> that serves many of the same functions in contemporary society that
> Christian and other religions did in their time.[12]

I share the concern of many regarding the impact of globalization on the environment and the poor and will discuss these concerns in more depth. However, my greatest concern is the values impact of globalization. A growing chorus of voices express concern that our new global economy is taking

---

[11]Benjamin R. Barber, *Consumed: How Markets Corrupt Children, Infantilize Adults, and Swallow Citizens Whole* (New York: W. W. Norton, 2007), p. 180.

[12]Robert H. Nelson, *Economics as Religion: From Samuelson to Chicago and Beyond* (University Park: Pennsylvania State University Press, 2001), p. xv.

on the character of empire. Historically one of the characteristics of empires is that they define the reigning view of reality for those living under their rule, much as religion does. What I believe we are witnessing is the global economy also taking on something of the character of a religion by defining for people everywhere what is ultimate. At the core of the modern worldview underlying globalization is the assertion that the ultimate in human experience is defined primarily in economic terms.

Not only does this imperial global economy claim to define what is ultimate, I believe it is increasingly colonizing the imaginations of peoples all over our planet to buy in to its notions of what constitutes the good life and better future. No wonder that many of Islamic faith are concerned. And we should be too.

While our Christian faith fully embraces the material and economic world, we know that for those working from a Christian worldview, the ultimate is never defined primarily in economic terms. We affirm that the ultimate will only be found in a different reality and a different dream for the global future, defined by the restoration of our relationship to the creator God. It is a dream in which the ultimate is found in seeing broken lives restored. It is a dream in which justice finally comes for the poor, wholeness for God's good creation and shalom for the nations.

One of the most remarkable accomplishments of this new global economy in the past fifteen years is the creation of borderless, Westernized, global youth culture. Young people from India and Bangladesh to Mexico and Kenya are all wearing the same jeans, watching the same MTV programs and buying into the same Western values. They have more in common with the North American and British youth than with the cultures from which they come. I believe that we are in a "religious" battle for the hearts and minds of the next generation.

Leaders in the emerging, missional, mosaic and monastic streams, as well as many in traditional churches, are interested in the intersection of faith and culture. Let's look at the ways in which this new global economy not only magnifies the values of modern and postmodern culture, but also seeks to increasingly define for people everywhere what is important and

what is of value. Let's take a closer look at the better future we are being
invited to come home to.

JOIN THE CONVERSATION

- What are some of the challenges and opportunities of becoming increasingly a part of a new global future in a post-9/11 world?

- What are some of the values assumptions that globalization works from
  that seem to be in tension with some of our biblical assumptions?

- Imagine one new way we might respond to the problems and possibilities of globalization.

COMING HOME TO THE
GOOD LIFE OF THE GLOBAL MALL

Is it possible that we allow the images of the global mall instead of the images of biblical faith to define our notions of the good life and better future?

Four attractive young women on the TV screen sit on the beach at a luxury resort obviously enjoying the surf, sun and one another. Suddenly, a small plane appears overhead, trailing a huge sign, which says in large letters, "ANNA WILL YOU MARRY ME?" Anna's friends immediately embrace her and excitedly jump up and down, celebrating this surprising wedding invitation. The plane makes a second pass over the beach. This time the trailing sign is extended to read, "ANNA WILL YOU MARRY ME . . . & PAY OFF ALL MY CREDIT CARDS?"

Obviously Anna's suitor knew exactly the future he wanted to come home to: life with Anna without any of his accumulated debt. What images come to mind when you think of coming home? What kind of future do you want to come home to?

When I think of coming home, my mind flashes back to my grandparents' farm in Blackfoot, Idaho. I am five years old again, sitting splayed-legged on the grass by the white rose arbor, playing with a parcel of kittens. I can smell homemade bread baking in my grandmother's wood stove. My grandparents Sarah and Norman Geyer were devout Methodists. They didn't say much about it, but my, how they lived it! My earliest memories of God's love were Grandma Geyer's large welcoming arms enveloping me.

On the PBS TV series *Homecoming*, which featured remembrances of black farming history, a woman named Yolanda reflected on life on her

BEGINNINGS

Home is both a place of origin and a destination. All our lives are comprised of different stories, with different images of home as the destination toward which we either consciously or unconsciously direct our lives. These images largely define an array of different notions of what constitutes the good life and better future. I am convinced these images play a huge role in defining the direction of our lives as well as how we steward time and resources. They even play a major role in defining what we raise our young for. And yet I have rarely been a part of Christian discussion groups where we have discussed their influence on us. In this conversation we will examine to what extent we unwittingly allow the aspirations and values of modern culture and the global mall instead of the images of an ancient/future hope to define our sense of what we are on the planet for.

Really tough question: Is it possible we got our eschatology wrong? Is it possible we have embraced an eschatology that has very little connection to the urgent issues that fill our world or to the important decisions of our daily lives? Is it possible that many of us have subscribed to an eschatology that has very little influence in defining our sense of what constitutes the good life and better future?

grandparents' farm in Sylvester, Georgia, where they raised twelve children at the turn of the last century.

I can remember the fresh bacon, ham, eggs, the yeast rolls, biscuits and cane syrup . . . the long long picnic table that sat in the middle of the kitchen, so we could all eat at the same time. . . . The first time I set foot on the farm again, I wanted to get on my knees and kiss the ground. It was as if all the souls of those gone before were there to welcome me back.[1]

[1]Yolanda, "Your Stories," KCTS Homecoming Project, February 21, 2000, accessed January 26, 2007, at <www.pbs.org/itvs/homecoming/yourstories.html>.

Many twenty- and thirty-year-olds tell me that the film *Garden State* connects with both their longing for home and a longing for life direction. In the film twenty-six-year-old Andrew Largeman, who is motivated by his mother's death, finds his way back home to New Jersey. But this film is not just about a rootless guy returning home. It's about trying to define where his life is going. It is through a young woman who has discovered meaning through suffering that Andrew begins to find new direction for his own life.

"All of life is a coming home," reflects Robin Williams in the opening soliloquy of the film *Patch Adams*. "Salesmen, secretaries, coal miners, beekeepers, sword swallowers . . . all of us, the restless hearts of the world, trying to find a way home." He adds, "Home . . . the dictionary defines it as a place of origin or a goal or destination."

At the very center of our Christian story is the strong belief that the Redeemer God will bring all God's children safely home. In fact the Bible is filled with imagery of homecoming. I will show in this conversation and the next that many of us have unwittingly embraced a narrow, spiritualized eschatology that is so other worldly that it has almost no influence on shaping our notions of what constitutes the good life and better future in the here and now. As a consequence too many of us have allowed the storytellers of the global mall to largely define our sense of what is important and of value.

Christians have had an ongoing discussion about the relationship of faith to culture that often revolves around the discussion in the seminal book *Christ and Culture* by Richard Niebuhr. The major options he offers us are "Christ above culture," "Christ against culture" and "Christ transforming culture." I am drawn, as theologian John Stackhouse is, to a fourth option that has had less discussion: "Christ and culture in paradox." Stackhouse writes, "God has called us to lives of difficult paradox, of painful negotiation between conflicting and competitive values, of seeking to cooperate with God wherever he is at work. Such a position, full of ambiguity and irony, is also full of faith and hope: 'In all these things we are more than conquerors' (Rom. 8:37)."[2] As we struggle to live our lives in the difficult

---

[2]John G. Stackhouse Jr., "In the World, but . . ." *Christianity Today,* April 22, 2002.

paradox of competing values, we still have the biblical responsibility to define where values of faith and culture seem to be in tension. My intent is not to revisit this lengthy discussion about faith and culture but instead to focus narrowly on a single question: to what extent have we allowed modern culture, as magnified through the global mall, to define our notion of what constitutes the good life and better future?

DANCING WITH CULTURE: RELEVANT OR RESISTANT?

Lauren Winner, author of *Girl Meets God*, asks the very important question, "How do you simultaneously attend to the culture and be a pocket of resistance?"[3] Emerging church leaders are frequently brilliant at finding innovative ways to engage certain segments of modern and postmodern culture. But many offer little critique of how the culture shapes our lives and values. A number seem to operate as detached curators of worship, borrowing intriguing cultural bits without fully recognizing how we are all being significantly shaped by that culture.[4] Scott Bader-Saye, in an article in *The Christian Century* called "Emergent Matrix," adds a key insight: "The emerging church, to be anything more than a hip blip on the radar of American religion, will need to live the tension of 'relevant-resistant' no less than it lives the tension of 'ancient-future.' "[5]

A number of missional church scholars offer thoughtful intellectual critiques of modern culture and the ways that economic globalization influences the values of believers everywhere. However, very few churches that fly under the missional church banner seem to feature discipleship resources any different from those used by either traditional churches or megachurches. These resources rarely mention altering either our cultural values or our lifestyles to become a more missional people.

Writers in the mosaic stream offer a much more robust critique of the

---

[3]Lauren Winner, *Girl Meets God: A Memoir*, as quoted by Scott Bader-Saye, "The Emergent Matrix: A New Kind of Church?" *The Christian Century*, November 30, 2004, p. 25.

[4]In fairness, I do have friends in the emerging stream, such as Mark Scandrette, who do vigorously deconstruct the dominant culture.

[5]Bader-Saye, "Emergent Matrix," p. 25.

dominant culture. Manny Ortiz reflects, "Like our Euro-American brothers and sisters, we too have assumed that the 'good' aspect of being an American is the Christian part, and that becoming more a part of Middle America is to be more Christian."[6]

Efrem Smith, pastor of Sanctuary Church in Minneapolis, says he struggles with at least three ways the Euro-centric American dream influences people in his multicultural congregation. First, he struggles with the white values of individualism, privilege, consumerism and buying a home in a "safe" neighborhood. Second, he is troubled by the fact that the driven consumerism of the dominant culture is celebrated by a number of African American congregations that have bought into the prosperity gospel. Finally, he grapples with the materialism and bling bling of hip-hop celebrity culture that influences many of his young people.

Many in the monastic stream, since they often live with the poor, involve themselves in ancient spiritual practices and live simpler lifestyles. They tend to be outspoken regarding the pervasive influence of the global consumer culture and its impact on their lives, the poor and the environment. For example, Shane Claiborne states that the story about the rich young ruler is not about whether God welcomes rich folks home or not. It is a description of the character of God's new kingdom. God's "economy is diametrically opposed to that of the world. Rather than accumulating stuff for oneself, followers of Jesus abandon everything, trusting God alone for providence."[7] Like Shane, we need to learn to use Scripture not just for our spiritual lives but to decode the bogus cultural messages that the good life will be found in accumulating more.

DECODING THE REIGNING MYTHOLOGY

As we struggle to find our way home to the best God has for us, it is important to recognize that all of our lives are connected to complex networks of

---

[6]Manuel Ortiz, *The Hispanic Challenge: Opportunities Confronting the Church* (Downers Grove, Ill.: InterVarsity Press, 1993), p. 107.
[7]Shane Claiborne, *The Irresistible Revolution: Living as an Ordinary Radical* (Grand Rapids: Zondervan, 2006), p. 174.

stories and cultures. There is not space to deal with how these many different stories shape who we are or how God will redeem parts of our stories and the cultures to which we have belonged. My concern is that some of these stories, born of modernity and powerfully marketed into our lives through the imperial mall, begin to eclipse the ancient story and the future hope to which we have allegedly given our lives.

I find very few resources to help those of Christian faith decode the messages being transmitted into our lives, congregations and communities about what constitutes the good life—a life worth coming home to. To respond to this need, Christine and I created a little exercise called "high status/extreme cool" to assist different generations in discovering how their notion of the good life and better future are shaped by mythmakers of the global marketplace. We divide the group by age, asking the over-forties to make a list of what is "high status" in their community, and the under-forties to list what is "extreme cool" among their peers. It is always immediately apparent to participants that we are asking them to define notions of what constitutes the good life across the generational divide.

We have found that the good life for the over-forties tends to focus more on palatial display and symbols of success and status. Their list typically includes gargantuan trophy homes with at least a four-car garage on the water's edge, second homes at resort locations, Jaguars, Mercedes, SUVs and luxury motor homes, memberships in the local country club, and holidays on the Riviera or cruise holidays to the Bahamas. Of course, their young are enrolled in prestigious academies and universities and are free to wander the world on their parents' plastic.

For the under-forties, the good life, not surprisingly, has more to do with edgy postmodern experiences, image, style and ever-expanding consumer choice. They mention living downtown in a loft in the middle of the active nightlife of upscale restaurants, concerts and theater. They drive everything from customized Mini Minors to Hummers, buy the latest tech toys, like iPhones and BlackBerries, and do extreme sports in New Zealand or the Alps. They have a passion for fashion, image and brands—from retro-garb, piercings and tattoos to Abercrombie & Fitch,

Tommy Hilfiger, Old Navy and celebrity-look-a-like apparel.

When we conduct these sessions in churches, we are very surprised to discover, in virtually every case, that this was the first time participants had ever talked about "cultural stuff" at church. The other thing that always happens is that as people make their lists, the energy level in the room visibly soars. Some people virtually levitate. Even though most of the participants don't own a lot of this stuff, it is clearly important to them. Why is this? Didn't someone once say something about where our hearts are?

CULTURE CRITIQUE, A BLIND SPOT?

Why don't we discuss the influences of the values of the dominant culture at church? Why don't we discuss the stories so many of us buy into and their influence on us and our kids? Why don't we explore the major role these stories play in defining our notions of the good life to which we aspire to come home?

I think part of the answer is that the Western church has historically taken a limited view of conversion. In most churches we are taught that following Christ involves transforming our spiritual lives and our moral values and helping us with our relationships. We rarely hear that God might want to transform our cultural values too. Part of the reason for this is that too many of us have been conditioned to unconsciously baptize those values instead of question them.

Let me give you one concrete example. Christian parents want what's best for their kids. No problem there. However, because of the huge influence of modern culture, most parents tend to define "what's best" primarily in economic terms. As we have worked on college campuses, the number-one barrier students report that restrains them from going into missions, believe it or not, is their Christian parents. The message is, "I did not spend $80 thousand on your education for you to head off to a refugee project in Ethiopia. You get your career under way, buy your home, your car, start investing in retirement accounts, and then after you are established, you can visit mission projects in Africa during your vacation."

TWO COMPETING VISIONS OF COMING HOME

Many sincere Christians succumb to two very different images of the future they want to come home to, neither of which is biblical. The first is making our home in the new global mall and getting "a piece of the rock" while the getting is still good. The second is waiting for our souls to be rescued when things go bad. The first image lacks a vision that calls us beyond ourselves. The second is a Greek vision of coming home as individual disembodied souls being rescued for a nonmaterial existence in the clouds. Lesslie Newbigin asserts, "For a biblical writer, continued existence as a disembodied soul is not something to be desired but feared with loathing."[8]

My concern is that the imagery of "individual soul escape" disconnects eschatology from daily life and the urgent challenges that fill God's world. These images may motivate some to try and get more souls into the lifeboats, but rarely do they seem to motivate followers of Jesus to engage the urgent societal issues troubling the planet. Many who embrace this vision of coming home as disembodied spirits also gravitate toward a compartmentalized private faith largely disconnected from real life. Since passively waiting for soul rescue gives very little motivation for our daily lives, it is understandable that numbers of Christians would be inclined to live into other stories that offer more immediate opportunities to experience the notions of the good life advertised by the global mall.

Glen Stassen and David Gushee, in their foundational work *Kingdom Ethics*, argue that

> when Jesus' way of discipleship is thinned down, marginalized or avoided, then churches and Christians lose their antibodies against infection by secular ideologies that manipulate Christians into serving some other lord. We fear precisely that kind of idolatry now.[9]

---

[8]Lesslie Newbigin, "Cross-currents in Ecumenical and Evangelical Understandings of Mission," *International Bulletin of Missionary Research* 6, no. 4 (1982): 149.
[9]Glen H. Stassen and David P. Gushee, *Kingdom Ethics: Following Jesus in Contemporary Context* (Downers Grove, Ill.: InterVarsity Press, 2003), p. 11.

Rodney Clapp traces the roots of this compartmentalized piety back to the inauguration of the Christendom Church in the time of Roman emperor Constantine, and the easy accommodation that fourth-century Christians made with both culture and the state. "In a real sense, then, it becomes fine and commendable for professing Christians to participate in the state and other realms of culture as if the Lordship of Christ made no concrete difference."[10] Clapp goes on to suggest that the reformers "were emphatically right to appeal to the scriptural Word," but they failed to question this "Constantinian synthesis itself and thus inadvertently 'created modern secularism.'" What this means, to borrow from the words of theologian John Milbank, is that the Reformation "completely privatized, spiritualized and transcendentalized the sacred."[11]

EMBRACING A SECULAR ESCHATOLOGY?

Those who, over the centuries, were nurtured in a more "privatized, spiritualized and transcendentalized" view of the "sacred" became more open to embracing much of the worldview of modernity to make sense of life in the "real" world. The Enlightenment not only offered a compelling new myth to make sense of our world, but it also offered us new imagery of the better future we are invited to come home to—a new secular salvation.

In fact the optimistic imagery of a better future of never-ending economic, technological and social progress at the center of Western culture is a product of modernity and the Enlightenment project. Essentially the storytellers of the Enlightenment took the vertical quest for God's kingdom, which had been a centerpiece of European culture, and turned it on its side. It became the horizontal pursuit of Western progress, technological mastery and economic growth. This optimistic view of progress is an integral component in neoliberal economic theory and, of course, the vision that powers the imperial global mall. In his critique of conservative American economists, Robert Nelson writes, "Economic progress is so

---

[10]Rodney Clapp, *A Peculiar People: The Church as Culture in a Post-Christian Society* (Downers Grove, Ill.: InterVarsity Press, 1999), p. 26.
[11]Ibid., pp. 28-29.

important because progress is seen as the path to the attainment of a heaven on earth, to a secular salvation."[12] I am certain that he is right. We call this vision of a better future the Western Dream or the American Dream.

Since this vision for the better future is defined primarily in economic terms, it shouldn't be a surprise that God's creation and, indeed, humanity are both seen largely in economic terms as well. God's good creation is seen as nothing more than provision of the resources needed to achieve this dream. In this view persons are seen as largely deriving our sense of identity, self-worth and even life purpose in economic terms—how well we play our roles as producers/consumers. Since the ultimate is defined largely in economic terms and because economic forces run the world, there is obviously little room left for God. Those of us who choose to believe in God are encouraged to view him as an absentee landlord who may come to our Bible studies and prayer meetings but who doesn't have a great deal to do with what is happening in the "real" world.

Brian Walsh and Sylvia Keesmaat see diverse messages "all telling the same story. . . . Economic growth is the driving force of history, consumer choice is what makes us human, and greed is normal. If we live in an empire, it is an empire of global consumerism."[13] To the extent we give our lives to images of the good life fashioned for us by global consumerism, we not only miss God's best for our lives but often become caught up in what the Old Testament calls idolatry.

In the helpful book *Christianity Incorporated: How Big Business Is Buying the Church*, Michael Budde and Robert Brimlow argue convincingly that the Western church has largely become a chaplain to modern culture and the global economy, tending to sanction its aspirations and values instead of questioning them. "We see the transformation of the church into a caricature of its best self . . . a church that has bent to capitalism and economic

---

[12]Robert H. Nelson, *Economics as Religion: From Samuelson to Chicago and Beyond* (University Park: Pennsylvania State University Press, 2001), p. 9.
[13]Brian J. Walsh and Sylvia C. Keesmaat, *Colossians Remixed: Subverting the Empire* (Downers Grove, Ill.: InterVarsity Press, 2004), p. 85.

power so long that its own practices and beliefs become shaped by the corporate form and spirit."[14]

Of course the most pronounced expression of the church being domesticated by modern culture is the prosperity gospel movement—an American invention that has, regrettably, been exported all over the planet. I am convinced that the real origin of the prosperity gospel is not found primarily in Scripture or the church but rather in the writings of Ben Franklin, who wasn't a Christian but a deist. Franklin was deeply committed, as evidenced in his autobiography, to the vigorous pursuit of wealth. He offered his own story of rising from rags to riches as one that others should seek to emulate. In his *Poor Richard's Almanac*, which was read by more people in the American colonies than any other work except the Bible, he offers a new secular set of moral teachings that had remarkable influence in society, including among those of Christian faith. Franklin criticized the Puritans because they taught that the goal of life is virtue; in his secular revision of their teachings he insisted that virtue isn't the goal of life but the "means." If one is virtuous then one will achieve the "real" goal of life—wealth and prosperity. Sound familiar?

Please understand that the part of the prosperity gospel's message to those at the margins that expresses God's love for them and his desire to see their circumstances improve is biblical. The part I struggle with is the tendency of many prosperity preachers to uncritically promote the notions of the good life and better future heralded by the global mall. Essentially what I think they are doing is asserting that when Jesus promises us an "abundant life," he really means we should expect God to give us all the goodies in the modern global mall as an expression of his love for us. This gospel tends to baptize the Enlightenment value of the pursuit of self-interest instead of calling us to give our lives and resources in service to God and others. The lives of wealthy preachers become blazing advertisements for the global mall instead of the gospel of the cross and kingdom. Obviously lifestyles of affluence also siphon off huge amounts of resources

---

[14]Michael L. Budde and Robert W. Brimlow, *Christianity Incorporated: How Big Business Is Buying the Church* (Grand Rapids: Brazos Press, 2002), pp. 1-24.

that could be invested in enabling our poorest neighbors to achieve a decent way of life for themselves and their families.

It is important to recognize though that not only those involved in the prosperity gospel but many of the rest of us in the church have uncritically embraced the Western dream as God's dream. Somehow we haven't realized that it enshrines individualism and the pursuit of self-interest, defining the good life in largely economic terms, as the individual pursuit of more—more economic upscaling, more choices and more experiences.

Postmodernity calls into question many of the fundamental assumptions of modernity and is more open to considering the spiritual nature of our world. However, I find that those operating from a postmodern viewpoint are often just as caught up in the consumer culture as everyone else, albeit for different reasons. Steve Taylor, in his thoughtful book *The Out of Bounds Church?* writes about the postmodern experiential understanding of life in the global mall:

> Identity and lifestyle walk hand-in-hand through the malls that define contemporary culture. . . . It is at the mall that you pick and mix your lifestyle. At the same time, the selection isn't as individualized as it sounds. The choices are still pre-selected by powers outside of our control.[15]

In a million different ways, the storytellers of this global mall seek to convince us that making our home in their stories will satisfy our needs for love, acceptance, community, significance, self-worth and even meaning.

COMING HOME TO THE WORLD OF HIGH FASHION

The fashion industry is at the forefront of this campaign to influence us and our young to more fully buy into their fables. The film *The Devil Wears Prada*, for example, brilliantly profiles the stratospheric world of high fashion. Andrea, a small-town girl right out of college hoping to ultimately receive a recommendation that will allow her to work for any mag-

---

[15]Steve Taylor, *The Out of Bounds Church? Learning to Create a Community of Faith in a Culture of Change* (Grand Rapids: Zondervan, 2005), p. 25.

azine she chooses, lands a job that many of her peers would kill for: she is hired as an assistant to Miranda Priestly, the highly successful, highly demanding editor of *Runway* magazine.

From her first day on the job, her stylish coworkers take every occasion to communicate to Andrea that she looks like a fashion disaster. She clearly doesn't fit in this story. Slowly Andy responds by not only catching up but surpassing many of her colleagues at *Runway*. She rises to every work challenge and endures the incredible abuse Miranda dishes out twenty-four hours a day.

As the film ends, Andrea realizes the cost of her aggressive career pursuit. She is near total physical and emotional burnout. Suddenly she realizes that by succumbing to the relentless seduction of life in a story that insists her worth is defined by style and image, she has unwittingly put her relationships and soul at risk. She became all she despised by making her home in this alien story.

When Miranda learns Andrea is quitting, she asks incredulously why she would want to do that. "Everyone wants this," says Miranda. "Everyone wants to be us!" As fashion and style is successfully marketed in small towns and even to the very young, growing numbers want to call this kind of life home.

COLONIZING THE IMAGINATIONS OF THE YOUNG

The Merchants of Cool, a *Frontline* documentary, reveals that corporations have mounted an unprecedented campaign "to colonize" the imagination of the largest teen generation in American history—32 million strong. This generation reportedly controls $450 billion in spending. The documentary portrays the huge investment corporations make to study and carefully dissect this generation.

The elitist world of high fashion is seeking to get a grip on this generation through TV shows like *Project Runway*. It pulled 3.4 million viewers for its second season finale in 2006.[16] Growing numbers of even the Christian

---

[16]Ann Oldenburg, "TV Brings High Fashion Down to the Everyday," *USA Today*, July 12, 2006, p. 1.

young are choosing to make their home in the illusory world of high fashion that is often connected to the seduction of celebrity culture. They seem
to accept the message that their sense of value is largely defined by their appearance, style and image. *The New York Times Style Magazine* candidly reports, "These days our identities hang by a thread, which may be why the
pull of fashion on our imaginations is stronger than ever and why celebrity
stylists have become our latest gurus."[17]

A major vehicle for influencing the young all over the planet to aspire to
image, style and adoration of the global celebrity cult is the TV show *American Idol. Idol* now airs in thirty-nine countries and on every continent except
Antarctica. The franchise has logged over two billion votes for its contes-
tants.[18] It is an integral part of the borderless global youth culture mentioned earlier.

The young from Brazil to China aspire to enter the illusional world of
pop culture as its new celebrities. " 'Performer heroes' are, in the end, all
about us. They don't summon us to serve a cause. . . . In the final rounds,
a fan becomes an idol; the ultimate dream of our age comes true before our
eyes and in our hearts."[19] Is the good life really fifteen minutes of fame or
shame on some reality show?

One of the hottest trends among the marketers of cool is called "age
compression." Sex, style and violence are pitched to kids at a younger age
than ever before. Violent video games are marketed to younger and younger
boys. Clothing for preschool girls focuses on appearance, fashion, style
and sexuality, often using young female celebs to demonstrate how to
flaunt it. The message in this story couldn't be clearer: your appearance,
your body and your sexuality matter most if you want to succeed with boys
and in an increasingly appearance-obsessed society.

Just how did these merchants of cool, these storytellers of the global

[17]Daphne Merkin, "Baby Got Back Hair," *The New York Times Style Magazine*, August
27, 2006, p. 186.
[18]Lorraine Ali, "'Idol' Airs in Every Continent But Antarctica," *Newsweek,* July 2-9,
2007, p. 67.
[19]Thomas de Zengotita, "Why We Worship 'American Idol,'" *Christian Science Monitor,* February 17, 2006, p. 9.

mall, so successfully shape the tastes of our young? *The Merchants of Cool* reveals that corporations have mounted an unprecedented campaign to "colonize" the imagination of the teen generation, investing heavily into studying and carefully dissecting youth culture to discover how to influence them to spend their money.

"Cool hunters," like anthropologists, search youth cultures and use the early teen trendsetters to design new products and fashion new marketing schemes to hook the young. The average American teen is blitzed with three thousand ads a day—ten million by the time they reach age eighteen. They are bombarded by TV, the web and "viral" ads; meanwhile corporate films flood public and private schools, even beaming their commercials into our kids' classrooms.

Increasingly the merchants of cool find new, stealth techniques to both influence and encircle our young. They use their friends, acquaintances, buzz groups, sleepovers and even youth groups to display examples of the latest glam fashions, cosmetics and technologies. Then they pay cool kids to persuade their friends to become "cool insiders" by purchasing the cool products. Marketers even use stories of rebellion and anarchy to sell their wares.

In her important book *Born to Buy*, Juliet Schor observes, "Marketers have defined cool as the key to social success, as what matters for determining who belongs, who's popular, and who gets accepted by peers."[20] While undoubtedly the desire for social acceptance is a central theme for all kids as they grow up, the marketers in this story elevate social acceptance to be essential to one's very existence. They unhesitatingly use the threat of social exclusion as a club to influence the young to conform and buy their "cool" brands. "'Cool' is the opiate of our time. . . . We have grown dependent on it to maintain our identities of inclusion."[21]

If you watch their ads, you see that merchants of cool don't just market the opportunity to be an insider. They also communicate that the young

[20]Juliet B. Schor, *Born to Buy: The Commercialized Child and the New Consumer Culture* (New York: Scribner, 2005), p. 47.
[21]Kalle Lasn, *Culture Jam: How to Reverse America's Suicidal Consumer Binge, and Why We Must* (New York: Quill, 2000), p. 113.

can find their sense of identity, self-worth, life purpose and even spirituality by living in the fictional stories these corporate storytellers of cool
create for them.

"Marketers convey the view that wealth and the aspiration to wealth is
the new cool. Material excess, having lots of money, career achievement,
and a lifestyle to go with it are all highly valued in the marketing world's definition of what's hot and what's not," writes Schor.[22] The fashion industry
is on the forefront of institutions that attempt to persuade the young toward more extravagant luxury tastes.

Is this definition of cool as the pursuit of a life of wealth and material
excess actually influencing our youth? According to an annual snapshot of
the views and values of freshmen entering college in the United States, it
certainly has an impact. Reportedly three in four freshmen "now consider
it 'very important' or 'essential' that they become 'very well off financially.'
That is nearly double the number that expressed the view in 1970. Finding
'a meaningful philosophy of life' was the big winner among students back
then."[23] If these storytellers of cool succeed in influencing the young to
make their homes in the make-believe world of glam fashion, celebrity
look-alikes and material excess, then selling them their wares will be a
piece of cake.

MARKETING COOL TO ALL GENERATIONS

The marketers of this new global economy haven't studied adults quite as in-
tensively as the young, but you would be amazed at how much information
they collect, on everything from our car preferences to our political views.
They even place us in cluster groups of consumers with similar preferences
such as "suburban settlers." They know exactly how to get our attention, stir
up our envy, and influence us to buy into their stories and products.

Essentially the marketers of McWorld are seeking to convince adults

---

[22]Schor, *Born to Buy*, p. 48.
[23]David G. Myers, "The Disconnect Between Wealth and Well-Being: It's Not the
Economy Stupid," *Edge: The Third Culture*, accessed January 26, 2007, at
<www.edge.org/3rd_culture/story/54.html>.

everywhere on the planet to embrace a new definition of the good life as one of high status, high fashion and high living. We are invited to live into a story where we enjoy the luxurious lifestyles once reserved for the super-rich, whether we can afford it or not. And it is working.

I find a growing number of Christians are as caught up in living as palatially as their neighbors, with very little concern about its impact on the environment or on how these lifestyle choices draw both their time and resources away from the work of God's quiet conspiracy.

Michael Silverstein, author of *Trading Up: The New American Luxury*, predicts, "We're convinced that this market will grow from $440 billion to $1 trillion by 2010 and that it's recession-proof. Consumers tell us that when times are bad, it's more important to have two or three luxury goods."[24]

The marketers of McWorld use the same stories to hook adults that merchants of cool use on our young. First they seek to persuade us that they alone can help us find the sense of self-worth, status and esteem we seek if we buy into their notions of what constitutes the good life and a better future. However, as with our young, there are costs to those who succumb to these fables. One of the greatest costs of succumbing to these messages, in addition to becoming more involved in new technologies, is the creation of an increasingly hyper-individualistic society in which concern for others is being seriously eroded.

Australian authors Clive Hamilton and Richard Denniss caution that we will wind up becoming not only more individualistic, but more insecure as well. We will also tend to have less healthy relationships and a declining sense of well-being. "In modern Australia, the gap between our actual selves and ideal selves is widening. We are urged to aspire to a better, slimmer, richer, more sophisticated real self, and that ideal self is increasingly becoming an exterior one."[25] And this "ideal self" is constantly being told

---

[24]Quoted in Kate Betts, "Luxury Fever," *Time Magazine Online*, September 14, 2004, accessed January 26, 2007, at <www.time.com/time/magazine/article/0,9171,995123,00 .html>.

[25]Clive Hamilton and Richard Denniss, *Affluenza: When Too Much Is Never Enough* (Crowns Nest, Australia: Allen and Unwin, 2005), pp. 13-15.

it needs to be at the front of every pack to inspire peer envy. Juliet Schor points out the inherent problem of trying to consume our way to the front of the pack: "The difficulty is the dynamic aspect of keeping up: the emulation process never ends."[26]

"Despite the barrage of advertising that tries to tell us otherwise, the more materialistic we are, the less free we are," insist Hamilton and Denniss. "Why? Because we must commit more of our lives to working for our material desires. And the more acquisitive people derive their sense of identity and their imagined place in society from the things they own, yet the symbols that confer that self-worth and status are at the whim of external forces—of fashion."[27]

COMING HOME TO A FABRICATED FUTURE
In the early moments of the 1998 film *The Truman Show*, Truman Burbank is living a very familiar portrayal of the good life. He seems very much at home in this idyllic island community. Later we discover that a corporation adopted him at birth to offer the public the pinnacle achievement of reality TV: every intimate moment of Truman's life is on display, scripted around a whirl of product placements and endorsements.

Slowly Truman discovers that something is seriously awry when he tries to leave his idyllic home. He wakes up to find his life is manipulated in ways he never imagined, and he finally escapes the world that was scripted for him. Cristoff, the fictional producer of the television show has a telling line: "We accept the reality of the world which we are presented."

I suspect that many of us are, like Truman, largely oblivious to the fact that much of life is scripted more than we recognize. I am not suggesting anything sinister or conspiratorial. I am certain, however, that there is a direct link between declining religious participation of Western Christians and the growing investment of our lives and resources into these fables that others have fashioned for us. In the film *The Matrix*, Morpheus

---

[26]Juliet B. Schor, *The Overspent American: Why We Want What We Don't Need* (New York: Harper Perennial, 1998), p. 98.
[27]Hamilton and Denniss, *Affluenza*, p. 15.

warns Neo that "a reality is being pulled down over your head and you don't even realize it."

TAKING BACK OUR IMAGINATIONS

In other days advertisers simply gave us information as to why their product was better than their competitors, and consumerism was seen as simply making a rational choice to purchase the better product. British sociologist Colin Campbell argues that marketers over the years recognized that people need transcendence and meaning, and moved beyond simply trying to sell us commodities to colonize our imaginations. They created fictional narratives around their products and invited us to live in these mythical tales.[28]

The CEO of Gucci, for example, declared luxury items are "more than goods. . . . They give people the opportunity to live a dream."[29] In other words, if we make our homes in these dreams, we will we finally attain the sense of significance and self-worth we long for.

Decoding culture. Several years ago, I asked a conference of U.S. Christian publishers, "Who are the other 'educators' who are educating our youth? What are their messages, what are their methods, and how successfully are they shaping the identities, desires, values and dreams of our young people?"

Given the huge and expanding influence of the merchants of cool in the lives of our young, I seriously question how much real formation we do an hour or so a week in Sunday school, or even with a little more time in our youth groups. If we are serious about the formation of our youth, we will need to enable them to become much more skilled in decoding the messages from the mall. But we will need to spend much more time in doing formation that enables them not only to grow spiritually but also to discover how God can use their mustard seeds to make a little difference in the world.

---

[28]Colin Campbell, *The Romantic Ethic and the Spirit of Modern Consumerism* (London: Blackwell, 1987).
[29]Ibid, p. 13.

There are a few Christian groups that offer us and our young resources to decode the messages coming at us from the global mall. For example, one that those in the monastic stream love is *Geez Magazine*, produced in Manitoba, Canada. This magazine prophetically challenges the aspirations and values of the imperial economy in a range of ways. In its issue on consumerism, "The Lighter Side of Less," readers are reminded of the extraordinarily high costs of our constant pursuit of more in our own lives, in the lives of our poorest neighbors and in creation itself.[30] Check out Geez's campaign "To Make Affluence History" (www.geezmagazine.org/affluence/).

Alternatives for Simple Living (www.simpleliving.org) not only provides resources to decode messages from the mall, the organization also provides a host of alternative resources for worship and celebration on themes of social justice and creation care, plus alternative Christmas celebrations. I am surprised how few emerging leaders have found this resource.

I hope you understand by this time that I am not simply attempting to persuade Christians to consume less. I am inviting followers of Jesus to do the hard work of decoding the cultural influences in our lives and the lives of our young. But I am also concerned at how the marketers of McWorld are even seeking to shape our views of spirituality.

Challenging the imperial claim to define reality. In her classic *No Logo*, Naomi Klein suggests that the marketers of our new global economy are not only the arbiters of cool, but increasingly they are also "brokers of meaning." She argues that as corporations moved into the era of branding, they intentionally infused their brands with a sense of transcendence in order to sell their products. And it worked. More and more frequently, we purchase everything—from tennis shoes to iPods—that offers us a new way of life, a new experience, a sense of meaning or a purpose to live that transcends the ordinary.[31]

Vincent Miller, in his important book *Consuming Religion*, states this should be a serious concern for those of Christian faith. "By exploiting the

---

[30]"The Lighter Side of Less," *Geez: Holy Mischief in an Age of Fast Faith* 2 (Spring 2006).
[31]Naomi Klein, *No Logo* (New York: Picador, 2000), p. 21-23.

human desire for meaning and belonging, marketers could be said to be positioning their products to compete with religion."[32] The merchants of the imperial mall have invaded the sacred groves of religion often, even appropriating and reinterpreting our own religious symbols to sell us their wares.

A central characteristic of every empire, from the military empire of Rome to the cyber-empire of the global marketplace, is the need to fashion "powerful myths" about the nature of reality and human destiny. Empires ancient and modern have always sought to influence God's people to give our lives to a story and a destiny that is clearly at counterpoint to the biblical story.

To counter the imperial colonization of our imaginations, we need poets, prophets and artists to help us create subversive imagery that challenges the reigning reality. Walter Brueggeman reminds us that the people of Israel challenged the powerful myths of the Babylonian Empire by the subversive power of poetic imagination and began to conjure a very different vision of the future. "The outcome of such poetry is hope. It is hope that makes community possible on the way out of the empire."[33]

Alan Roxburgh, who works with both emerging and missional leaders, observes that, as a direct result of living in exile in the Babylonian Empire, the Jews reentered "their primary stories and traditions from a radical new perspective. . . . Only in this ambiguous location did they discern both the nature of God and the possible future God intended for them."[34] As those living in exile in this global empire, we too can find our way home by reentering our ancient story and rediscovering a new vision of our future hope.

Brian Walsh and Sylvia Keesmaat remind us,

Israel understood the dynamics of empire and imagination and always had a counterplan. In the shadow of empire, Israel's prophets

---

[32]Vincent J. Miller, *Consuming Religion: Christian Faith and Practice in a Consumer Culture* (New York: Continuum, 2004), p. 88.
[33]Walter Brueggemann, *Hopeful Imagination: Prophetic Voices in Exile* (Philadelphia: Fortress Press, 1986), p. 196-97.
[34]Alan J. Roxburgh, *The Sky Is Falling: Leaders Lost in Transition* (Eagle, Id.: ACI Publishing, 2005), p. 74.

wrote evocative and subversive poetry that wove together images of homecoming [and] restoration . . . and a coming Messiah who would do a new thing.[35]

In the next conversation, we will explore the biblical imagery of home-coming and restoration by reentering God's story. We will encounter the coming of a Messiah who does a surprising new thing that both heals the past and offers hope for our turbulent future.

JOIN THE CONVERSATION

- In what specific ways have you seen the marketers of the global mall influencing the aspirations and values of both youth and adults in your congregation or community?

- What are some of the specific notions of the good life and better future promoted by the global mall?

- Imagine one creative way to help either youth or adults to decode, with humor, the messages being sent to us by the global mall.

---

[35]Brian J. Walsh and Sylvia C. Keesmaat, *Colossians Remixed: Subverting the Empire* (Downers Grove, Ill.: InterVarsity Press, 2004), p. 82.

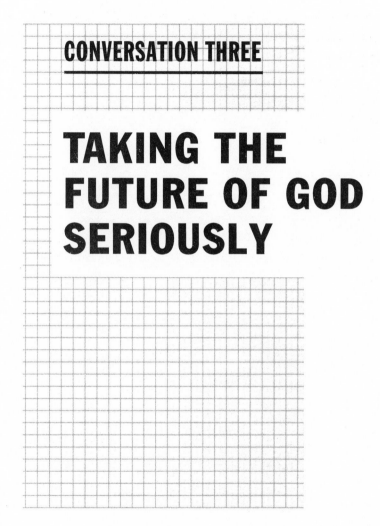

CONVERSATION THREE

TAKING THE FUTURE OF GOD SERIOUSLY

COMING HOME TO
THE GOOD LIFE OF GOD

Is it possible that the Bible's imagery of coming home to the kingdom of God is not simply a theology we salute on Sunday but a new reason to get out of bed on Monday—a new "cultural" vision of the good life and better future that reflects God's loving purposes for a people and a world?

Since the tragedy of September 11, 2001, immigrants from Ireland have been returning to their homeland in record numbers from the United States and other countries. Many are illegal immigrants and find they are under much more scrutiny since 9/11. Irish immigrants have also been motivated to return home by the booming economy in Ireland, which is part of the global economic lift-off.

One of the places feeling the impact of this exodus is a small, improbable Irish village in the Bronx. Some immigrants actually cure Irish bacon in their basements. You can find chives bramble jelly in their shops, but you can't find nearly as many Irish in this village's pubs as even a couple of years ago.[1]

The Padded Wagon, a container-moving firm that serves those returning home to Ireland, reported that some of the returnees are in such a hurry that they are afflicted by near terminal memory loss. One couple completely packed their container, and the Padded Wagon transported it to the shipping dock. Just before it was due to be loaded, the couple discovered that they had inadvertently packed their passports in the container. They had to

---

[1]Ellen Berry, "Irish Are Returning Home," *Gulf News*, March 9, 2006, accessed January 26, 2007, at <http://archive.gulfnews.com/articles/06/03/09/10024085.html>.

BEGINNINGS

Earlier I quoted Patch Adams: "All of life is a coming home." As we have seen, the storytellers of the new global economy are seeking to influence us not only to live into their fables but to accept their destination for our lives. They want us to embrace their notions of the good life and better future.

In this conversation we'll go back to the Bible to rediscover new imagery of coming home to the kingdom of God—not simply as a theology we salute on Sunday but as a more motivating reason to get out of bed on Monday. I will urge you to rediscover the kingdom as a new "cultural" vision of the good life and better future that reflects something of God's loving purposes for a people and a world.

I will also attempt to offer an eschatological vision that much more directly connects to the urgent issues filling our world and more intentionally informs the direction and daily decisions of our lives. I will argue that to the extent we embrace this vision, we will have the possibility of experiencing a more vital whole-life faith. We will also find our lives much more caught up in the conspiracy that is quietly changing our world.

I am not attempting to do in-depth theological work in this conversation, but rather am taking a more of a narrative approach, seeking to highlight and contemporize some of the important biblical images of the world that is breaking into and redeeming this one.

---

rush down to the loading dock and completely unpack and repack the container to reclaim their passports. Flaming expletives could be heard along the entire length of the wharf as they dug through their container.

Since the great potato famine of the late nineteenth century, no other people in Europe have left home in such large numbers as the Irish. Their music is filled with lyrics longing for home. Plays like *The Long Journey Home*, by Eugene O'Neill, capture that sense of almost mystical reverence for return to Eire. Now Ireland's record-breaking economic boom is leading the European Union and making it possible for many to return home and reconnect with their families.

A surprising number of South Africans are also trying to find their way home. A website called Homecoming Revolution celebrates and welcomes people who return to South Africa to be a part of the "miracle" that began with the leadership of Nelson Mandela and the remarkable work of the Truth and Reconciliation Commission. Colin Hundermark, a repatriate of this homecoming revolution, is particularly concerned with South African children either orphaned by or infected with AIDS.

I knew I couldn't make a difference in the lives of South African children from London. Most people can give money, but that wasn't enough for me. I wanted to make a difference that I could see with my own eyes, touch with my own hands and feel with my own heart! South Africa's future is as promising as you want to make it. You have to be here to make dreams for South Africa come true.[2]

Some people are trying to find their way back home to reconnect to family. Some are trying to capitalize on economic opportunities, while others are returning home to try and make a difference.

TAKING ESCHATOLOGY SERIOUSLY

As I suggested in the last conversation, I suspect numbers of us have been nurtured in a highly spiritualized eschatology that focuses on escape to a nonmaterial world "up there." As a consequence we tend to wind up with an eschatology that is largely divorced from the urgent issues that fill our world and a pietism largely disconnected from the important decisions of our real lives. Not surprisingly, Christians of this persuasion tend to have a very limited view of the language and imagery of God's kingdom.

I find many are searching for a biblical alternative to the popular "end times" imagery of coming home as disembodied spirits—leaving clothes

[2]"Homecomers: Colin Hundermark," Homecoming Revolution, accessed January 26, 2007, at <http://www.homecomingrevolution.co.za/index.php?page=2&category_id=35&related_id=138>.

behind on airplane seats. I also find that Christians are weary of giving their lives to the mad economic race to the top. I think even those outside the faith are searching for a different dream—a dream that calls us beyond ourselves.

Numbers of those involved in the emerging, missional, mosaic and monastic streams offer us a much broader kingdom vision. Eddie Gibbs and Ryan Bolger state that a focus on the kingdom of God is a major characteristic of both the U.S. and U.K. emerging church movements.

> The idea of a kingdom focus instead of a church focus is a major paradigm shift, one that does not come easily. But emerging church leaders are getting the message across. The gospel of emerging churches is not confined to personal salvation; it is social transformation arising from the presence and permeation of the reign of Christ.[3]

Deep within us is a longing to return home to the best we can remember and the best we can dream. Frederick Buechner reflects that our longing to return home is inherent: our "first home foreshadows the final home, and the final home hallows and fulfills what was most precious in the first."[4] If we are to find the best God has for us, then we need to pay attention to the compelling images of our destination—that "final home" at the center of the story of God. We also need to recognize that through the resurrection of Christ, that "final home" is already here; God is at work through the mustard seed challenging the imperial powers and transforming lives and communities.

To rediscover a more compelling biblical vision of that "other world that is already here," we need to begin with a question we first heard asked in Australia: "What is God on about?" What are God's purposes for a people and a world? What is the good life of God that is found in the imagery of our "final home"?

---

[3]Eddie Gibbs and Ryan K. Bolger, *Emerging Churches: Creating Christian Community in Postmodern Cultures* (Grand Rapids: Baker Academic, 2005), pp. 62-63.
[4]Frederick Buechner, *The Longing for Home: Recollections and Reflections* (San Francisco: HarperSanFrancisco, 1996), p. 3.

"HEAVEN IS NOT OUR HOME!"

"Heaven is not our home!" N. T. Wright declared at a faculty luncheon at Seattle Pacific University on May 19, 2005. The bishop of Durham's startling assertion completely arrested everyone's attention. Wright went on to offer an alternative biblical vision of coming home to God's resurrected future, drawing on his book *Resurrection of the Son of God*. His comments stirred an animated discussion.

One cannot read the book of Acts or examine the history of the early church (before Constantine) without recognizing that following Christ means not only a change of heart but also the embrace of a new vision for the human future. As these communities of "resident aliens" spread through Imperial Rome, they rejected the empire's reality and its claim to define the future. Clearly, they believed they weren't called to passively wait, but to actively work to express God's new order in the here and now. As Wright makes clear, they not only lived in hope of the bodily resurrection and the transformation of the world, they gave their lives to see something of God's kingdom come in their own place and time.[5]

Kingdom language, however, doesn't connect well to life in the twenty-first century. In an article in *Sojourners* magazine and again in his book *The Secret Message of Jesus*, Brian McLaren tries out some alternate images: "the dream of God," "the revolution of God," "the mission of God" and the "dance of God." Elsewhere he calls on musicians to write songs that capture the spirit of the prophet Isaiah, using themes of "the celebration, peace, justice, and wholeness towards which our dismal, conflicted, polluted, and fragmented world must move."[6] He writes, "The universe was created to be an expression and extension of the dance of God."[7] I like that. As followers of Jesus, we are invited to dance, celebrate and give compassionate expression to that other world that is already here!

---

[5]N. T. Wright, *The Resurrection of the Son of God,* vol. 3, Christian Origins and the Questions of God (Minneapolis: Fortress Press, 2003), p. 3.
[6]Brian McLaren, "An open letter to Worship Songwriters," <www.clba.org/resources/pdfs/Open_Letter_McLaren.pdf>.
[7]Brian McLaren, "Found in Translation," *Sojourners* (March 2006), pp. 14-19.

READING THE BIBLE FROM THE UNDERSIDE

I find it very difficult as a privileged, white, American male to fully appreciate the meaning the biblical images of hope must have for the powerless, excluded and suffering with whom we share this planet. Bob Ekblad invites us
to learn to read the Bible from the perspective of the powerless. In his provocative book *Reading the Bible with the Damned*, Bob shares how he learned
to understand a whole new perspective of Scripture by studying it with Latino
and Hispanic men incarcerated in the Skagit County Jail.[8] Similarly, while I
was working in Haiti on a community development project for World Concern, Christians there began to help me read the Scriptures with new eyes.

Dr. Martin Luther King Jr. found ways to share the powerful prophetic
images of the coming of God's new order in ways that ignited the imaginations of the excluded and inspired them to give themselves sacrificially to
see that dream become a reality in this world. Dr. King's compelling restat-
ing of those images and his call to change the world through nonviolent
love have brought about amazing societal transformation, not only in the
United States but in nonviolent initiatives in many other nations as well.
His message still resonates in a world divided by race, class, culture and religion. I remember his historic address on August 28, 1963, as it rang out
across our divided nation: "I have a dream that one day, on the red hills of
Georgia, the sons of slaves and the sons of former slave owners will be able
to sit down together at a table of brotherhood."

On the eve of his assassination on April 3, 1968, Dr. King delivered another message, called his "Mountaintop Speech," that brought alive the
biblical theme of homecoming and tragically turned out to be prophetic.
The telling line goes, "He's allowed me to go up to the mountain. And I've
looked over. And I've seen the promised land. I may not get there with you.
But I want you to know tonight, that we, as a people will get to the promised
land."[9] Dr. King brought the power of these ancient images alive in a way

[8]Bob Ekblad, *Reading the Bible with the Damned* (Louisville: Westminster John Knox, 2005).
[9]"Mason Temple Church of God in Christ," accessed January 26, 2007, at <www.cr.nps.gov/nr/travel/civilrights/tn1.htm>.

that called us all to break down walls and open doors. The need to give fresh expression to these ancient images is ongoing. We all need to join at the margins and seek to reimagine what God is on about—that connects to the hurting world in which we live.

THREE IMAGES OF THE INBREAKING OF THE FUTURE OF GOD

I will now take you through three different sets of images of what the inbreaking of God's new order might look like in our world today. These images come from the imaginations of three different people: Anthony, a kid from the Bronx; Bruce Cockburn, a subversive poet and songwriter; and my own struggling efforts to reimagine God's great homecoming.

Reimagining homecoming in the Bronx. One of America's poorest communities is a part of the Bronx called Mott Haven. Forty-eight thousand of New York's poorest people live jammed tightly together in this run-down ghetto. It is two-thirds Hispanic and one-third black. Kids not only have to contend with grinding poverty but also with drugs, violence, HIV/AIDS and the struggle to believe that there is anything for them to look forward to in the future. Jonathan Kozol has dedicated his life to spending time with poor kids, listening to their fears, dreams, and even their hope for life beyond life.[10] Kozol asked some of these children to share their images of heaven. Anthony, age thirteen, was one of the first to respond. "God's kingdom," reads the title.

> God will be there. He'll be happy that we have arrived.
>
> People shall come hand-in-hand. It will be bright, not dim and glooming like on earth. All friendly animals will be there, but no mean ones.
>
> As for television, forget it! If you want vision, you can use your own eyes to see the people that you love. No one will look at you from the outside. People will see you from the inside. All the people from the street will be there. My uncle will be there and he will be

---

[10]Jonathan Kozol, *Amazing Grace: The Lives of Children and the Conscience of a Nation* (New York: Harper Perennial, 1996), pp. 3-6.

healed. You won't see him buying drugs, because there won't be money. Mr. Mongo will be there too. You might see him happy for a change. . . .

No violence will there be in heaven. There will be no guns or drugs or IRS. You won't have to pay taxes. You'll recognize all the children who have died when they were little. Jesus will be good to them and play with them. At night he'll come and visit at your house.

God will be fond of you.[11]

Isn't Anthony's description brilliant? No clouds here. He has instinctively connected God's loving purposes to the real people and tough streets where he lives. Anthony understands that the gospel is intended to transform real lives and real communities in the real world.

Reimagining homecoming in Pinochet's Chile. Bruce Cockburn is a Canadian songwriter, musician and singer who, in his lyrics, constantly struggles between the harsh realities of the world we call home and the abiding belief that there is something more. Richard Middleton and Brian Walsh see in his lyrics the idea that "the embrace of pain is the door to hope."[12] In his song "Broken Wheel," Cockburn confesses the brokenness of our world and our own complicity in that brokenness:

On the rim of a broken wheel,
Way out on the edge of the galaxy
The gifts of the Lord lie torn
Into whose charge the gifts were given
Have made it a curse for so many to be born
This is my trouble—
These were my fathers
So how I am supposed to feel?
Way out on the rim of a broken wheel.

---

[11]Ibid., pp. 237-38.
[12]J. Richard Middleton and Brian J. Walsh, "Theology at the Rim of a Broken Wheel: Bruce Cockburn and Christian Faith in a Postmodern World," *Grail* 9, no. 2 (1993): 15-39.

It certainly seems to be true "that the embrace of pain is the door to hope" for Bruce Cockburn. In "Santiago Dawn," Cockburn imagines citizens of Chile coming home to a future and a hope that stands in stark contrast to the brutality of Pinochet's Chile.

I've got a dream and I am not alone
Darkness dead and gone
All the people are marching home
Kissing the rush of dawn
Santiago sunrise
See them marching home
See them rising like grass through cement
In the Santiago dawn.[13]

Middleton and Walsh state that Cockburn's anger at injustice and suffering, like the oppressive military dictatorships in Latin America in the eighties, "opened him up to the possibility of an alternative future, to hope in a vision of a better world rooted in the loving action of God."[14]

Like Anthony's imaginings, these are not images divorced from the real world, but "like grass through cement," it is God breaking through the rock-hard horror of our world with surprisingly small blades of life and promise. Any vision of God's homecoming future must include more than middle-class Christians looking forward to their souls being redeemed and making it safely home to God. It must also include imagery, as Anthony's and Bruce Cockburn's visions do, of God's love changing the lives of our poorest neighbors and transforming the brutal conditions under which they live.

Reimagining coming home to a new mountain and a new city. Join me as I work impressionistically with a few ancient images, largely from the

---

[13]Bruce Cockburn, "Broken Wheel" and "Santiago Dawn," quoted in J. Richard Middleton and Brian J. Walsh, "Theology at the Rim of a Broken Wheel: Bruce Cockburn and Christian Faith in a Postmodern World," accessed January 26, 2007, at <www.things.org/music/bruce_cockburn/articles/grail.html>.

[14]Middleton and Walsh, "Theology at the Rim of a Broken Wheel."

prophet Isaiah, to imagine a future hope. I will attempt to connect these images directly with the real world we know and experience. I also invite you to connect these images to both your best memories of coming home and your strongest hopes of the day of welcoming into that other world that is already here.[15]

> I have just arrived in a vast wilderness, arid and desolate. As I get my bearings, the forbidding silence of the place engulfs me. The landscape is as flat as the surface of the moon. As far as the eye can see, not a single blade of living grass. The heat of the scorching sun radiates off the rocks and scattered bones as I walk toward the distant horizon with my back to the sun.
>
> Unexpectedly the skies quickly darken. Cannonades of threatening clouds rumble across the heavens. Violent lightning and slashing rain surround me as I quickly whip on my poncho. The earth begins convulsing under my feet like a woman in labor. Suddenly a gigantic mountain erupts from the valley floor directly in front of me. It is as lifeless and forbidding as the desert that surrounds it. I feel unsettled. As quickly as the downpour started, it ends. The desert and mountain settle into a deep silence. I lie down under a gigantic slag at the foot of the peak to spend the night.
>
> I awaken to the song of a single bird. Incredibly, it smells like the first morning of spring. I am surprised to find myself surrounded by a field of blossoming plants that were not here yesterday. As I climb up on top of the slag, I look out at the wasteland now bursting with life. It is hard to grasp.
>
> Looking to the horizons, I spot small dark specks—millions of small specks. The radiating of the sun against the horizon makes it look like these specks are moving. As I focus my eyes, I realize they

---

[15]Jesus seemed to draw from Isaiah more than any other source. There are, of course, three different parts of the writings of Isaiah, but I am drawing images on the assumptions that the message of Isaiah as whole is integral. I view these passages through the filter of the life, death and resurrection of Jesus Christ, who I believe directly connected these images to his life and his call to seek first the kingdom.

are actually moving toward me like huge armies of ants coming from all directions. As they come closer, I realize they are people converging on the mountain—people from all over the world. Most of them look very poor, but clearly they are oblivious to everything but their destination. I climb up the foothills to get a better view.

I watch some of the travelers stop at the river to drink. Young and old, they come. Children in arms, they come. Carts and walkers, they come. Hand in hand, they come. Singing songs of thanks to God in a hundred different languages, they come. They slowly move toward the mountain with evident anticipation.

Looking up the mountain, I see the pathways lined with fruit trees. I see a small child from Haiti pick and devour a huge blood orange, the juice running down his torn T-shirt. Some teenagers, who look as though they might be from Latin America, help an aging black couple over some rocks as they start up the mountain. A family with three kids, hockey logos on their shirts, push their bikes up the trail; they are obviously from Canada.

As I join the trek, I notice some wheelchairs abandoned beside the trail. To my surprise, beyond the wheelchairs, I see a tall slender man from Iran throw down his hand-made crutches and begin to run up the trail. Moments before he had begun the climb with great difficulty because his left leg was withered.

A gaunt woman from Darfur tries to pull her shawl over her emaciated baby to protect it from the sun, even though she knows her little girl died hours earlier during the trek across the valley. She seems confused by the singing. As she starts up the trail, a child's cry is heard above the singing. A large family from the Philippines realizes what has happened and sweeps the mother and infant up into their celebration, almost carrying them up the trail.

Together with many others, I finally make it to the top of the switchbacks. A vast plateau opens before me. As I look out over the plateau, I am almost blinded by the brilliant skyline of an enormous city.

There are fountains everywhere. Remarkably, they look like they are fabricated out of rocket launchers, the front end of recycled Hummers and huge plastic corporate logos. They provide a vast array of spectacular water displays in the open pavilion.

As the masses approach, we see that the glistening entry arch is covered with banners welcoming us home in every language imaginable. Moms and dads, sons and daughters, grandparents reunite after many years. Everyone seems grateful to be safely home at last. As I join in the spontaneous singing, it is as though someone has removed a blindfold from my eyes. I see the people around me with new eyes.

I feel as though I were five years old again on my grandparent's farm in Idaho. I can almost smell my grandmother's bread baking in her old wood stove and feel her arms around me . . .

Amazingly there are animals of all descriptions wandering with the crowds, and no one seems to mind. It is like a simultaneous combination of a family reunion, a circus and a meeting of the United Nations.

I join the crowds singing and dancing into an enormous square the size of two dozen huge airfields joined together. It is filled not only with fountains but also with trees festooned with garlands of flowers. The huge square looks like a wedding reception waiting to happen. Streamers and colored lights hang above large oak tables that stretch in all directions.

The crowd hushes as the festivities begin. The guests of honor are introduced. Not a celebrity or political, corporate or religious leader in the lot. The honor roll is comprised entirely of the poor and forgotten ones and those martyred for their faith. A tall, dark Middle Eastern man, with a towel wrapped around his waist, seats each of the honored guests with a particular graciousness.

My parents, Tom and Katherine, appear suddenly out of nowhere. Surprised, I hug them both so hard they almost holler. Tears streaming, we just keep hugging each other. I can't remember ever being so happy to see anyone. We sit down at the first table we come to. My folks always loved good food, and the spread is incredible. We recall some of our best stories over some of our favorite foods.

Before us is a feast gathered from every part of the world. Everyone immediately becomes aware of savory aromas from their own home-land. The spread includes pita, hummus and olives from Lebanon; kimchi from Korea; tamales from Mexico; mangos, papaya and star fruit from Costa Rica; large skewers of beef, pork, chicken and fish barbecued Brazilian-style; rice and beans from Haiti; roasted pota-toes, carrots and onions from the U.K.; asparagus and mushrooms sautéed in sherry from France; rich salads loaded with antipasto from Italy; cheese fondue from Switzerland; Sichuan eggplant from China; sushi from Japan; sadza and gravy from Zimbabwe; freshly roasted coffee from Ethiopia. The finest wines from all over the world are served with each course of this lavish fare. Suddenly, I spot my son Clint among those who have artfully prepared the feast, and we strongly embrace for what seems an eternity.

God's presence is palpable, and we sense his generous welcome. Emissaries from all over the world bring their cultural riches from many nations to honor God and to enrich us all. As we receive these remarkable gifts, somehow we are aware that while we retain our cul-tural uniqueness, we can still appreciate the gifts from many different cultures. Somehow the best of human creation, from over many ages, is embraced and integrated into this huge celebration.

A voice rings out above the crowd, "On this mountain the LORD Al-mighty will prepare a feast of rich food for all peoples, a banquet of aged wine—the best of meats and finest of wines. On this mountain he will destroy the shroud that enfolds all peoples, the sheet that cov-ers all nations; he will swallow up death forever. The Sovereign LORD will wipe away the tears from all faces; he will remove the disgrace of his people from all the earth. The LORD has spoken. In that day they will say, 'Surely this is our God; we trusted in him, and he saved us. Let us rejoice and be glad in his salvation'" (Is 25:6-9).

Another voice calls out, "I saw Heaven and earth newly created. Gone the first Heaven, gone the first earth, gone the sea. I saw Holy

Jerusalem, new created, descending resplendent of Heaven, as ready for God as a bride for her husband. I heard a voice thunder from the Throne: 'Look! Look! God has moved into the neighborhood, making his home with men and women! They're his people, he's their God. He'll wipe every tear from their eyes. Death is gone for good—tears gone, crying gone, pain gone—all the first order things gone.' . . . 'Look I'm making everything new'" (Rev 21:1-4 *The Message*).

These images remind us that God cares not only for us but for all those with whom we share this earth and, indeed, all of God's good creation. These images should also remind us that God is interested not just in transforming a spiritual part of our lives but every area of our lives and God's world. Our faith is intended to be much more than a devotional add-on to our "real lives." It is an invitation to give our lives to a very different dream than the one offered us by the global mall.

In the story *The Last Battle*, C. S. Lewis imagines the resurrected future of God as a homecoming. As Narnia ends and the children come home to God's new creation, Lewis writes, "It's only the beginning of the real story. All their life in this world and all their adventures in Narnia had only been the cover and the title page: now at last they were beginning Chapter One of the Great Story, which no one on earth has read: which goes on forever and forever; in which every chapter is better than the one before."[16]

We are all only at "the beginning of the real story." But the images we have briefly looked at give us a glimpse of the future that is to come. What is God on about? Clearly God intends to bring us safely home as a great resurrected, multicultural community to a restored creation. This is vastly different from the imagery of individual disembodied souls coming home to the clouds. It also offers us radically different imagery of the good life and better future than the one offered us by the marketers of McWorld.

However you related to my struggling efforts to imagine, contemporize and concretize ancient images, I have tried to offer you a broader, more

---

[16]C. S. Lewis, *The Last Battle* (New York: Collier Books, 1956), p. 184.

compelling imagery of God's purposes for a people and a world. Next we'll explore the biblical basis for this hope-filled imagery.

JOIN THE CONVERSATION

- What images of the future of God were you nurtured in? How do you feel about those images today?

- What is your response to the imagery of the future of God in which we come home as a great resurrected community to a restored creation?

- Imagine one creative way you could give expression to these images in your daily life, in your church and in response to needs in your community and God's world.

ANOTHER WORLD
THAT IS ALREADY HERE

*Is it possible that the imagery of God's new order, which the
Bible tells us we will one day come home to, has implications
for spiritual, social, economic and political transformation of
our world today?*

In his book *Living the Resurrection*, Eugene Peterson reminds us that even
though the four Gospel accounts of the resurrection of Christ are all a bit
different, they share "a sense of wonder, astonishment, surprise."[1] I am certain that we will be at least as filled with astonishment and wonder when we
come home as a resurrected community as the first disciples were when
they encountered the risen Christ.

A number of New Testament scholars believe the Scriptures teach that
as Christ was resurrected from the dead, we, at the return of Christ, will be
bodily resurrected to the world as God intended it to be. According to
Paul's writings in I Corinthians 15, we will be bodily resurrected with transformed bodies—immortal, but real.

> If corpses can't be raised, then Christ wasn't, because he was indeed
> dead. And if Christ weren't raised, then all you're doing is wandering
> about in the dark, as lost as ever. It's even worse for those who died
> hoping in Christ and resurrection, because they're already in their
> graves. If all we get out of Christ is a little inspiration for a few short

---

[1]Eugene H. Peterson, *Living the Resurrection: The Risen Christ in Everyday Life* (Colorado Springs: NavPress, 2006), p. 14.

years, we're a pretty sorry lot. But the truth is that Christ has been raised up, the first in a long legacy of those who are going to leave the cemeteries. (1 Cor 15:16-20 *The Message*)

BEGINNINGS

In this section I will examine the biblical basis for the belief that at the return of Christ we will be bodily resurrected and come home to a new heaven and a new earth. I will also describe some of the implications of the coming of God's new order not only for spiritual but also for social, economic and political transformation.

"When Paul said 'resurrection,'" N. T. Wright states in *The Resurrection of the Son of God*, "he meant 'bodily resurrection. . . . What the creator God did for Jesus is both the model and the means of what he will do for all Jesus' people."[2]

Wright further explains Paul's teaching on believer's resurrection in *The Challenge of Jesus*. He states "emphatically" that the Christian living and the Christian dead can look forward to coming home to an "embodied" future. The present body, Paul teaches, "is a [physical] body animated by a 'soul'; the future body is a [transformed physical] body animated by God's Spirit."[3]

> "Heaven" for Paul . . . is not so much where people go after they die . . . but the place where the divinely intended future for the world is kept safely in store, against that day. . . it will come to birth in the renewed world, "on earth as it is in heaven." . . . Jesus knows . . . the new creation, whose central feature is bodily resurrection, is being "prepared," and that he is a part of it.[4]

---

[2]N. T. Wright, *The Resurrection of the Son of God*, vol. 3, Christian Origins and the Questions of God (Minneapolis: Fortress Press, 2003), pp. 314-16.
[3]N. T. Wright, *The Challenge of Jesus: Rediscovering Who Jesus Was and Is* (Downers Grove, Ill.: InterVarsity Press, 1999), pp. 143-44.
[4]Wright, *Resurrection*, pp. 368-69.

Jürgen Moltmann has written as convincingly about a Christian view of hope as any author I know. Looking forward to a resurrected future, he writes,

> Because . . . the resurrection hope sees a future for those who are gone, those who are living in the present gain courage for the future. Because of the great hope of overcoming death and transience, our little hope for the future, better times gain strength, and do not fall victim to resignation and cynicism. In the midst of an age of anxiety, we hope "against hope" and still do not give ourselves up to despair.[5]

The best that has been will be alive again. We will come home as a great resurrected community with those we have loved that have gone before us. We will not only be transformed spiritually, but those who are disabled will be healed and we will finally grasp what God is up to. We will know as we are also known.

Isaiah 65 offers the panoramic view of what God intends:

> Pay close attention now: I'm creating new heavens and a new earth. All the earlier troubles, chaos and pain are things of the past, to be forgotten. Look ahead with joy. Anticipate what I am creating: I'll create Jerusalem as sheer joy; create my people as pure delight. I'll take joy in Jerusalem, take delight in my people: No more sounds of weeping in the city, no cries of anguish . . . neither animals nor humans will hurt or kill anywhere on my Holy Mountain. (Is 65:17-19 *The Message*)

Not only will we be welcomed home and transformed in every aspect of our being, but Scripture makes clear that society will be transformed as well. Justice will come for the poor, instruments of war will be transformed into implements of peace, the walls that divide us will be broken down, and "the knowledge of the Lord will cover the earth as the waters cover the sea."

---

[5]Jürgen Moltmann, "Progress and Abyss: Remembering the Future of the Modern World," in *The Future of Hope: Christian Tradition Amid Modernity and Postmodernity*, ed. Miroslav Volf and William Katerberg (Grand Rapids: Eerdmans, 2004), p. 19.

REIMAGINING ANCIENT IMAGES OF HOPE

Anyone who has traveled to the Holy Land knows that even by Kansas's standards, Mount Zion is barely a hill. In Isaiah 2, the author focuses specifically on our homecoming not only to a new heaven and a new earth but also to a new mountain and a new city. Watch how Zion is transformed into a peak that transcends all other mountains. Also watch who comes home to this mountain and see the imagery of God's purposes being realized.

> In the last days, the mountain of the Lord's temple will be established as chief among the mountains; and all the nations will stream to it. Many peoples will come and say, "Come, let us go up to the mountain of the Lord to the house of the God of Jacob. He will teach us his ways, so that we might walk in his paths." The law will go out from Zion, the word of the Lord from Jerusalem. He will judge between the nations and settle the disputes for many peoples. They will beat their swords into plowshares and their spears into pruning hooks. Nation will not take up sword against nation and will not train for war anymore. (Is 2:1-4)

What we are witnessing is God's intention to bring God's faithful people from all over the world safely home, not as disembodied souls but as a great bodily resurrected, multicultural community. Walter Brueggemann, in his commentary on Isaiah, states "In time to come . . . Jerusalem will be like a magnet, drawing all the nations of the world."[6]

Look to the horizon again and see others God is drawing home to the New Jerusalem.

> What's that we see in the distance,
>> a cloud on the horizon, like doves darkening the skies?
> It's the ships from distant islands,
>> the famous Tarshish ships.
> Returning your children from faraway places,
>> loaded with riches, silver and gold,

---

[6]Walter Brueggemann, *Isaiah 1-39*, Westminster Bible Commentary (Louisville: John Knox Press, 1998), p. 24.

And backed by the name of God, The Holy of Israel,
   showering you with splendor.
Foreigners will rebuild your walls,
   and their kings assist you in the conduct of worship.
When I was angry I hit you hard.
   It's my desire now to be tender.
Your Jerusalem gates will always be open
   —open house day and night!—
Receiving deliveries of wealth from the nations,
   and their kings, the delivery boys! (Is 60:8-14 *The Message*)

We will all be enriched as we share the gifts of many different cultures.
Richard Mouw, in his stimulating book *When the Kings Come Marching In*,
offers his insights into this passage:

> When the end of history arrives, then, there is something to be gath-
> ered in—diverse cultural riches to be brought into the Heavenly City.
> . . . The citizens of the renewed Jerusalem will be "fed" by the pres-
> ence of many peoples bearing diverse gifts. "Red and yellow, black
> and white"—and all that these labels designate—will be precious to
> God and to all of his saints.[7]

One of God's purposes that is clearest in the imagery of Isaiah was to
end the oppression of the poor and powerless and bring down the powerful. Ched Myers, who writes convictingly on this subject, points out that
the Old Testament instructions on the Jubilee and Sabbath year included
debt relief, the purpose of which was to reduce the tendency of human communities to concentrate power and wealth in the hands of a few, creating
hierarchical societies where the poor are more easily victimized.

> The prophet Isaiah railed against the process of economic stratifica-
> tion by which wealthy creditors "add house to house and field to field,
> until there is room for no one but you" (Isaiah 5:8). He saw it as a be-

---

[7]Richard J. Mouw, *When the Kings Come Marching In: Isaiah and the New Jerusalem*
(Grand Rapids: Eerdmans. 1983), p. 48.

trayal of Israel's vocation to be "God's pleasant planting; God expected justice, but saw bloodshed" (Isaiah 5:7).[8]

In Isaiah 35:7-9, we see the in-breaking of the shalom of God. The creator God intends to bring wholeness not only to those who are broken but also to God's good creation. Again, try to imagine this as today's reality in the lives of those you care for and also in many areas of our environment that desperately need restoration.

Wilderness and desert will sing joyously, the badlands will celebrate and flower—Like the crocus in spring, bursting into blossom, a symphony of song and color. . . . Energize the limp hands, strengthen the rubbery knees. Tell the fearful souls, "Courage! Take heart! God is here, right here, on his way to put things right and redress all wrongs. He's on his way! He'll save you!" Blind eyes will be opened, deaf ears unstopped, lame men and women will leap like deer, the voiceless break into song. Springs of water will burst out in the wilderness, streams flow in the desert. Hot sands will become a cool oasis, thirsty ground a splashing fountain. Even lowly jackals will have water to drink, and barren grasslands will flourish richly. (Is 35:1-7 *The Message*)

The Beatitudes in Luke always challenge me as one who lives in a society of remarkable affluence. Christ described God's lavish banquet, like so many Gospel images, as an inverted celebration where the poor and excluded are the ones who are the honored guests. Jesus tells the poor who weep and hunger that they will laugh and be satisfied, but Jesus warns those of us who are rich and well fed to take serious stock of our lives. In Isaiah 25:6-9, we are given a preview of the homecoming feast God is planning. Consider how you might set it to music or create a celebration to bring it to life

On this mountain, God . . . will throw a feast for all the people of the world. A feast of finest food, a feast of vintage wines, a feast of seven courses, a feast with lavish gourmet desserts. And here on this moun-

---

[8]Ched Myers, "God Speed the Year of Jubilee!" *Sojourners,* May 1, 1998.

tain, God will banish the pall of doom hanging over all peoples, the
shadow of doom darkening all nations. Yes, he'll banish death forever. . . . "Look at what's happened! This is our God! We waited for
him and he showed up and saved us! Let's celebrate, sing the joys of
his salvation. God's hand rests on this mountain!" *(The Message)*

Throughout the prophets, imagery of the world being transformed spiritually, politically and economically is present. The God of the Jews is a God
who intends to bring us home to a future of righteousness, justice and shalom. In Isaiah 9:2-7, we are shown a day when God will make all things new.
Watch what happens to the rod of the oppressors, military boots and uni-
forms soaked in blood from warfare at the coming of the Prince of Shalom:

> The people walking in darkness have seen a great light; on those liv-
> ing in the land of the shadow of death a light has dawned. You have
> enlarged the nation and increased their joy; they rejoice before you as
> people rejoice at the harvest, as men rejoice in dividing the plunder.
> For as in the day of Midian's defeat, you have shattered the yoke that
> burdens them, the bar across their shoulders, and the rod of their op-
> pressor. Every warrior's boot used in battle and every garment rolled
> in blood from the warfare will be fuel for the fire. For unto us a child
> is born, to us a son is given, and the government will be on his shoul-
> ders. And he will be called Wonderful Counselor, Mighty God, Ever-
> lasting Father, Prince of Peace [Shalom]. Of the increase of his
> government and peace [shalom] there will be no end. He will reign on
> David's throne and over his kingdom, upholding it with justice and
> righteousness from this time on and forever. The zeal of the Lord al-
> mighty will accomplish this. (Is 9:2-7 NIV)

The film *Antwone Fisher* is based on the true story of a young man whose
father was violently killed before he was born, and whose mother abandoned him shortly after birth. He grew up in an abusive foster home and yet
was determined to live his life with integrity against tough odds. In the
Navy, he works with a Navy psychologist, Dr. Davenport (played by Denzel
Washington), after getting into fights. In the film we see yet another meta-

phor of what the homecoming pictured in Isaiah might look like.

Dr. Davenport encourages Antwone to discover if he has any family and, if so, to try to connect with them. After a difficult search, he succeeds in finding his birth mother, only to discover that she isn't interested in restoring contact. He also connects with his father's family, who invite him to stop by before going back to his Navy base. When he comes through the door, he is greeted and welcomed by a huge community of family he never knew he had. The table is loaded with a huge spread of home-cooked delights, and Antwone is visibly overwhelmed by the welcome. Isn't this the kind of welcome we can expect when we come home to loved ones and everything that God has promised? Won't this homecoming transform not only our lives but also the larger society in ways that reflect God's purposes for a people and a world?

JOIN THE CONVERSATION

- What views regarding the resurrection and God's purposes for the future were you nurtured in?
- What is your response to the discussion of coming home as a bodily resurrected community? How do you respond to the imagery from Isaiah?
- Imagine one way you might give expressions to these ancient images by creating celebrations and forms of societal transformation that reflect something of God's loving purposes for a people and a world.

COMING HOME TO A
TRANSFORMED HUMAN FUTURE

Did Jesus come simply announcing the new empire of God,
or did he come inviting us to join him in making it real in the
turbulent world where we live?

When Jesus arrived on the scene, Israel was ruled by yet another imperial power—the Roman Empire. Jesus traveled down the back roads of Galilee and the main streets of Jerusalem with a very startling message: "Good news, good news . . . the empire of God has arrived!" This message directly challenged the "illusions of authority" of both the Roman Empire and the Jewish religious establishment.

One thing is immediately apparent about Jesus' announcement, according to Brian McLaren: "This kingdom throws down a direct challenge to the supremacy of the empire of Caesar."[1] It is an empire from the underside that challenges the pretensions of all other empires. N. T. Wright reminds us that Jesus' announcement was an integral part of the story and dreams of Israel. In fact, he writes, "Jesus believed . . . Israel . . . was the means through which the world would be saved." This would be accomplished through God finally bringing "his love and justice, his mercy and truth, to bear upon the whole world, bringing renewal and healing to all creation."[2]

Jesus' empire of the mustard seed is directly connected to the Old Testament imagery of homecoming. In Christ's mustard seed parable, the image

---

[1]Brian D. McLaren, *The Secret Message of Jesus: Uncovering the Truth That Could Change Everything* (Nashville: W, 2006), p. 17.
[2]N. T. Wright, *The Challenge of Jesus* (Downers Grove, Ill.: InterVarsity Press, 1999), p. 35.

of birds nesting in a gigantic mustard tree is a metaphor for many nations coming home to the welcoming care of the creator God. It appears that the parable was inspired by Ezekiel's vision of the birds of the nations finding a sheltering welcome in the boughs of a lofty cedar (Ezek 17:23). Craig Blomberg explains that in Ezekiel's parable, the birds symbolize the Gentiles of the world coming home to the festive welcome of the God of Israel.[3]

Jesus believed his unique vocation was to actually be the good news of the in-breaking of this shalom future of God. He stood up in his hometown and read from Isaiah, "The Spirit of the Lord is upon me, / because he has chosen me to bring good news to the poor. / He has sent me to proclaim liberty to the captives / and recovery of sight to the blind, / to set free the oppressed / and announce that the time has come / when the Lord will save his people"(Lk 4:18-19 TEV). He then quietly handed the scroll back to the attendant, sat down and announced, "Today this scripture is fulfilled in your hearing" (Lk 4:21). Through the life, death and resurrection of Christ, God's new world has indeed broken into this one. And that is very good news!

BEGINNINGS

As one reads the gospels, it becomes evident that very few people, including the followers of Jesus, had any idea what this announcement of good news actually meant. But it certainly got people's attention. Just what is this new empire he heralded, and how are we invited to be part of it?

THE MUSTARD SEED EMPIRE OF JESUS

John Howard Yoder, in his classic *The Politics of Jesus*, persuasively argues that Jesus wasn't only the inaugurator of God's new order, but also the realization of everything Jubilee promised for the poor and marginalized in ancient Israel.[4]

---

[3]Craig L. Blomberg, *Preaching the Parables: From Responsible Interpretation to Powerful Proclamation* (Grand Rapids: Baker Academic, 2004), p. 123.
[4]John Howard Yoder, *The Politics of Jesus* (Grand Rapids: Eerdmans, 1972).

If you want to see what the shalom future of God looks like, look at
Jesus. Every time we see Jesus heal the disabled, open the eyes of the
blind, hug the kids, feed the hungry, set the possessed free, forgive
the sinner and raise the dead, we are shown a glimpse of what God's
purposes are for the human future.[5]

In Jesus, God's new order has actually broken into our troubled world.
We are invited to be a part of this good news and follow Jesus by passionately living into that new world that is already here, not just with our spiritual lives but with our entire lives.

Jesus not only demonstrated the compassion of God's new order, he embodied the right-side-up values of that order in an upside-down world. One
of the first things Jesus did was to create a new countercultural community—a living, breathing example of the right-side-up aspirations and values
of God's new order. Those first disciples discovered that following Jesus
was a call to a whole-life faith that would change their lives spiritually, mor-
ally and culturally.

Let me clarify. When we join this movement, we are not building God's
new order on earth through our own efforts. Through the life, death and
resurrection of Christ, God is actively at work in our world today, using our
ordinary lives in ways we have never imagined to give expression to God's
new order, in anticipation of that great homecoming day when all things
will be made new.

Remember that Jesus' empire was not ushered in with pomp and circumstance. It had its origins with a baby born in a cow stall in an undistin-
guished village in the Roman Empire. When Jesus began teaching, he made
clear that his new empire would be unlike any empire the world had ever
seen. It came on a donkey's back. Its "imperial council" was comprised of a
handful of unemployed fisherman, a couple of I.R.S. agents, a prostitute
and some other hangers-on. Jesus demonstrated how to wield his imperial
power by washing feet, telling stories and playing with kids. Jesus' empire
is based on the absurd values that the last should be first, losers are winners

---

[5]Tom Sine, *The Mustard Seed Conspiracy* (Waco, Tex.: Word, 1981), p. 101.

and the most influential in this empire should clean the toilets.

Members of this empire are instructed to love their enemies, forgive their friends, always give twice as much as people ask of them and never pursue power or position. Jesus insisted that those who are a part of his empire shouldn't worry about finances, but simply trust God. The resources to run this empire were basins, towels and leftover lunches. This empire also developed a reputation for constant partying—almost always with the wrong kind of people.

Seriously, is this any way to run an empire? Imagine what would happen if you ran a political, economic or even religious institution with these bizarre values. Clearly, it wouldn't have much of a future. These values might even get the leader assassinated. It is essential we remember that this unlikely empire is destined to defeat the evil that victimizes our lives and brutalizes God's world.

TAKING EVIL SERIOUSLY

One only has to reflect on the horrors of Rwanda or the starvation in Darfur, witness demonic powers in Haiti, or lose a loved one to addiction to realize we aren't wrestling with flesh and blood but are up against brutal spiritual powers of evil intent on our destruction. In his life and ministry, Jesus confronted the powers of darkness head on and demonstrated the power of God's new order over Satan and all evil.

Pentecostals, particularly in majority countries, seem to take evil much more seriously than some of us who have a more intellectual Western faith. These believers regularly engage demonic powers by often seeing their prayers for deliverance and supernatural healing answered by the power of God.

Walter Wink is correct when he reminds us evil is not just personal. It is also structural. Principalities and powers have been embedded in every human empire from Babylon and Rome to the global economic empire that has such huge influence over our world today.[6] These powers of evil perme-

---

[6]Walter Wink, *Naming the Powers: The Language and Power in the New Testament* (Philadelphia: Fortress, 1984), p. 135.

ate every human institution, regrettably, even the church. And part of our work is to unmask evil and help people reduce its influence in our lives, our institutions and the larger world.

A friend of ours named Bill was out walking with his ten-year-old daughter, Courtney, and her small barkless African dog, Savannah. Suddenly, the neighbor's pit bull advanced in a dead run to attack his daughter's dog. Bill immediately picked up Savannah and put her on the roof of a car to get her out of harm's way, but the pit bull jumped onto the hood of the car, then onto the roof, and savagely grabbed the small dog by its left hind leg. Bill saw the pit bull release its powerful jaws in order to go for the neck of the smaller dog to kill it.

Bill immediately reached into the pit bull's mouth with his right hand, grabbed it by the tongue and refused to let go. The pit bull bit down on Bill's hand, but he held firm. He told us, "I wasn't about to let that beast kill my daughter's dog!" After a few moments of struggling to get free, the pit bull's owner came running over and hurriedly took the pit bull back home. Bill went to his home and patched up his injured hand.

In very much the same way, Jesus Christ reached down into the throat of evil on our behalf, not just subduing it, but destroying it forever. In his brutal death and his powerful resurrection, Jesus Christ forever defeated the spiritual forces of evil that beset our lives and trouble God's world. "The lions may roar and growl, / yet the teeth of the great lions are broken" (Job 4:10).

In Mark, demons asked Jesus if he had come to destroy them. As Richard Hays observes in *The Moral Vision of the New Testament*, "The answer is yes: in the coming of Jesus, God mounted a decisive campaign against the powers of evil that oppress humanity. But the campaign is waged in a mysterious way that no one expected, culminating in the cross."[7] Jesus not only died to redeem us and forgive our sins, but to forever break the back of evil. Scripture reminds us that those of us who are in Christ are no longer sub-

---

[7]Richard B. Hays, *The Moral Vision of the New Testament: Community, Cross, New Creation* (San Francisco: HarperSanFrancisco, 1996), p. 89.

ject to the power of the enemy. Paul writes, "The Lord Jesus Christ . . . gave himself for our sins to set us free from the present evil age, according to the will of our God and Father" (Gal 1:3-4).

However, until we come home to God's restored creation, we continue to live in a world that is victimized by Satan and the powers of darkness. Therefore, we must continue to do battle with the forces of evil in the lives of individuals and those we love. But we must also seek to unmask the work of the principalities and powers in our institutions and the global empire in which we live until that day when God's victory is complete.

The reason God will welcome us home to a restored creation in which there is no sickness, suffering, oppression, violence and death is that the forces of evil have been forever vanquished. I find such hope in the hymn "Joy to the World" by Isaac Watts

No more let sins and sorrows grow,
nor thorns infest the ground;
he comes to make his blessings flow
far as the curse is found.

As Luke reminds us, we are looking forward not only to the destruction of the works of the enemy, but to "the restoration of all things in Christ" (Acts 3:21). I love the words of the Phillips translation of Romans 819: "The whole creation is on tiptoes to see the wonderful sight of the sons of God coming into their own."

TAKING JUDGMENT SERIOUSLY

Miroslav Volf, speaking from his personal experience of the horrific violence and ethnic cleansing in the Balkans, makes a very persuasive argument that God's restoration cannot take place unless this evil is both exposed and judged by God. He insists, "There can be no redemption unless the truth about the world is told and justice is done. To treat sin as if it were not there, when in fact it is there, amounts to living as if the world were redeemed when in fact it is not." He adds that God's new order cannot be birthed without God judging those who have done evil. "God will judge, not because God gives people what they deserve, but because some people refuse to receive what no one deserves; if evildoers experience God's terror, it will not be because they have done evil, but because they have resisted to the end the powerful lure of the open arms of the crucified Messiah."[8]

In Christ's sacrificial death on the cross, the creator of the universe acts not only to redeem us and forever destroy the power of evil but also to fully enter into our humanity, experiencing in his own body our pain, suffering and death. He particularly identifies with those who suffer most in our world. Puerto Rican scholar Orlando Costas wrote, "Jesus not only did justice on the cross by standing in the place of the weak and poor. . . . He continues to do justice standing in the place of those who suffer . . . identifying himself with their suffering, and condemning all acts of injustice and oppression."[9]

Therefore, in choosing to follow this God, revealed in Jesus, we are to become people for others; we are to enter into the "fellowship of his suffering." The call to follow Christ is a call to look beyond our narrow self-interests and give ourselves to the "otherness" of the gospel of Jesus, to join him in making God's shalom homecoming a reality in the lives of others right now. René Padilla urges us to take Scripture seriously, since Jesus "laid down his life for us . . . we ought to lay down our lives for one another" (1 Jn 3:16). Padilla insists that faithful discipleship requires us to set aside our personal ambitions and become a part of God's conspiracy that focuses on the well-being of others. He writes, "God's love expressed in the cross must be made visible in the world through the church."[10]

TAKING AN ACTIVIST GOD SERIOUSLY

The biggest lie of our modern global empire is that no God is present in the world. Of course the empire allows us to worship a God, if we choose, as long as we recognize that the God who shows up during worship and at our

---

[8]Miroslav Volf, *Exclusion and Embrace: A Theological Exploration of Identity, Otherness, and Reconciliation* (Nashville: Abingdon Press, 1996), pp. 294-99.

[9]Orlando E. Costas, *The Church and Its Mission: A Shattering Critique from the Third World* (Wheaton, Ill.: Tyndale House, 1974), p. 66.

[10]C. René Padilla, *Mission Between the Times: Essays on the Kingdom* (Grand Rapids: Eerdmans, 1985), p. 24.

Bible studies has little power to actually change our world. The message is clear: The world is governed by the forces of the global free market, political and economic power, and random mutations of nature—period.

In spite of this message, I am finding growing numbers of Christians who believe the God of the mustard seed empire is actively at work in our world. Our wild outrageous hope is that through the death and resurrection of Christ, our God (who is the author of this story) will write the final chapter and make all things new, not just personally and spiritually but also culturally, economically and politically; he will transform every dimension of our global society.[11] In *Wild Hope*, circa 1991, I argued that the God of Jesus and the prophets is alive and well and actively involved in our world. I wrote that the dance on the Berlin Wall was the dance of God. The songs sung in the streets of Soweto at the release of Nelson Mandela were the songs of God. And the prayers raised by many in the Middle East for the peace of Jerusalem were the prayers of God. The movements toward peace in Northern Ireland, the campaign to make poverty history and the battle against global warming all reflect something of God's influence in our world today. We need to be vigilant, watching for the fingerprints of God so we can join what God is doing through God's conspiracy from the underside.

TAKING THE GOOD LIFE OF GOD SERIOUSLY

Clearly the good life of God isn't about enabling individuals to endlessly consume more or to patiently wait to have their souls rescued. We will never find happiness by pursuing it. John Hayes reminds us that Jesus' teachings consistently have a theme of reversal at their core. "We find it in sayings— for example, 'Whoever would save his life will lose it; and whoever loses his life for my sake and the gospel's will save it'" (Mark 8:35 RSV).

In other words, Jesus teaches that, paradoxically, "it is in losing life" in service to God and others that we find life, not in seeking it. Therefore, the good life of God will be found only as we join followers of Jesus all over the world

---

[11]Tom Sine, *Wild Hope: Crises Facing the Human Community on the Threshold of the 21st Century* (Waco, Tex.: Word, 1991), p. 1.

in discovering how God can use our ordinary little mustard seeds to give compassionate, creative expression of that new world that is already here.

Case Western Reserve University has sponsored over fifty studies in fifty-four universities by scientists in a broad range of disciplines that all conclude "that love and caring expressed in doing good for others lead people to healthier, happier and even longer lives."[12] In other words the way we find a happy, fulfilling life is not by pursuing it. It is only in Jesus' paradoxical teachings of forgetting about ourselves and caring for others that we will ever discover the good life that God has for us.

If we choose to more fully live into that world that is already here, then it is essential that we learn to pay more serious attention to the challenges facing us and particularly our poorest neighbors. To the extent we can anticipate even a few of the coming challenges, then we have lead time to imagine and create new compassionate responses that provide a glimpse of God's future of reconciliation, justice and shalom.

JOIN THE CONVERSATION

- In what ways is Jesus' invitation to seek first God's kingdom an invitation to join him in creating new forms of countercultural communities?

- What might be the consequence of joining Jesus in losing our lives in service to God and others?

- Imagine one creative way God might use your mustard seed if you joined others in discovering that the good life of God is the life given away.

---

[12]Jane Lampman, "Science Finds Giving Leads to a Healthier, Happier Life," *Christian Science Monitor*, July 25, 2007, p. 13.

TAKING TURBULENT TIMES SERIOUSLY

TAKING THE FUTURE SERIOUSLY

How might it change our lives, congregations and communities if we both anticipated and creatively responded to even a few of the coming challenges?

Do you know the median age of your donor base?" I recently quizzed board members of Habitat for Humanity. The CEO had asked me to outline some of the challenges likely to face Habitat in the next ten years. I shared about new economic challenges facing the global poor as well as escalating urban land costs in the United States. I also shared with the board members some challenges facing their donor base of which they were not aware: "The median age of your donor base is sixty-five years of age!"

The bells and whistles immediately went off as these able board members realized the implications for future funding. During the discussion board and staff started exploring creative ways to cultivate a younger constituency, including reaching out to the thousands of college students that help Habitat build houses during spring break every year.

In 1981, in *The Mustard Seed Conspiracy*, I predicted a "galloping conservatism" in America with a dramatic increase in the influence of the political right and the religious right. I also stated we would see the gap widen between U.S. rich and poor as we headed into the 1990s. Both took place. (I also forecasted that gas prices would soar to over $2.00 a gallon by the end of the nineties. I was a bit early on that one.)[1]

TAKING OUR LOCAL FUTURES SERIOUSLY

No business leader would ever do strategic planning without first trying to

---

[1]Tom Sine, *The Mustard Seed Conspiracy* (Waco, Tex.: Word, 1981).

anticipate how his or her market context might change. It is rare, however, to find a Christian organization that researches how the context in which they do mission will likely change before it does strategic planning.

BEGINNINGS

In this conversation I will make a strong case that we in traditional churches, as well as those in the emerging, missional, mosaic and monastic streams, need to learn to lead with foresight and make a greater effort to pay attention to the coming waves of change that will impact our lives and the lives of our poorest neighbors, as well as create new ways to respond.

Then I will take you on a quick tour of both a changing world and a changing church to give you a heads-up regarding some of the new challenges and opportunities we will likely face as we race into the second decade of the twenty-first century. To the extent we can anticipate some of the waves that will buffet our lives, congregations and God's world we will have lead time to create imaginative ways to address those new challenges before they fully arrive while advancing the purposes of God's resurrected future.

In the final conversation I will present a broad range of creative ways the new conspirators, as well as traditional churches, can be a difference and make a difference for God's kingdom.

Most Christian churches, denominations and mission organizations do long-range or strategic planning. The irony is that they plan as though they are frozen in a time warp—as though the future will simply be an extension of the past. Pastors in both conventional and experimental churches are often unaware of the challenges facing their members in our new global society. So it shouldn't be surprising that they offer little help in dealing with those challenges. Similarly, those who work with Christian college students at Christian colleges or through campus ministries seldom alert them to new challenges or creative alternatives facing them upon graduation. As a consequence, students are not adequately prepared to live and serve God in a rapidly changing world.

Those in the mosaic and monastic streams are often sensitive to issues that impact the poor, but they still rarely look down the road to identify new directions in social policy or projected changes in funding to assist those at the margins. Likewise, many emerging church leaders are skilled at assessing a local cultural population they are attempting to engage, but even here I find many of them aren't aware of problems on the horizon that are likely to impact those they work with.

Recently I met with Hot House, a group of emerging and missional church planters who meet monthly here in Seattle. James B. Notkin is planting a chocolate café gathering place through the Presbyterian Church (U.S.A.). He and his compatriots have done excellent research regarding the profile of their target community, the South Lake Union neighborhood, not only for today but for tomorrow as well. South Lake Union is a light industrial area that is quickly becoming a high-tech center. The district includes restaurants, shops and a rapidly growing number of condos for the high-tech young who are relocating there. The median age is thirty-one and the median income is $80,000 per year. There are also a growing number of empty nesters, aged fifty-five to sixty-five, moving into this neighborhood.

James B.'s congregation reflects this spread, having virtually no middle-agers with kids. They are focused on creating ways to reach these two populations, but their research has alerted them to the fact that this profile could dramatically change in the next ten years. Today a one-bedroom condo costs about $300,000. But given the high inflation rate in housing in this area, prices could soar to double that amount and beyond the reach of the young high-tech crowd. That could require shifting focus to the wealthy retiring set.

When Christine and I work with local churches, we encourage them to ask (1) How is your community likely to change in the next ten years? (2) How is the age profile of your congregation likely to change in the next ten years? (3) What will be some likely congregational needs? We don't just look at projected changes in housing prices, but we also consider who is likely to move in and what their needs are likely to be. For example, one suburban church predicted a rapid increase in single-parent families in their neighborhood in the next ten years. In response, the leadership proactively created a new educational ministry focused on financial, parenting and support resources for this new population—before they fully arrived.

Leaders in a church plant in Sherwood, Oregon, determined that in ten years they would be swamped with teens because they currently have a huge preschool population. During our futures workshop, they suddenly realized that they don't have to wait for that new teen population to arrive. They can start designing an innovative youth ministry now to enable their teens to live and serve God in a world that is very different from the one in which their parents grew up.

TAKING OUR GLOBAL FUTURES SERIOUSLY

Over some thirty years, I have done futuring seminars with leaders in a number of different denominations and mission organizations, such as Tearfund U.K. and the Mennonite Central Committee, as well as with university students at gatherings like the Urbana Student Missions Convention. I believe it is essential for those involved in global mission to identify some of the new perils and possibilities facing our poorest neighbors and God's good creation so we have lead time to create new ways to respond.

Last year I conducted a two-day scenario forecasting seminar to help prepare World Concern for the possibility of a global avian flu pandemic. This was a daunting but important exercise. World Concern flew staff in from all over the world, and I worked them through two different scenarios: one based on the 1959 pandemic and one based on the much more devastating 1918 flu pandemic. By the end of the second day the staff had successfully developed three-stage strategic plans to deal with possible pandemics in Thailand and Kenya. Unlike other agencies that haven't considered this possibility, World Concern has now proactively designed strategic responses in all twenty-two countries where they serve for a pandemic we pray never comes.

Leaders in global mission need to ask two important questions if they are to lead their organizations with foresight: (1) How is the context in which you minister likely to change in the next ten years and what are likely to be new areas of human need? (2) How is the economic support base of your missions organization likely to change?

Global warming, for example, is likely to decisively alter the kind of agriculture farmers will be able to do in the Tropics. Therefore, organizations like World Vision Europe and TEAR Fund New Zealand need to effectively research these changes and help farmers alter their crops and farming practices to be ready for rising temperatures. These agencies also need to help people prepare for increasing weather-related disasters.

These leaders also need to assess how the retirement of the baby boomers is likely to impact the funding base of Western ministry organizations. During a scenario session with World Relief staff, one person proposed doing massive will and estate planning with the aging boomer population so that mission organizations will have some resources on hand to help buffer them through the tough time as the boomers retire.

Of course we can't begin to anticipate all the change rushing toward us in turbulent times. But to the extent we can anticipate even some of the new challenges in our lives, congregations, communities and God's larger world, we have lead time to proactively create new ways to respond.

Next I am going to take you on a tour of our global future and sketch some of the dramatic ways the landscape of tomorrow's world is likely to change. Some of these changes may seem a bit overwhelming. It is important to remind ourselves again that even in these uncertain times God hasn't lost control. For followers of Jesus, all these challenges are really opportunities to create imaginative responses that reflect something of God's loving purposes for a people and a world. I urge you to keep your Palm Pilot and notebook handy as you read so that you can list your creative responses to these challenges in your own life, congregation and ministry with others.

JOIN THE CONVERSATION

- What are some practical ways you could anticipate a few of the challenges that your church or community is likely to face?

- What are some new challenges that you believe are likely to impact your own life, family, congregation and community in the next five-to-ten years?

- Imagine one creative way to respond to one of the challenges you listed above.

TRAVELING TOGETHER ON A SHIP OF FOOLS

If economic globalization is a major driving force for change in our post-9/11 world, what are some of the challenges it presents for our lives, our churches, our poorest neighbors and God's world?

The ship of this world is on its journey to eternity." Katherine Anne Porter used this fifteenth-century allegory as the basis of her bestselling 1962 novel *The Ship of Fools*.[1] The 1965 film version makes our growing reality vivid: all humanity is traveling into an uncertain future on a single, crowded vessel.

In the novel we find ourselves traveling in 1933 from Mexico to Germany just before World War II. The privileged elite in connoisseur class dine with the captain in luxury every evening as though there is not a care in the world. The cabin class, who operate the ship, are all but invisible, as many in our middle-class societies are today. Below deck in the cattle cargo area are six hundred impoverished laborers who have lost their plantation jobs in Cuba. The owners of the plantation, wanting to receive a better price for their sugar on the global market, decided to burn their fields rather than sell them with apparently little regard for the human cost of their decision.

I will use the "ship of this world" as a metaphor to remind us how deeply interconnected our lives are to one another and to the fragile earth vessel

---

[1]Marie Rose Napierkowski, ed., "Ship of Fools: Introduction," in *Novels for Students*, vol. 14 (Detroit: Gale, 1998), accessed January 18, 2007, at <www.enotes.com/ship-fools/20442>.

on which we travel together. We will seek to identify how the new challenges of the next ten-to-fifteen years will influence the various classes, and we'll explore creative ways we might join other conspirators in responding to these challenges as we cruise into some turbulent seas.

BEGINNINGS

We will begin this cruise by exploring some of the perils facing our imperiled planet. Then we will visit those who live on all three levels of the ship. We will start by visiting the people of privilege and wealth who travel in connoisseur class. Then we will visit those traveling in cabin class and identify some new challenges and opportunities facing those in the middle class. Next, we will seek to identify some of the problems and possibilities facing the huge population in the cargo hold—the global poor and their families. Finally, we will identify challenges facing the church and creative ways both traditional and experimental congregations will need to change to face all these new challenges.

CONFRONTING A VESSEL IN PERIL

My second conversion was on the first Earth Day in 1970. Dr. James Dator came from the University of Hawaii to the college where I was working on Maui and spoke not only about new environmental challenges, but also the future of literally everything, including the possibility of engineering transgenetic creatures. It was through his deeply disturbing presentation that I discovered part of my vocation: to try to help others make sense of our rapidly changing future. It also began my own personal journey to try to live a little more lightly on the earth as a part of that first environmental movement.

In 1981, in my book *The Mustard Seed Conspiracy,* I expressed serious concerns about sustainability and limits to economic growth on our finite planet. "How much growth and what kinds of growth can our planet sustain? What impact will a world of shrinking resources have on the burgeoning poor with whom we share this planet?"[2] These questions about sustainability are even more urgent in the twenty-first century as the rapid growth in the global economy is dramatically accelerating the rates at which we are both using up finite global resources and polluting our small planet. I also urged readers to conserve energy and explore using alternative forms of energy, which weren't nearly as promising in 1981 as they are today.

Economic globalization is the major driving force accelerating the rate at which we are polluting our Earth-home. Increasingly we are reading about troubling die-off levels of frog and bee populations. Scientists don't seem to be clear regarding either the causes or the long-term consequences. We are also witnessing a serious reduction in wild fish stocks and a concerning loss of species and habitats. Many parts of the world, like Australia, will be facing serious water shortages as well. No one knows what the tipping point will be before there are major ecological collapses in regions of our world. But Bill McKibben reports in his important book *Deep Economy*,

> In the spring of 2005, a panel of 1,300 scientists assembled by the United Nations issued a "Millennium Ecosystem Assessment" report. They found that "human actions are depleting Earth's natural capital, putting strain on the environment and the ability of the planet's ecosystems to sustain future generations can no longer be taken for granted." . . . This is the planetary equivalent of the doctor clearing his throat and asking you to sit down.[3]

On October 9, 2006, the Global Footprint Network reports, the world moved into ecological overdraft. Our ecological footprints are measured both by how much we consume of the earth's resources and how much we pollute. By the Network's measure, we have used up the ecological capacity of the planet. We can borrow against the future carrying capacity of the planet for a time, but clearly it is not sustainable over the long term. Recent research increasingly links many health conditions, particularly cancer and

---

[2]Tom Sine, *The Mustard Seed Conspiracy* (Waco, Tex.: Word, 1981), pp. 23-24.
[3]Bill McKibben, *Deep Economy: The Wealth of Communities and the Durable Future* (New York: Times Books, 2007), p. 189.

heart disease, to all the toxic compounds we ingest through our air, water and food. All of us on this ship of fools are paying a high human price in our personal health for our growing affluence. Tragically our children and grandchildren will have to pay the largest bill for our profligate lifestyles.

The Live Earth Concert of the summer of 2007 was touted as the largest concert event in history. It specifically called people all over the planet to combat global warming. Al Gore's film *An Inconvenient Truth* has made many aware of the serious threat posed by global warming, and it seems as though even the business community is beginning to get involved, in part because of the growing economic opportunities that are being identified to combat global warming.

In 1991 I warned that global warning "could increase the risk of forest fires, cause major droughts . . . and even cause oceans to rise." I asked, "Since the potential impact is so significant, would it not be reasonable to take the threat seriously until the theory is either proved or substantiated?"[4] Today there is widespread recognition that it is a serious mistake to wait any longer. The increase in global warming could have apocalyptic implications. A recent report commissioned by the British government "predicted apocalyptic effects from climate change, including droughts, flooding, famine, skyrocketing malaria rates and the extinction of many animal species during the current generation if changes aren't made soon."[5]

Researchers at the University of Arizona showed that we could see sea levels rise from one to six meters during this century if global warming is not curtailed. A one-meter rise would put cities like Hamburg, London, Miami, New York and New Orleans in serious peril. Bangladesh, Egypt, Vietnam and coastal portions of China would also be threatened by this rise.[6]

At its core this is not just an ecological issue but a justice issue as well. The United States is the world's largest producer of greenhouse gases, con-

---

[4]Tom Sine, *Wild Hope: Crises Facing the Human Community on the Threshold of the 21st Century* (Dallas: Word, 1991), p. 23.

[5]Heather Timmons, "Britain Warns of High Costs of Global Warming," *The New York Times*, October 31, 2006, p. A8.

[6]John Young, "Blackwater Rising: The Growing Global Threat of Rising Seas and Bigger Hurricanes," *World Watch Magazine* 19, no. 5 (2006): 30.

tributing some 25 percent even though we are only slightly more than 4 percent of the world's population. We Americans use almost twice as many resources as our European counterparts.[7] The average North American needs 9.6 hectares or 23.7 acres of land to sustain life while the average African needs only 1.4 hectares.[8] If everyone on the planet were to adopt an American lifestyle, we would need five planets to support us.

In fact the people who will pay the highest price for the SUV lifestyles of the world's affluent are the world's poor. The reason for this is that they live in regions that will be most seriously impacted by global warming. "The inequity of this whole situation is really enormous if you look at who's responsible and who is suffering as a result," stated chairperson of the United Nations climate council Rajendra K. Pachauri.[9]

As China's appetite for coal and oil dramatically increases in the next ten years, we are likely to see a dangerous increase in global warming. Dr. Norm Ewert, an economist at Wheaton College, has told me that we will reach peak oil capacity by 2010 or 2020. After that we will face a difficult time of adjustment: a postpetrol future for industrialized countries and soaring prices for oil everywhere.

McKibben states that not only is there a huge sucking sound coming out of China for oil but for other commodities as well. The swelling middle class is developing an enormous appetite for meat and alcohol. Beef, pork and chicken are, of course, heavily dependent on grain production, as is alcohol. McKibben points out that global grain production actually plateaued in the mid-eighties. Per capita grain production is considerably lower than a generation ago. The United States and other countries are significantly increasing their production of ethanol which is causing corn prices to soar. Wholesale prices for grain escalated 32 percent from 2005 to

---

[7]"North America's Ecological Footprint: Summary," accessed January 16, 2007, at <www.oneplanetliving.org/northamerica/ecofootprint.html>.

[8]Ian Sample, "World Moves into Ecological Overdraft Today, Says Study," *The Guardian*, October 9, 2006, accessed January 16, 2007, at <www.guardian.co.uk/uk_news/story/0,,1890834,00.html>.

[9]Andrew C. Revkin, "Poorest Nations Will Bear the Brunt as World Warms," *The New York Times*, April 1, 2007, pp. 1, 6.

2007 in part because of increased production of ethanol. Experts predict that not only will the poor have to pay significantly more for grains but relief agencies will have a much smaller buffer in the future to deal with relief disasters.[10] A dramatic increase in China's demand for grain could raise food prices all over the world.[11] This could have further disastrous consequences for our poorest neighbors.

As followers of Christ, we need to live our lives and influence policies that reflect our unqualified commitment to creation care. We need to join those who are finding creative ways to influence global energy and environmental policies. But I suspect that we can exert more influence than we realize by helping shape local environmental policies.

GREENING OF SOCIETY

As I wrote in *The Mustard Seed Conspiracy*, the least expensive energy is always the energy we conserve where we live. There are myriad ways that most of us can, in our communities, churches and homes, significantly reduce both the amount of carbon we put into the air and the amount of energy we use. While our national government is slow to act, a small number of people in city and state governments in the United States (particularly in California) have successfully raised the bar on carbon emissions significantly above those set by the federal government. Consequently, states like California have the potential to become global pacesetters in carbon reduction.

A part of this strategy needs to be the growing advocacy and use of energy alternatives like solar, tidal and wind energies. We need to also support the development of new technologies that have the capability of not only reducing carbon emissions but actually removing carbon from the atmosphere.[12]

Growing numbers of people are finding ways to reduce their emissions

---

[10]Mark Trumbull, "Rising Food Prices Curb Aid to Global Poor," *Christian Science Monitor,* July 24, 2007, pp. 1-2.

[11]McKibben, *Deep Economy,* p. 18.

[12]One of the best resources for those who want to be much more involved in both environmental advocacy and innovation is the Grist website <www.grist.org>. For information on green construction or remodeling check out the website for Built Green <www.builtgreen.net>.

by purchasing green energy technologies for their homes and businesses. For example, households in the U.K. are purchasing their own renewable energy sources such as rooftop wind generators. The British government pays 30 percent of the cost of a wind generator and solar water heaters and 50 percent for solar panels.[13] While some political leaders in the United States are concerned about the costs of global warming, other leaders see environmental challenges as a huge economic opportunity. For example, in Britain it is estimated that manufacturing green technologies could mean $55 billion worth of business over the next ten years.[14]

Advocates such as Bill McKibben and Wendell Berry urge us to rediscover the "economics of neighborliness." Hyper-individualism—one of the cardinal virtues of the global economy—has been a major force in undermining our values of neighborliness, community and mutual care. The rise of big box stores and big corporate agriculture have, over the years, seriously undermined local communities in North America. Nevertheless, "Localism . . . offers a physically plausible economy for the future."[15]

There were only 340 farmers' markets in the United States in 1970 when we celebrated that first Earth Day. By 2004 there were 3,700. The first community-supported agriculture project began in Massachusetts in 1985. Today there are more than 1,500.[16] Growing numbers of us are discovering the delight of growing our own urban gardens. We are trying to do our bit at The Mustard Seed House by growing approximately 60 percent of our vegetables on our urban lot in Seattle. There is nothing quite as luscious as a Brandywine tomato right out of the garden.

Surprising numbers support these local agricultural initiatives by attempting to purchase food grown within one hundred miles of where they live. If this trend caught on, it could significantly reduce the fuel used to transport foodstuffs internationally and the carbon dioxide emissions that

---

[13]Kendra Norton, "In Britain, Wind Turbines Offer Homespun Electricity," *Christian Science Monitor*, November 30, 2006, pp. 13-15.

[14]Mark Rice-Oxley, "Never Mind Aaltruism: 'Saving the Earth' Can Mean Bucks," *Christian Science Monitor*, October 25, 2006, p. 4.

[15]McKibben, *Deep Economy*, p. 122.

[16]Ibid., p. 81.

are a consequence of that transport, and it would strengthen economic systems as well as foster community and mutual care.

There is a whole new movement afoot to create wealth and do good by creating "corporate hybrids." For example, a small restaurant chain called Farmers Diner has committed to secure 65 percent of its food within a range of seventy miles of its restaurants. Another firm, Trans-Forms, was started in 2005 to produce removable wall décor. The firm decided to do its manufacturing in the United States instead of China, even though labor is more expensive, in order to create jobs. Trans-Forms also offers training for disabled people that leads to employment within the company. This hybrid was designed in a way that directs a portion of corporate profits into a foundation that supports social projects.[17]

GREENING OF THE CHURCH

The monastic and emerging streams tend to be most directly involved in initiatives to care for God's good creation. But we find Christians in traditional churches starting to become involved as well. Michigan Interfaith Power & Light, a coalition of over one hundred congregations in Michigan, offers energy assessments of church buildings, energy conserving appliances and technologies, and energy education for members of their churches. St. Elizabeth Catholic Church in Wyandotte, Michigan, a coalition member, has sharply reduced energy use and emissions of carbon dioxide by installing two solar panels and a small windmill. "We're all a part of God's creation," said Father Morris, "If someone like me doesn't speak out its care, who will?"

Regrettably, there are a large number of those on the religious right in the United States who are still in denial about the reality of global warming. With the leadership of Rich Cizik at the National Association of Evangelicals that has changed. "Last February, 86 evangelical Christian leaders backed an initiative to combat global warming, a move that broke the evangelical

---

[17]Stephanie Strom, "Make Money, Save the World: Businesses and Nonprofits Are Spawning Corporate Hybrids," *The New York Times,* May 6, 2007, pp. 1, 8.

movement's broad silence on the issue, but exposed stark divisions."[18]

When churches ask new monastic leader Shane Claiborne to speak, he has a "carbon reduction request." Someone from the inviting church forgoes using their car to offset his share of carbon output in a flight to and from the speaking destination. Shane says that the first thing he does when he begins his presentation is to thank that person by name.

Restoring Eden has twelve chapters on Christian college campuses; its executive director Peter Illyn organizes students to lobby against global warming and find creative ways to care for God's creation. Chris Elisara runs a high-quality program on environmental education called the Creation Care Study Program with study centers in Belize, New Zealand and Samoa. In Britain two different organizations speak out regarding creation care: A Rocha U.K., an international conservation organization devoted to caring for God's world, and Christian Ecology Link, a multidenominational Christian organization for people concerned about the environment. In the United States, *Creation Care* magazine is also a major resource.

The environmental challenges facing us are huge. If we as individuals make a serious commitment to live more lightly on the ship that carries us, it can make an enormous difference. But we also need to influence international organizations, our governments, businesses, churches and community organizations to operate as though the environment mattered. If we can make necessary changes by 2020, then I think our Earth home has a hope. Change must begin with the wealthy and the rest of us reducing our appetite for more.

JOIN THE CONVERSATION

- What challenges facing our fragile planet particularly concern you?
- What is a biblical basis for Christians to be involved in caring for creation?
- Imagine one creative way you could influence environmental policy and one creative way you could change your own lifestyle in order to reduce your footprint.

---

[18]Neela Banerjee, "Citing Heavenly Injunctions to Fight Earthly Warming," *The New York Times*, October 15, 2006, p. 19.

CHALLENGES FACING
THE GLOBAL RICH

How are the wealthy affected by the new global economy?
What is their responsibility to those on the lower decks of our
crowded craft?

There must be more to life than everything" quipped Maurice Sendak. However, a number of the very wealthy traveling in connoisseur class can't imagine that is true.

CRUISING IN CONNOISSEUR CLASS

How well does this new global economy work for the wealthy? The short answer is that we have seen an explosion of wealth for the global rich in this new economy. In fact we have seen the creation of more millionaires and billionaires in the last ten to fifteen years than at any time in human history. *Forbes* magazine, in its annual 2007 report on the global wealthy, celebrated the news that there are now 946 billionaires in the world, up from 793 the previous year. The total wealth of these 946 billionaires grew by 35 percent in the past year, topping $3.5 trillion in U.S. dollars.[1]

In an article titled "Wealth Goes Supernova," *The Sunday Times* of London trumpets, "Wealthy people in Britain have never had it so good. . . .The combined wealth of the top 1,000 has soared by £59 billion. . . . This near 20% rise over 2006 is one of the highest annual increases in wealth we have recorded

---

[1]Luisa Kroll and Allison Fass, eds., "The World's Billionaires," Forbes.com, March 8, 2007, accessed October 11, 2007, at <www.forbes.com/2007/03/07/billionaires-worlds-richest_07billionaires_cz_lk_af_0308billie_land.html>.

BEGINNINGS

As we continue to cruise together on this ship of fools we are going to visit those on the upper decks who seem to be acquiring "everything." We are going to ask two questions: (1) How well does this new global economy work for the wealthy in this post-9/11 world? (2) How can the rich help the poor secure the skills and resources they need to participate in this new global economy?

since our list was first published in 1989."[2] According to Merrill Lynch's Tenth Annual World Wealth Report, the number of millionaires in our world soared to a record 8.7 million people in 2005, up from 4.5 million in 1996. This burgeoning class of millionaires collectively controls $33.3 trillion of the world's wealth, up from $16.6 trillion in 1996,[3] "while income levels for the lower 55% of the world's 6-billion-strong population declined or stagnated."[4]

Clearly this new global economy seems to work exceedingly well for the world's wealthy, but the future of the global wealthy is not without its challenges. Part of what has accelerated the explosion of wealth for those at the top in the United States is the extravagant inflation of CEO salaries. Median pay for the CEOs of the top 350 corporations was $6.8 million in 2005. "According to the Wall Street Journal, that's 179 times the pay of the average American worker."[5] This has contributed to a new class war between the super-rich and the merely rich.

[2]Philip Beresford, "Wealth Goes Supernova," Times Online, April 29, 2007, accessed May 13, 2007, at <http://business.timesonline.co.uk/tol/business/specials/rich_list/article1708616.ece>.

[3]"Merrill Lynch and Capgemini Unveil 10th Anniversary Edition of World Wealth Report," accessed May 13, 2007, at <www.ml.com/?id=7695_7696_8149_63464_67074_67212>.

[4]James Petras, "Is There a Global Ruling Class?" The Progress Report, accessed May 13, 2007, at <www.progress.org/2007/wealth02.htm>.

[5]Teresa Tritch, "The Rise of the Super-Rich," *The New York Times,* accessed October 11, 2007, at <http://select.nytimes.com/2006/07/19/opinion/19talkingpoints.html?_r=1&oref=slogin>.

THE SUPER-RICH LEAVE THE MERELY RICH IN THE DUST

Among the merely rich in Britain is the well-paid professional class. On average these workers earn 500,000 pounds a year ($1 million). They live in expensive homes, take regular foreign holidays and send their children to exclusive private schools. The new super-rich in the U.K. and elsewhere live at an entirely different level. These people think nothing of spending several million pounds on a party, having their children picked up from their private schools by helicopter and taking exotic holidays in their private jets.[6] Surprising numbers of the super-rich are trading in their small private jets for Boeing 787 Dreamliners that they transform into lavish flying yachts.

This same phenomenon is taking place in the United States. The merely rich in America, like their counterparts in the U.K., earn around $1 million a year while the super-rich earn at least $4.5 to $20 million a year. Reportedly there is no love lost between the two groups, and the merely rich are struggling with a serious case of wealth envy.[7] Numbers of the super-rich feed this wealth envy by the display of what is called "Mogul Style."

Mogul Style is less about conspicuous consumption and more about the giddy spending of money—sometimes shareholders' money—and it results not in pleasure of ownership, or connoisseurship, but in the succulent gratification of making other moguls quake in their Gucci loafers.[8]

For this new mogul set, birthdays and weddings typically cost between $150,000 and $3 million. "Mogul style is . . . a way of showing off the peacock feathers to inspire awe in other moguls. . . . 'It's display behavior,' [says Richard Coniff]. . . . 'You're supposed to walk in and be impressed and think: "Good grief! What a way to spend your money." But in the end it is supposed to make you feel a little cowed.'"[9] You can be sure this kind of display captures the attention of many of the merely rich, and I suspect they do feel a little cowed.

---

[6]Sarah Vine, "The Haves and Have Yachts," Times Online, December 4, 2006, accessed January 21, 2007, at <http://women.timesonline.co.uk/article/0,,17909-2482054 .html>.
[7]Ibid.
[8]Alex Kuczynski, "Lifestyles of the Rich and Red-Faced," *The New York Times*, September 22, 2002, p. 9:1.
[9]Ibid., pp. 9:1-2.

HERALDING A NEW TRANSNATIONAL COMMUNITY OF
THE SUPER-RICH

What we are witnessing is another byproduct of globalization: the creation of a new transnational community of the super-rich. Those in this new community frequently have more in common with one another than with the national cultures they come from. They frequent the same lavish resorts. They often travel to the same boutique international health-care centers. They keep the same highly paid plastic surgeons in these centers very busy correcting the ravages of time and the "mistakes" of nature.

One of the members of this new transnational community is Roman Abramovich, a Russian who is worth 7.2 billion pounds. He, his wife, Irina, and their three kids own a selection of super-sized homes, including a forty-five-acre estate in West Sussex, a Knightsbridge mansion, a luxury dacha outside of Moscow, and resorts in Nice, St. Tropez, Austria and Russia. On top of this, they own three luxury yachts, including the Pelorus, which is worth 72 million pounds and has a full-time crew of forty. They own a private jet and two helicopters to travel between their many different dwellings. Oh yes, and Roman also owns the Chelsea Football Club in the U.K.[10]

You can find this new class of the super-rich from dot-comers in Europe and hip-hop celebrities in the United States to tycoons from China and Australia. In 1999 media sensation Diddy spent $375,000 on a new Bentley. As a consequence Bentleys became very popular among rappers, as have $300,000 Maybachs and other luxury vehicles. Increasingly, their tastes are soaring into what is called "ghetto fabulous," which includes such uptown labels as Escalade, Burberry, Gucci, Prada and Louis Vuitton. "Many of the high-end companies are feeling a bit uneasy. . . . Hip hop's embrace can mean a windfall, but executives are concerned about long-term damage to their brands because of rap's sometimes unsavory aspects."[11]

As a result of the global economic boom of the 1990s, there has also been an explosion of wealth in China. Now there are over ten thousand Chi-

---

[10]Rachel Oldroyd, "7.2 Billion," *The Mail on Sunday*, March 7, 2004, p. 3.
[11]Johnnie L. Roberts, "The Rap of Luxury," *Newsweek*, September 2, 2002, pp. 42-44.

nese businessmen who have assets valued at over $10 million each. They too are flaunting their mogul lifestyles, buying large numbers of luxury vehicles, including Maybachs and Rolls Royces, as well as Bugattis, which can cost as much as $900,000. A Beijing real-estate developer named Zhang Yuchen re-created a three-story seventeenth-century French chateau (covering 157,000 square feet on the main floor alone) on the outskirts of Beijing. Zhang also created a replica of the Garden of Versailles on his estate, complete with Greek mythological statues. The entire estate is surrounded by a moat. Other wealthy Chinese are invited to purchase real estate and create their own super-sized mansions on the 1.5-mile estate. The losers in this spectacular display of new wealth in China are the poor farmers who lost their land.

This story is really a metaphor for what is happening thoughout China. The gap is dramatically widening between the very wealthy and the rural poor. China's egalitarian society is rapidly returning to a hierarchical feudal society, all in the name of economic progress. This troubling trend could destabilize China's future.[12]

THE HIGH COSTS OF HIGH LIVING

It is important to remember that life for the super-rich isn't simply one long extravagant party. Life for the super-rich can come unraveled too. *Forbes* reports the deadly impact of the dot-com bust on thousands of the newly wealthy, but many of the newly wealthy experience dramatic increase in other life pressures. A thirty-year-old dot-com executive lost his entire $20 million fortune in four months and became suicidal. A Beverly Hills portfolio manager lost half his net worth and most of his clients. He not only started having panic attacks but was unable to drive on Southern California freeways.[13]

Stephen Goldbart, psychologist and cofounder of San Francisco's Money, Meaning and Choices Institute, stated, "Never has financial success

[12]Joseph Kahn, "China's Elite Learn to Flaunt It While the New Landless Weep," *The New York Times*, December 24, 2004, p. 1.
[13]Kroll and Fass, "World's Billionaires."

and self-esteem been so co-mingled." When the rich crash and burn they don't just lose their wealth "but their identity and their image."[14] Our new imperial global economy has persuaded not only the super-wealthy and the merely rich but many in the middle class as well to increasingly derive our sense of identity, self-esteem and even our life purpose from our success in the marketplace of more.

LUXURY LIVING IN A POST- 9/11 WORLD

The very rich and those who cater to them were seriously impacted by the horrific terrorist attack on September 11, 2001, just like the rest of us, but in different ways. Immediately after the attack, the remaining fashion shows in New York City were canceled and the entire luxury industry was briefly sent scrambling in all directions, wondering out loud how to market ostentation, luxury and envy in the midst of horror.

It didn't take these clever purveyors long to reposition their pitch. Tom Ford, the designer for Gucci, held one of the first fashion shows after the attack. He rationalized, "More than ever, there is a need for beauty in the world. . . . I think we should all cry for beauty. That may be the only way to get through this."[15] Amazing! Ford is advocating that the way to make it through terrorist attacks is to focus on indulging ourselves in luxury consumption.

In *Living It Up: Our Love Affair with Luxury*, James Twitchell argues that indulging in luxury goods not only brings beauty into our lives, but also creates a cohesive social bond that cuts across a number of societal divides. In a world where religion is used to justify terror and ethnicity is used to justify mass murder, Twitchell contends, "If Americans can't share God, why not Gucci?"[16] Why not indeed? I am ready to join the super-rich and blow

---

[14]Leigh Gallagher, "Having It All—but Needing a Grip," *Forbes*, October 8, 2001, p. 112.

[15]Lynn Hirschberg, "Luxury in Hard Times," *The New York Times Magazine*, December 2, 2001, p. 124.

[16]James B. Twitchell, *Living It Up: Our Love Affair with Luxury* (New York: Columbia University Press, 2002), reviewed by Kathleen Madigan, "Gucci Is Good," *Business Week*, July 8, 2002, p. 15.

my small savings on outrageously expensive junk to help create a cohesive social bond, aren't you?

Many of the very wealthy have an absolute aversion to the kind of uncertainty that was a part of the aftermath of recent terrorist attacks. In fact, many of the super-rich have purchased elegant estates in parts of the world that are much less likely to experience terrorism. An architect in Australia told me that he had designed a very expensive home in a secluded forest in Tasmania for a super-rich American. It was his client's sixth home, and he only plans to use it two weeks a year . . . unless there is a terrorist threat.

While some business tycoons in China and some entertainers in America are purchasing the most expensive automobiles available, most of the Western super-rich are not. David Cole, chairman of the Center for Auto Research, states, "Flashing your wealth 'is a dangerous thing to do.'" The super-rich are trading in their luxury cars for less ostentatious brands and having them rebuilt with heavy-duty armor.[17]

In the film *A Ship of Fools*, the wealthy in connoisseur class have dinner with the captain every night and are totally preoccupied by their own self-involved lives, clearly all but oblivious to the huge number of poor farm laborers jammed in the cargo hold below deck.

Let's seek to answer the second question—how should the wealthy use their resources to enable the poor to participate in this new global economy? Nineteen billion dollars a year between now and 2015 could end global starvation and malnutrition. An additional $12 billion per year over the same period could provide education for every child on the planet. An additional $15 billion a year would translate into access to clean water and basic sanitation to everyone traveling on this vessel with us.[18] Thankfully, there are those among the very wealthy today who have been able to focus beyond their own wealth, comfort and security to offer new possibilities to some of the global poor.

---

[17]"Conspicuous non-consumption," *The Economist*, January 8, 2005, p. 57.
[18]Claude Rosenberg and Tim Stone, "A New Take on Tithing," *Stanford Social Innovation Review*, Fall 2006, accessed May 13, 2007, at <www.ssireview.org/articles/entry/a_new_take_on_tithing/>.

FUTURES OF THE RICH REIMAGINED

Growing numbers of the swelling ranks of the wealthy are becoming serious philanthropists. An organization called The New Tithing Group, which
encourages wealthy Americans to give more to charity, paid the I.R.S. to
pull detailed information on the giving patterns of the top four hundred
wealthy Americans. They posted their findings and analysis on the Internet
to influence the wealthy to increase their generosity.[19] If top earners in the
United States gave at the same level as the middle class or the working poor,
charitable giving would increase by $25 billion a year. If the wealthy gave
what they could afford based on conservative charitable benchmarks, they
could give $100 billion a year.

The giving of the top four hundred earners in America increased 80 percent from $93 million in 1997 to $174 million in 2000. Bill Gates, the cofounder of Microsoft, is doing some of the most intelligent philanthropy in
the world today through the Bill and Melinda Gates Foundation. For example, the foundation is seeking to expand access to basic immunizations for
the 27 million children in our world today who have no access to them.
Through the Grand Challenges Initiative, the Gates Foundation is attempting to use scientific research to improve vaccines for children, find ways to
stop the spread of malaria and develop more nutritious staple crops to help
two billion of our neighbors combat malnutrition. Super-rich Warren Buffet and others have invested generously in this important effort.

A number of Christians in many countries have been successful in making money. The question I want to raise is: How much of the money God
has entrusted to us do we need to spend on our own needs and wants? Many
of us who are wealthy and not so wealthy could significantly increase our
giving to empower those at the margins without feeling any pain.

Harvest Time provides a community for wealthy Christians to help one
another discern together how to use their money to advance God's kingdom. For example, Nancy and Howard Thurston, a part of a Harvest Time

---

[19]David Cay Johnston, "The Very Rich, It Now Appears, Give Their Share and Even
More," *The New York Times*, January 1, 2004, pp. C1, C3.

small group in Portland, Oregon, felt led to purchase an apartment to be available for both hospice care and hospitality for those in need. Howard and Nancy are stewards of that apartment for their group.[20]

One wealthy family in the U.K. created some imaginative ways to be a part of the quiet conspiracy. Kim Tan states his vocation is "making wealth to distribute wealth." He is the son of a Malaysian businessman who emigrated to the U.K. sixteen years ago. Shortly after his arrival, he came to vital faith in Christ. Kim immediately plunged himself into a university education, through which he became convinced that God cares for every part of life on this planet.

He and his wife, Sally, residents of Surrey, England, developed the policy of giving away 50 percent of their income, plus any surplus at the end of the year. Kim and Sally collaborated with two Christian leaders in the U.K., Roger Forster and Alan Kreider, to create a new form of Christian venturing, the Transformational Business Network, to encourage entrepreneurs to start small businesses in poorer countries where there is high unemployment.

The Tans also started a creative venture in rural South Africa, setting up a wild game park in a malaria-free area. He is training sixty-five workers to fence the park and is helping them start their own fencing business in the process. These people were not only well-paid for the work they did, but they were also well-trained in construction and literacy skills.

Kim states, "The liberator God provides a mechanism for a fresh start and the generous delegator God wants people to be able to take responsibility. In the Jubilee, the means to wealth is re-distributed back to the people. This is not a charity mentality but a stewardship mentality."[21] In the next section, we will look at the stewardship opportunities and challenges facing those of us in cabin class as we cruise into this new global future together.

---

[20]For ideas on how you can more faithfully steward your resources, contact Rose Feerick at Harvest Time <www.harvesttime.cc>.

[21]Mark Greene, "Rich Christian in a World of Need," *Christianity and Renewal,* August 2004, pp. 46-48.

JOIN THE CONVERSATION

- What do you anticipate will be some of the consequences of our wealthiest neighbors receiving a growing share of global income?

- What do you believe Scripture calls all of us in the West who are affluent to regarding our poorest neighbors?

- Imagine one way that you or some of your wealthy friends might creatively use some of your resources to empower the poor.

CHALLENGES FACING THE
VULNERABLE MIDDLE

How well is the new global economy working for the middle class? How can we join God's conspiracy by creating new ways to serve others?

As Christine and I arrived in Melbourne at the Dangerous Stories Conference sponsored by Alan Hirsch and The Forge, we were immediately impressed by the age range and creativity of those we met. There was a broad spectrum of emerging, missional and traditional church leaders working together in a way we hadn't seen before. There was also a frank discussion of concerns facing a new generation of church planters.

During one panel discussion, an Anglican priest stood and expressed concern about two twenty-year-old church planters she had met the week before at an emerging church conference in the States. These young leaders "were sinking like rocks in their personal finances." One had run up a credit card debt of $34,000 to stay alive during his first year of church planting. The other had run up $17,000 on his cards. Both were facing plastic meltdown and had no idea what to do. "How can we help young emerging church planters find the resources they need to stay alive while they are seeking to create new expressions of the church?" the priest asked the panel.

"Christians have always had to sacrifice for the ministry of Christ and that's the way it's always been," responded a middle-aged denominational executive who was on the panel with me. I countered, "It's not the way it has always been!" Many conscientious leaders don't seem to realize that the middle-class young are hitting the global economy at a much tougher time than their parents or grandparents did. Young leaders today are facing a much more demanding financial challenge than any prior generation because of a major economic age shift.

BEGINNINGS

In the last section I asked: How well is this new economy working for those in connoisseur class? We discovered it seems to be working exceedingly well for the rich (in economic terms) and especially for the new super-rich. Now we will ask: How well does this new global economy work for those of us in the middle class—and particularly for those just getting started? As you will see, even though a number in the middle class are benefiting from the boom economy, this certainly is not true for everyone. We will also ask: How can we in the middle class create new ways to both deal more effectively with the challenges facing us and become much more a part of God's compassionate conspiracy in the lives of others?

MOUNTING TIME PRESSURES

How well is the new global economy working for those of us in cabin class? Clearly numbers of us in the middle class are making more money than we were ten or fifteen years ago. But others are seeing jobs disappear overseas or retirement savings suddenly evaporate. Many of us are awash in cheap consumer goods from China, while others struggle with soaring housing costs. A handful of the under-thirty-five crowd has joined the ranks of the newly rich, but many more will struggle just to keep their noses above water.

When Christine and I work in churches in the U.K., Australia, New Zealand and North America, we ask, "How many of you are working harder and longer than you were five years ago?" Invariably, at least 70 percent of the hands go up. One of the major reasons for this growing sense of time crunch is that this new global economy is obsessed with the pursuit of greater efficiency. As a consequence, there is mounting pressure on workers everywhere to work harder and longer. Many people in Britain, Australia and particularly the United States are putting in more hours at work than even a decade ago. Also, Americans have much less vacation time than our counterparts in most other Western countries.

An Obstacles to Growth Survey studied 20,000 Christians in 139 countries over 5 years to discover how busy they are. They discovered that the levels of busyness were extremely high in the lives of Christians, particularly in countries like the United States and Britain, and particularly for pastors. Dr. Michael Zigarelli, at Charleston University School of Business, described the problem as "a 'vicious cycle' prompted by cultural conformity." He added that this extremely high level of busyness results in God being marginalized in our lives and "Christians becoming even more vulnerable to adopting secular assumptions about how to live, which leads to more conformity to a culture of busyness, hurry and overload. And then the cycle begins over again."[1]

One of the new creations of the global economy is the 24/7 workweek. Growing numbers of people in our churches and communities are on call twenty-four hours a day, seven days a week, and functionally never leave their work. That's new. This pressure to work harder and longer is likely to only get worse. Add to it the stunning growth of new hybrid technologies that will increasingly blend flat-screen TVs with our computers and iPods to create an expanding and tantalizing array of entertainment options. Plus with the advent of Internet-based producer technologies being described as Web 2.0, huge numbers of us are spending a growing portion of our time both producing and consuming DVDs, podcasts and other media.

Bottom line: as we see growing pressure to spend more time at work and more time consuming and producing media, we will have less time for other things, among them family, friends, church, prayer and Scripture—and certainly less time to be involved in serving others.

---

[1]Audrey Barrick, "Survey: Christians Too Busy for God," *Christian Today*, July 31, 2007, accessed at <www.christiantoday.com/articledir/print.htm?id=11977>.

Therefore, those in leadership in the emerging, missional, mosaic and monastic streams as well as those in traditional churches need to recognize that the people they work with need help! We need to find or create practical resources to help people more effectively steward their time and resources to insure they have time for the things that we claim, as followers of Jesus, matter most. We also need to model a less driven way of life in which we are much more present to God and those with whom we are in community.

One of the most unusual aspects of this new global economy is that some in the middle class are being lured to pursue extreme wealth while others are in danger of falling into extreme poverty. I will share two very different stories of middle-class families struggling with these extremes. See if you can relate to either of these stories.

IN PURSUIT OF EXTREME WEALTH

Karen Adey wakes up every morning in her modest suburban home dreaming she will own a multimillion-dollar business, vacation on the Riviera, shop in Paris and purchase a huge trophy house. Karen is one of a swelling number in the middle class who deeply envy the lifestyles of both the rich and the super-rich. She is convinced that if she can decode the Rosetta Stone of wealth and privilege, she can transport herself, her husband and her two teenagers into the luxurious lifestyles of the super-wealthy. Karen has already spent thousands of dollars attending motivational sessions at Madison Square Garden, where Anthony J. Robbins has participants walk on hot coals and pump their hands in the air while singing along with Tina Turner's song "Simply the Best" in order to "awaken the giant within."

Karen has fully invested herself in this passionate quest for more. "Leadership is the capacity to significantly influence the thoughts and actions of others. . . . I am dissatisfied with being excellent. I want to be outstanding." Her husband, who is a computer technician, grew up on a farm in Pennsylvania and has a different vision for the future than Karen: he wants to retire to a small farm. Karen observed, "You can't take care of animals when you are on the Riviera," to which he replied, "I won't be going to the Riviera."[2]

Imagine Karen hanging out of a porthole in cabin class with a grappling hook and a winch. Here's a woman who is absolutely determined to winch her family up to connoisseur class—whether they want to go or not!

In *Luxury Fever*, Robert Frank reports that luxury spending has been growing at four times the pace of overall spending.[3] Growing numbers of the middle class, like Karen, hanker for lavish lifestyles. Most of us don't have Karen's expectations to move on up. We simply want to indulge in luxury items that, until recently, were totally out of reach.

This new appetite for luxury goods is no accident. In the last couple years, the marketers of the global economy devised a new campaign called "the democratization of luxury." Sounds grand, doesn't it? That means even though most of us will never experience what it is like to fully enjoy the lifestyles of the rich and famous, marketers are seeking to persuade us that we are all entitled to a taste of it.

The message to women in the middle class goes something like this: Go ahead and buy your $100 casual outfit from the Gap. You are entitled to a little luxury in your life . . . indulge yourself . . . go ahead and buy a $5,000 Gucci purse to dress it up a bit. . . . You're worth it.

A host of companies who produce luxury items from BMWs and Gucci to luxury resorts and spas are seeking to seduce those of us in cabin class to develop an appetite for luxurious living, even though we will never be able to afford to relocate to connoisseur class. And it is working! Recently, a young woman we met at a camp observed that "luxury has become ordinary" in her suburban community in California. Arnold Schwarzenegger, the governor of California, reminds those aspiring to live like the very rich that money doesn't happiness make. "I now have $50 million, but I am just as happy as when I had $48 million."[4]

---

[2]Chris Hedges, "Seeking the Path to Riches: It's Not About Coveting, It's Unlocking the Inner Tycoon," *The New York Times*, December 24, 2002, p. A22.

[3]Robert Frank, *Luxury Fever: Money and Happiness in an Era of Excess* (Princeton, N.J.: Princeton University Press, 1999), p. 18.

[4]Geoff Tibballs, *The Mammoth Book of Zingers, Quips and One-Liners* (New York: Carroll & Graf, 2004), p. 352.

Increasingly, we are finding middle-class Christians not only in the United States, Canada and Australia, but also in the U.K. and New Zealand, who are indulging in everything from McMansions and luxury cars to expensive cruises and spa holidays. Many people don't seem to realize that purchasing monster houses from five thousand to twenty thousand square feet is not only costly economically, but also costly for the environment. As a consequence, communities from Silicon Valley to the Rocky Mountains are imposing energy restrictions on super-sized dwellings. In Los Altos, California, the typical megahome is larger than the town's 8,500 square-foot city hall.[5]

More of us are indeed being seduced to spend a growing share of our limited resources on luxuries, which means we have less left over to pay our daily bills but also less to invest in the work of God's new order.

I want to introduce you to another family who have absolutely no interest in moving on up to connoisseur class. They simply don't want to lose their grip on life in cabin class.

IN PERIL OF EXTREME POVERTY

Arnold and Sharon Dorsett and their three kids Zachery, Dakota and Jessica reside in Camby, Indiana, and are treading as hard as they can to simply keep their heads above water. It is not working. Zach, who is now eight years old, has had a series of health problems since he was an infant, including two bouts of pneumonia. Belatedly, his parents discovered that he has a serious immune system disorder that requires monthly infusions of immune globulin. Their health insurance covers 90 percent of their doctor bills, but the copays are eating them alive. Since their son was an infant, they have been accumulating bills of $12,000 to $20,000 a year.

Arnold, who works on commercial heating and air conditioning systems, has increased his hours at work to eighty to ninety hours a week, earning a

---

[5]Joan Lowy, "Communities Rising Up Against McMansions," *HGTV*, accessed January 22, 2007, at <www.hgtv.com/hgtv/rm_home_building_other/article/0,,HGTV_3727_3529761,00.html>.

good income of $68,000 a year. With the long hours he puts in, he has very little time with his kids, and still the Dorsetts haven't been able to keep ahead of the constant stream of bills for Zach's treatments. Sharon does her part doing child care, but it doesn't bring in a lot of money. They tried to manage by relying on their credit cards and ran up nearly $30,000 in debt. When they fell behind in their payments on their primary card, the company raised their interest rates from 2.9 percent to 14 percent, which only compounded their problems.

Friends encouraged them to turn to the church, but they weren't comfortable asking for help. They refinanced their small home to pay off their credit cards, but that didn't solve their problems. They found the higher monthly mortgage payment and their monthly car payment were beyond their ability to pay. With great reluctance, Arnold and Sharon decided to file for bankruptcy in an effort to get their noses above water.

It was extremely difficult for Arnold to tell his father that he had filed. "I make good money, and I work hard for it. When we filed for bankruptcy, I felt I failed." His dad had worked two or three jobs during hard times and had always been able to pay his bills. Arnold makes more money than his father, but it just doesn't seem to go as far. Even though their bankruptcy takes them out of debt for the moment, the Dorsetts have lost their home, and Zach's medical bills keep rolling in. There is no assurance they won't slip into the chilly waters again.[6]

How is it possible that growing numbers of middle-class families like the Dorsetts, who work hard, play by the rules and care for their kids, find themselves in such impossible situations, while other middle-class families like Karen's have the possibility of moving up to connoisseur class? How can those of us in cabin class deal with both the increasing seduction of luxury and the increasing peril of financial calamity? We need to be much more aware of both "the great risk shift" facing all generations and "the great age shift" that is facing a new generation.

---

[6]John Leland, "When Even Health Insurance Is No Safeguard," *The New York Times*, October 23, 2005, pp. 1, 20.

THE GREAT RISK SHIFT

I grew up in the 1950s. Clearly, we are enjoying consumer goodies now that we couldn't even have imagined back then. Many are heralding our new economy today as a wondrous celebration of happiness and delight, and most of us do have much more stuff: from computers to DVD players, from satellite-guided car-computers to iPhones. However, research shows that we aren't any happier than we were in the 1950s.

In 2005 the *Wall Street Journal* announced, "The Miracle Continues," celebrating this season of booming economic growth and new consumer goods. However, most Americans don't believe the miracle even exists.[7] The Economic Policy Institute, a Washington, D.C., think tank, stated that between 1979 and 2000, while those in the top fifth of incomes in the United States saw their incomes increase by 70 percent, the top 1 percent increased by an incredible 184 percent, the middle class saw only a small increase, and the lowest fifth of incomes in the United States grew by a meager 6.4 percent, a rate that doesn't begin to keep pace with inflation.[8] Yale economist Robert Shiller expresses concern that this new "casino economy" seems to be contributing to an economic winner-take-all effect, in which a tiny fraction of the population earns most of the money—and a large fraction doesn't earn very much at all.[9]

Even though most Americans are still optimistic about their economic futures, they don't seem to realize that the upward mobility machine doesn't work very well these days. In fact, Jacob Hacker writes, "There is more social mobility in European nations, such as Sweden, than in the United States, and in fact only South Africa and Britain have as little mobility across generations."[10] In other words, inequality is growing.

Hacker raises another concern: "The instability of American families' in-

---

[7]See Jacob Hacker's important book *The Great Risk Shift: The Assault on American Jobs, Families, Health Care, and Retirement and How You Can Fight Back* (New York: Oxford University Press, 2006) for a thorough analysis.
[8]"Ever Higher Society, Ever Harder to Ascend," *The Economist*, January 1, 2005, p. 22.
[9]Robert J. Shiller, "American Casino: The Promise and Peril of Bush's 'Ownership Society,'" *The Atlantic Monthly* 295, no. 2 (2005): 34.
[10]Hacker, *Great Risk Shift*, p. 24.

comes has risen substantially faster than inequality of families' incomes. The chance that families will see their income plummet has risen." He explains that income instability was five times as great at its peak during the boom of the late 1990s as it was in the early 1970s. In 2002, it was three times greater than in the early 70s.[11] Jacob Hacker lists the reasons for this growing instability. First, workers in this new global economy in Britain, Australia, New Zealand and North America are much more susceptible to job layoffs for longer periods of time than in the sixties, seventies and eighties. When workers do find work, it is often at a much lower wage than the job they lost. Many people have lost all their retirement benefits from corporations defaulting on their retirement programs.

In addition, both businesses and government in the United States are increasingly shifting the costs of health care and retirement back to our families and to us. In other words, we are seeing the safety nets that used to be provided by businesses and government slowly being shredded. This means that those of us in the middle class and our young are increasingly going to need to create our own economic safety nets.

Political and economic conservatives around the world are lobbying for what they call "the ownership society." These advocates correctly observe that when people own their own homes, land and other investments, they tend to take a more responsible role in society. However, Robert Shiller points out that the kind of ownership society that is often advocated doesn't just encourage personal ownership, but significantly increases the levels of personal risk.[12] I believe that this kind of "ownership society" is really code language for shifting people back to living "on their own."

Hacker explains that advocates of this policy want to shift more of the risk back to workers and their families. They actually believe it is better for us to bear the full weight of the economic costs on our lives instead of having governments or businesses sharing the risks in areas such as health

---

[11]Ibid., pp. 12-18, 27.
[12]Shiller, "American Casino," p. 33.

care, unemployment benefits and retirement costs.

Unquestionably, we all need to set aside more for a rainy day. For example, private retirement accounts like 401K programs are a good idea. But there is no way most of us will ever make enough money to put away even a small percentage of what we will need to cover our health care, retirement and other protection that those in the middle class have come to expect.

Frankly, the only thing that kept many families in the middle class in the 1970s, 1980s and 1990s was wives going back to work. Elizabeth Warren, in her definitive book *The Two-Income Trap: Why Middle-Class Mothers and Fathers Are Going Broke*, documents that today even two-income families are having a hard time making ends meet—let alone sharing with those in need.

> The average two-income family earns far more today than did the single-breadwinner family of a generation ago. And yet, once they have paid their mortgage, the car payments, the taxes, the health insurance, and the day-care bills, today's dual-income families have *less* discretionary income—and less money to put away for a rainy day— than the single income family of a generation ago.[13]

According to *The Economist*, household savings rates plummeted from 7 percent at the beginning of the 1990s to less than 1 percent, not only for Americans, but for Canadians and Brits as well. Savings rates in Australia and New Zealand are actually negative; Aussies and Kiwis borrow to consume more than they earn.[14] Recently Americans also joined the negative savings-rate club, binging on borrowed money with gusto.[15]

Like the Dorsetts, growing numbers of us are in serious danger of losing our grip on the middle class and slipping down into cargo class, where economic uncertainty is a way of life. In fact, more and more middle-class

---

[13]Elizabeth Warren and Amelia Warren Tyagi, *The Two-Income Trap: Why Middle-Class Mothers and Fathers Are Going Broke* (New York: Basic Books, 2003), p. 8.

[14]"The Shift Away from Thrift," *The Economist*, April 9, 2005, p. 58.

[15]Jennifer Bayot, "Economy Was Showing Strain Before Storm," *The New York Times*, September 2, 2005, p. C5.

families in Western countries are only one paycheck away from economic disaster as economic storm clouds gather.

ESCALATING DEBT IN CABIN CLASS

Ironically, one of the major factors keeping the global economy growing is American consumer confidence. One needs to ask: How long are Americans going to be able to spend more than we earn to keep the global economy booming?

Levels of personal debt are soaring for many who live in Western countries. The rapid growth of credit card use in the United States is one of the reasons we are able to consume beyond our means. "Loaded up on expensive toys largely by borrowing and charging,"[16] Americans now owe $750 billion in revolving credit card debt. That is six times what it was two decades ago. Personal debt in Britain rose to £1,318 billion in March 2007—a dramatic increase from the 1993 total of £400 billion.

From 1989 to 2001, credit card debt carried by poor families increased 149 percent. Credit card companies sought to sell their wares to people whose credit history made it clear they would have difficulty using a credit card without making their situation worse. They then charged those customers an average interest rate of 13 percent and late fees that averaged $29.[17]

One of the most concerning new responses to growing debt is people borrowing against their homes. Economist Stephen Roach declares, "We have turned the American home into a gigantic ATM machine, where anytime you need money—to take trips or to buy DVD players made in China— you go to a friendly lender."[18] Incredibly, while debt is soaring, one of the most rapidly growing industries in America is the $17 billion storage industry. Apparently we need more space to store all those consumer delights that we don't really need and can't really afford.

The consequence of soaring consumer debt is, of course, soaring bank-

[16]Jennifer Steinhauer, "When the Joneses Wear Jeans: Signs of Status Are Harder to Spot, but Look Again," *The New York Times*, May 29, 2005, p. 13.
[17]"The New Loan Sharks," *The Atlantic Monthly* 293, no. 1 (2004): 48.
[18]Stephen Roach, "Paging Dr. Doom," *Money*, October 1, 2004, p. 72B.

ruptcy rates. Reportedly British bankruptcy rates increased 60 percent between 2006 and 2007.[19] Between 1983 and 2003, U.S. bankruptcy filings increased 500 percent.[20] If this trend continues, Elizabeth Warren predicts that bankruptcy filings for U.S. families will increase from about one million in 2003 to five million by the end of the decade, sending record numbers falling into the chilly waters of financial crisis.[21]

When people find themselves having to file for bankruptcy, they often lose their homes. Hacker reports that the U.S. mortgage foreclosure rate has escalated 500 percent since the early seventies.[22] With the mounting crisis in defaults in new variable-rate mortgages, the housing foreclosure rate could soar into the stratosphere.

New laws, clearly designed to protect the interests of credit card companies and other lending institutions, have been passed in the United States to make it more difficult for people to file for bankruptcy. Please understand that this doesn't mean credit institutions don't care about you, however: columnist Ann Landers wrote, "If you think nobody cares whether you are living or dead, try missing a couple car payments."[23]

In light of these new economic challenges, leaders in both traditional churches and new expressions need to provide practical resources to help people become more effective stewards of the resources with which God has entrusted us.

SOARING HEALTH-CARE COSTS IN CABIN CLASS

As Christine and I travel, we hear that the health-care systems in Britain, Australia, New Zealand and Canada are under severe economic stress. Many of our friends in these countries are supplementing their single-payer care system with private health-care insurance. Few have any idea what their health-care costs would be if they joined Americans and relied entirely on

---

[19]"Debt Statistics," <www.creditaction.org.uk/debt-statistics.html>.
[20]Bayot, "Economy Was Showing Strain Before Storm," p. C5.
[21]Elizabeth Warren, "The Growing Threat to Middle Class Families," *Brooklyn Law Review* 401 (April 2003): 3.
[22]Hacker, *Great Risk Shift*, p. 13.
[23]Tibballs, *Mammoth Book of Zingers*, p. 154.

private health-care insurance with escalating costs. For Christine and me it runs about $1,000 a month and is increasing at 5 to 7 percent a year.

In America we are headed for a health-care breakdown. The reason so many American families have so much more difficulty managing their finances today compared to earlier times is the cost of health care. According to Warren's study, between 46 and 54 percent of debt is a result of families having more medical bills than they can manage, just like the Dorsetts.[24] More than eight out of ten cite the major reasons that families with kids filed for bankruptcy were medical expenses, job loss and family breakup.[25] Michael Moore's documentary *Sicko*, though a bit over the top, documents many of the serious challenges facing us.

When the huge population of baby boomers begins retiring in 2010, demand for health care for the elderly is likely to accelerate dramatically, which will significantly increase the stress on all our health-care systems. But we in America are facing, by far, the most daunting challenge of all, because the costs of our free-market health-care system are soaring beyond the ability of growing numbers of us to pay.

Remember, the Dorsetts had health insurance that covered 90 percent of their costs, which is considered excellent coverage in the United States, but it wasn't enough. The number of Americans who lack any health insurance at all has increased with little interruption for the past twenty-five years as corporations have consistently shifted the costs back to workers. Today, over 45 million Americans live without health insurance. Over a two-year period, more than 80 million Americans have spent some time without any health insurance at all.[26]

The average American, with a median household income of $42,409, spends 21 percent of that amount on health-care insurance. Americans are often surprised to learn that our largely private model of health-care coverage costs twice as much per person as what our neighbors in other indus-

---

[24]Gail Russell Chaddock and Ron Scherer, "Bankruptcy Terms Toughen," *Christian Science Monitor*, March 10, 2005, p. 10.
[25]Warren, "Growing Threat," p. 13.
[26]Hacker, *Great Risk Shift*, pp. 13-14.

trialized countries pay for coverage through their taxes. In fact, in 2005, U.S. health-care costs climbed to $1.6 trillion, or 15 percent of the total U.S. economy.[27] Insurance costs increase at about 10 to 12 percent a year, about three times the rate of inflation, which means that insurance premiums for individuals and businesses will double in just over seven years.[28]

Clearly, most of us can't afford this rate increase, and health-care policymakers I have talked with predict that the American health-care system is headed for a major train wreck in the very near future. In spite of health-care proposals from both Democrats and Republicans, few see any viable alternatives on the horizon that will materialize in time.

Many people would love for the United States to adopt a single payer, tax-funded system like our friends in the commonwealth countries. The Massachusetts plan to require everyone to buy insurance could be a step in the right direction. But if costs continue to soar in the United States, adequate insurance could cost more than those in the middle class can afford to pay.

Globalization does offer some Americans a few surprising lower-cost options. Some health-care plans are actually flying Americans to India because surgical procedures are much less expensive there. In Southern California near Mexico, an American health insurance provider has contracted with fully qualified doctors, dentists and health-care facilities in Mexico to create "Access Baja," providing care for thousands of Americans at a cost of only $100 a month.

Unfortunately, most of us don't have access to these new global options. When Mennonites migrated to America generations ago, they created mutual care networks that included health care. It is time for followers of Jesus to create mutual care models of health care that are affordable for not only our members but also the vulnerable in our communities as well.[29]

---

[27]David R. Francis, "Why the Healthcare Crisis Won't Go Away," *Christian Science Monitor*, July 18, 2005, p. 17.

[28]Julie Appleby, "Health Insurance Premiums Crash Down on Middle Class," *USA Today*, March 16, 2004, accessed January 22, 2007, at <www.usatoday.com/news/health/2004-03-16-healthcost_x.htm>.

[29]The Hutterites, a communal branch of the Mennonite church, maintain a contemporary mutual care network.

THE GREAT AGE SHIFT

All of those under age forty, including those in the emerging, mosaic, missional and monastic streams, need to ask: How well does this new global economy work for those just getting started? Remember the two emerging church planters that we met? They are representative of an entire generation. As a direct result of what I call "the great age shift," those getting started today are having to pay a much higher proportion of their income for living expenses than their parents and grandparents did. While the consumer stuff from China is cheaper, young people are having to spend more for higher education, housing and health care in relationship to what they earn than prior generations.

I graduated from Cascade College in Portland, Oregon, in 1958. The cost of my tuition, room, board, fees and books was $700 for the entire year. I worked a summer job at $4 an hour (which was a good wage back then) as a janitor, and had no problem paying off the entire bill. As college students know today, a summer job hardly makes a dent in the costs of a private college education.

What happened? The cost of a private college education increased fortyfold from $700 a year in 1958 to around $30,000 today. But the summer job has only doubled or tripled in value, from $4 to $8 or $12 an hour during the same period. As a consequence, very few of my generation had any student debt; we could easily work our way through school.

Anya Kamenetz, the twenty-five-year-old author of *Generation Debt: Why Now Is a Terrible Time to Be Young*, says that this generation is running the highest rate of school debt of any generation in history, graduating with "a kind of a mini-mortgage on their backs." The situation is compounded because many student loans impose exorbitant interest rates. Fully two-thirds of students in the United States graduate with school debts of $17,600 to $23,000.[30] I have run into undergrads who have debts as high as $40,000 to

---

[30]Rachel Kramer Bussel, "Interview: Anya Kamenetz, Author, *Generation Debt: Why Now Is a Terrible Time to Be Young*," *Gothamist*, February 2, 2006, accessed January 22, 2007, at <www.gothamist.com/archives/2006/02/02/anya_kamenetz_a_1 .php>.

$50,000 and graduate students who are several hundred thousand dollars in debt. Only one in six African American and one in twelve Hispanic students are earning a college degree, but over half of those who graduate wind up with unmanageable levels of school debt.

Kamenetz further reports that the under-thirty-fives are also running an average credit card debt of $4,000.[31] A recent Citibank/Sony Visa campaign promoted credit cards to college students as the "Currency of Fun." They offered electronic gadgets as rewards for high levels of purchasing, implying that the more you spend the more "fun" you will have and the more "toys" you will receive.[32] One must ask, is this really a responsible approach to marketing to a generation already so laden with debt?

In addition, the job opportunities in this new global economy have changed significantly since the previous generation parents entered the work force. Many graduates today wind up working in dead-end, low paying service and contract jobs with no benefits. Of course, even the average school-debt loads seriously limit students' life options, particularly those who want to make a difference with their lives.

The cost of housing has soared for this generation as well. Most of us from the silent generation were able to live the middle-class dream on a single income, and few spent over 20 percent of a single income for rent or mortgage. I bought my first home in Portland, Oregon, in 1963 when I was on staff at Cascade College. An older couple had totally restored a 1920s two-story bungalow with a massive front porch. It was a four-bedroom, two-and-a-half-bath home with a full basement. The couple had redone the wiring and plumbing, added a modern kitchen and baths, and repainted it inside and out. The total cost in 1963 for this lovely restored home was $14,500. Even though the college paid me a salary of $4,000 a year, which was equivalent to being on public welfare, I had no trouble making that $100-a-month mortgage payment on a single income. Today, that same house would likely sell for over $700,000 and two young people with good

---

[31]Ibid.
[32]Robert D. Manning, "Credit Cards on Campus," *Enough!,* Fall 2003, p. 1.

incomes would have difficulty qualifying for a loan.

Again, the cost of the house has increased in value over forty-five times from 1963 to 2006. But the starting wage has only increased about seven or eight times from $4,000 to $30,000 a year. As a consequence of this age shift, large numbers of the under-forties we work with in Chicago, Los Angeles, Seattle, Toronto, London, Sydney and Auckland are often paying over 50 percent of two incomes for rent or mortgage.

Here's the problem for a new generation in a nutshell: The double whammy of higher school debt and higher housing costs seriously limits life options for those who want to make a difference with their lives. In other words, the age shift makes it much more challenging for a new generation to get started and even harder to free up time or money to invest in the work of God's mustard seed conspiracy. Those of us who are older need to help those in the four streams and recent grads find innovative ways to meet their essential needs without spending such a large share of their limited resources.

FUTURES OF THE MIDDLE CLASS REIMAGINED

While numbers in the middle class are making more money in this new economy, it clearly isn't all good news. In fact it looks as though we are heading into a future in which the pressures on our time and resources will only increase. We are also likely to see a continuing erosion of our safety nets as well.

Numbers of us in the West have come to see the single-family-detached lifestyle model as the norm, even though most of our forebears before World War II lived in extended or shared housing arrangements like many of the urban poor still do today. As we race into the twenty-first century, we are facing two conflicting trends. On one hand our global consumer culture and our growing involvement in the cyber world are influencing us to become much more individualistic. On the other hand, the cost of our individualistic lifestyle models is becoming increasingly more expensive than many will be able to afford. As a consequence, growing numbers of us will be pressured to consider shared and cooperative lifestyle models for economic reasons.

Frankly, I think it is time for middle-class Christians to reexamine our love affair with our individualistic lifestyles and explore community and cooperative based models. They could enable us to more authentically embody the values of our faith, provide a bit more economic security, and reduce our costs so that we have more time and money to invest in the work of God's new order. In fact, I propose that both our new expression churches and conventional congregations actively help members rediscover the gift of community and mutual care. I would urge that leaders even consider enabling them to create cooperative ventures to help us live less expensive and more faithful lifestyles.[33]

Brian McLaren is right: "everything must change."[34] Given these trends and the uncertain times in which we live, it will no longer be enough for churches to have a small rainy-day fund when families become unemployed or hit an economic crisis. We will need to revision the church less as an institution that we support and view it more like a large extended family that creates a range of cooperatives to care for one another and particularly those in need.

Cooperatives have been around for a long time and currently serve 120 million people in the United States. Co-ops are growing in popularity in this era of big box stores and corporate agriculture because they show special loyalty to their local communities. Co-ops create jobs and economic opportunities, enable us to reduce our ecological footprint, often help us create a bit of a collective safety net, and are both member-run and motivated by service rather than profit.[35]

There are 30,000 Hutterites living in large cooperative style communities in North America. Through creating cooperative living models, they significantly reduce their lifestyle costs. For example, they are able to build a home for a family of four in the Hutterite Community in Woodcrest, New

---

[33]Andrew McLeod has put together a very helpful Web resource on cooperatives called Book of Acts Project <www.bookofacts.info>.

[34]See Brian's book *Everything Must Change* (Nashville: Thomas Nelson, 2007).

[35]"Co-ops Generate Billions in Income While Supporting Community Causes Like Education and the Environment, Study Finds," Co-op Month <www.coopmonth.coop/toolkit/sample_article_nl.html>.

York, for around $50,000. It only costs about $1,000 a month to support a family of four because the community buys all its food, clothing and appliances cooperatively. Through a cooperative lifestyle, the health care and retirement costs of everyone in the community are covered, and generous support is provided to help the local poor and homeless.

While joining the Hutterites isn't an option for most of us, we can learn from them. Our congregations could become birthing centers for a host of new housing, food, health care, energy and even economic cooperatives. Robert Waldrop, the director of music at the Epiphany of the Lord Catholic Church in Oklahoma City, has started a large food co-op (www.plentymag.com) that specializes in organic locally grown food. Christians in Cambridge, U.K., have started The Daily Bread Co-op (www.daily-bread.co.uk), offering organic and fair-trade foods.

We can all create informal cooperatives that will enable us to live more faithfully. The Sojourners Community in San Francisco that is a part of the monastic network has had a car cooperative for a number of years that has significantly reduced members' personal costs. Each of the thirty-five members of the community spend a monthly amount, ranging from $50 for light use to $150 for everyday use, to have access to seven cars. This monthly amount covers the cost of purchasing, insuring and maintaining the vehicles.

Brent and Melinda, a Christian couple in Boulder, Colorado, came up with an imaginative way to both reduce their housing costs and create community in support of their ministry with college students. Instead of renting a small two-bedroom apartment that they could afford out of town and commuting, Brent and Melinda rented a larger six-bedroom house right in Boulder near their church and the University of Colorado. They share the house with three students and a young man who is employed in Boulder. Their community shares meals together, offers hospitality and divides up household responsibilities. This frees up time for spiritual practices such as lectio divina and engaging issues like the marketplace and world events. Currently, they are working with university students as part of Justice for Children International to advocate for children caught in sex trafficking.

Both traditional churches and new expressions need to reinvent our congregations to help those of us in cabin class deal more creatively with times of economic crisis and the growing pressures on both our time and our money. To the extent that we can create innovative new forms of community and new cooperatives, we can live more faithfully and be more a part of God's compassionate response to our neighbors traveling in cargo class.

JOIN THE CONVERSATION

- What are some of the economic and time pressures facing you, people in your church and your community?

- What biblical principles about mutual care might help a church more effectively care for people in need?

- Imagine one new form of a cooperative that could enable those in your church and community to both provide a little more mutual care while helping the most vulnerable in your community.

CHALLENGES FACING
THE WESTERN POOR

*What are the challenges that are likely to confront our poorest
neighbors? How can we help them survive and thrive in this
new global economy?*

The chanting was deafening as Christine and I viewed the Live 8 Concerts
on TV in Australia back in 2005 with a group of keen younger Christians.
The concert lobbying for the forgiveness of Third World debt was a huge
event there, as it was throughout Europe. We've been deeply impressed by
the significant number of young Christians we have met in Australia and
Great Britain who are working to make poverty history.

In one scene of the film *The Ship of Fools*, an immigrant worker living in
the cattle hold of the boat falls off one of the lower decks and is lost at sea.
An older wealthy couple in connoisseur class, preoccupied with their little
lap dog, greet the news of this loss of human life with the kind of chilling
indifference that is pervasive in our world today. Every day we awake to images: a mother with child in a refugee camp in Darfur, whose life is at risk
every day; a cluster of children huddled in a shanty in South Africa who just
lost their mother to AIDS; homeless people sleeping in doorways and under
viaducts of too many Western cities. Over time, we somehow seem to become numb to the images. But then we hear Christ's voice again, "as you
have done it to the least of these . . ."

Frankly, I have never fully recovered from my first trip to Port-au-Prince,
Haiti, in 1977. I had never seen that kind of wrenching urban poverty before. I supervised a community development project in Haiti and spent sev-

eral months on location each year for seven years. I learned more about the life of faith from my Haitian friends and coworkers than I have ever learned in church. They also taught me how to cook wonderful Haitian food.

Nelson Mandela believes we have reached a turning point in history: "Massive poverty and obscene inequality are such terrible scourges in our times, in which the world boasts breathtaking advances in science, technology, industry and wealth accumulation—that they have to rank along slavery and apartheid as social evils."[1] I am hearing a growing chorus of those who join Mandela in declaring this scourge will no longer be tolerated. Ian Cairns, a young American who works with us in Mustard Seed Associates, wrote, "Our generation will be judged by what we do about the extreme poverty in Africa." Before we look more closely at the extreme poverty of the global poor, let's look at the future of the poor in our own Western countries.

BEGINNINGS

Growing numbers of Christians share a commitment to make poverty history. But I find that those involved in the mosaic and monastic streams are particularly committed to this cause. In this section I will ask: How well does the new global economy work for the poor in our own communities and throughout the world? I will also ask: What are specific creative ways we can all be much more a part of God's compassionate response in empowering those at the margins?

TRAVELING WITH THE WESTERN POOR

Like the horrific terrorist attack four years earlier, the enormous catastrophe of Hurricane Katrina brought an immediate response of prayer and empathy from all over the world. As we look back, this crisis also raised serious questions for many of our global neighbors of the apparent deep divide between America's poor and the middle class.

---

[1]*Human Development Report 2005* (New York: United Nations Development Programme, 2005), p. 17.

Nearly one million Americans tried to flee the terror of Katrina. Most of the middle-class residents were able to escape the devastating flood in their cars, SUVs and RVs, but many of the poor weren't able to escape. Thousands in Gulfport, Mississippi, weren't able to get out of the hurricane's path. The "perfect storm of catastrophic weather, human error, socioeconomic inequity and bureaucratic dysfunction"[2] is documented in Spike Lee's CNN documentary *When the Levees Broke: A Requiem in Four Acts*. As I write, the Gulf States are gearing up for another hurricane season. Reportedly a number of regions are little more prepared than they were the last time a devastating storm rolled through.

Shannyake, a twenty-nine-year-old single mom, recounts her experience of trying to find a safe place to ride out Katrina with her three kids: George, age eight; Destiny, age six; and Cerkaria, age three. Their father is serving with the U.S. Army in Iraq. Weeks before the storm, Shannyake had been struggling to find work. A few days before the hurricane hit, she had landed a job as a clerk at a local gas station. She was hopeful that this low-wage job would help her begin to turn her life around.

Shannyake realized her apartment building wasn't safe. After frantic searching, she finally found some people who let her and her small brood hide out in their house to provide protection from the raging winds. In the middle of the night, during the height of the gale-force winds, a large pecan tree blew down, crushing the roof and nearly killing Shannyake and her kids. After the winds subsided, the family made its way back to their small apartment and found that they had lost all their earthly belongings, including the old 1985 Chevy.

Shannyake was able, with considerable difficulty, to get her kids to the fairgrounds in Jackson, Mississippi, with thousands of other displaced families seeking help. They waited long hours in the sweltering heat and discovered firsthand how slow the relief efforts were to address the needs of those who had lost everything, including a place to live.

[2]Joe Leydon, "Review: *When the Levees Broke: A Requiem in Four Acts*," *Variety*, August 17, 2006, accessed January 23, 2007, at <www.variety.com/review/VE1117931327.html?categoryid=1237&cs=1&query=requiem%2C+spike+lee>.

"Leaning forward with her hands pressed together between her knees, she says she'll never erase the terror of holding her children as the world crashed around them."[3] There are so many whose lives will be forever changed by the hurricane, but clearly the poor got the worst of it.

THE GREAT DIVIDE

"Seven in ten blacks (71%) say the disaster shows that racial inequality remains a major problem in the country; a majority of whites (56%) say this was not a particularly important lesson of the disaster," according to the Pew Research Center. "Most striking, there is widespread agreement among blacks that the government's response to the crisis would have been faster if most of the storm's victims would have been white; fully two-thirds of African Americans express that view. Whites, by even a wider margin (77%), feel this would not have made a difference in the government's response."[4]

There are reasons for this very different perception of the government's response to Katrina. Many of those in cabin class aren't aware that this new economy doesn't work nearly as well for those, like Shannyake, who reside in cargo class. Conservative commentator David Brooks, reflecting on Katrina, was deeply distressed at the way the poor and the black were left behind, "The first rule of the social fabric—that in times of crisis you protect the vulnerable—was trampled. Leaving the poor in New Orleans was the equivalent of leaving the injured on the battlefield. No wonder confidence in civic institutions is plummeting."[5] Images of the abandoned black and poor are reminiscent of some of the images in the film *Hotel Rwanda*, where

---

[3]Edward Robinson, "Gulfport Family, Escaping Katrina, Can't Find U.S. Aid," Bloomberg.com: News & Commentary, accessed January 22, 2007, at <http://quote.bloomberg.com/apps/news?pid=nifea&&sid=azRjaR1Pa_1s>.

[4]"Two-in-Three Critical of Bush's Relief Efforts: Huge Racial Divide Over Katrina and Its Consequences," The Pew Research Center for the People and the Press, September 8, 2005, accessed January 23, 2007, at <http://people-press.org/reports/display.php3?ReportID=255>.

[5]David Brooks, "The Bursting Point," *The New York Times*, September 4, 2005, accessed January 22, 2007, at <http://select.nytimes.com/gst/abstract.html?res=F30D17 F83F550C778CDDA00894DD404482>.

the white and privileged were transported out while the poor and black were left to fend for themselves.

Unlike many middle-class people, most of these folks have no insurance and absolutely no resources to begin their lives over again. While many of us in cabin class worry about our safety nets becoming frayed, many of our poorer neighbors are seeing theirs shredded.

One of the immediate consequences of Katrina was hundreds of thousands of Americans becoming homeless refugees in their own country. People like Shannyake and her children scattered all over the country. But quite apart from this kind of natural disaster, homelessness is becoming epidemic in a number of countries.

CONFRONTING AN EPIDEMIC OF HOMELESSNESS

There are between 3.5 and 5 million homeless people in the United States; 39 percent of them are children. According to the Urban Institute, shelter capacity in the United States has tripled in the past decade.[6] The people staying in shelters are those who have all but lost whatever safety net they might have relied upon.

Believe it or not, homeless shelters report that growing numbers of the middle class are joining the ranks of the homeless, in part because of the high price of housing. Another new homeless group in the United States is veterans coming back home from Iraq. Herold Noel, his wife and three kids found themselves sleeping on the streets or anywhere else they could find. "It's horrible to put your life on the line and then come back home to nothing. . . . I thought I was alone, but I found out there are a whole lot of other soldiers in the same situation."[7] With the soaring numbers of foreclosures on homes that families are buying with variable-rate mortgages, we could see the ranks of the homeless dramatically increase.

Confronting the growing crisis of the working poor. This increase in poverty

---

[6]The Urban Institute, "A New Look at Homelessness in America," February 1, 2000, accessed January 23, 2007, at <www.urban.org/publications/900366.html>.
[7]Alexandra Marks, "Back from Iraq—and Suddenly on the Streets," *Christian Science Monitor*, February 8, 2005, p. 2.

and homelessness came despite a season of strong American economic growth. Part of the problem is that growth in service jobs that often don't pay a living wage has been overwhelming. Growing numbers are being priced out of affordable housing.

Barbara Ehrenreich, a journalist with a Ph.D., decided to leave the comfort of her middle-class life to go undercover and join the ranks of the working poor. She was determined to demonstrate to herself that she could live frugally and make ends meet on a job in the service sector. She reported her findings in her book *Nickel and Dimed*. Ehrenreich landed her first job as a waitress at the Hearthside in the Florida Keys for $2.43 an hour, plus tips. She rented a single room with a hot plate for $500 a month.

For many of the working poor, the only housing they can afford is often a three- to five-hour daily commute from where they live, which takes a serious toll on family life and on their budget as transportation costs rise.

Ehrenreich enjoyed the staff she worked with and didn't mind the grinding work, but after two weeks, she realized that she simply couldn't make the numbers work. With tips, she was barely making the minimum national wage, which then was $5.15 an hour. Even though she had spent virtually no money on anything but very basic food, she suddenly realized that she wouldn't earn enough to make rent. Since she didn't want to wind up homeless and start sleeping in her old junker car, like her coworkers, she decided to seek a second job.

A surprising number of the working poor have to work virtually every waking hour at multiple jobs to keep their heads above water. Barbara got a second job waitressing at Jerry's, a greasy joint, from eight o'clock in the morning until two o' clock in the afternoon, with no breaks and no food. She then hustled to the Hearthside by 2:10 p.m. and worked until ten o'clock in the evening. An old back injury flared into painful spasms, so Barbara doped up with assorted pain pills and kept on trucking, just like many others who simply can't afford the luxury of being ill.

Barbara was thankfully making enough from her two jobs to make rent, but then things suddenly went up in flames at Jerry's. She quit and was back to a single job, feeling like a failure. She realized she had to decide whether to join the ranks of the homeless and start sleeping in her car, or to move on to another service job where she might do a little better.[8]

THE WESTERN POOR FALLING BEHIND

Here are the current economic realities in the United States: Those in the top 20 percent economically earn over 50 percent of the income in America, and their share of the pie is growing. The U.S. poverty rate has risen for the fourth consecutive year to 12.7 percent—thirty-seven million now live in poverty—meaning the average impoverished family of four is trying to get by on $19,000 a year. African Americans have the lowest median income. Regionally, the South has the lowest median income.[9]

The poor in America are having a tougher time making ends meet; their incomes have been largely stagnant, while costs for fuel and food continue to rise, shredding their safety net. Twenty percent of children in America are born into poverty—a higher percentage than any other Western country.

In Britain poverty rates have declined in recent years, but there are still more poor in the U.K. than in most other European countries. In 2004-2005 there were 11.4 million people living in poverty, compared to 14 million in 1996-1997; 3.4 million of those living in poverty are children. There are twice as many people from other cultures living in poverty as whites, a statistic that is similar to the situation in the United States.[10]

In Australia the Salvation Army states that about 2.5 million or 12 percent of the population lived in poverty in 2005. This is a 400,000-person increase since 2002. Again there were far more people from other cultures grappling with poverty and unemployment than the white population. In fact there are 3.8 times as many aboriginal and Torres Strait Islander Aus-

[8]Barbara Ehrenreich, *Nickel and Dimed: On (Not) Getting By in America* (New York: Metropolitan/Owl, 2001), pp. 11-49.
[9]Given this data, one can understand part of the reason that many African Americans responded so strongly in the Pew survey ("Two-in-Three Critical").
[10]"United Kingdom Indicators," The Poverty Site, accessed May 13, 2007, at <www.poverty.org.uk/summary/uk.htm>.

tralians unemployed as white Australians.[11]

Thankfully the U.S. Congress, after years of stonewalling, voted to raise the minimum wage from $5.15 to $7.25 an hour by 2009, to provide a bit of help for the working poor.[12] The government in Britain in 2007 raised the minimum wage to £5.35—equivalent to roughly $10.70 in U.S. dollars.[13] The problem is that given rising costs for life's essentials, even these increases don't provide a living wage in many regions of the Western world.

In this competitive global economic race to the top, I think we will see many Western countries attempting to reduce the drag on national economies by slowly whittling away at the safety net for not only the poor but even the middle class. Since Katrina the U.S. Congress whittled away at the minimal safety net for the American poor, including cutting back on funding for food stamps and Medicaid.[14] These same representatives lobbied to continue offering $70 billion in tax cuts for the wealthiest Americans. Some have called this "trickle up economics." I am convinced that both of these initiatives had a single goal: to shrink government regardless of the costs to the poor.

We are likely to continue seeing not only better-paying manufacturing jobs but also professional jobs being shipped overseas. As a consequence, the domestic poor will need to settle for jobs in the service sector that often don't pay a living wage.

The public education system contributes to the widening gap between rich and poor in the United States. In *The Shame of the Nation*, Jonathan Kozol documents that over the past twelve years, American public schools are

---

[11]"The Salvation Army and the National Coalition Against Poverty," accessed May 13, 2007, at <www.salvationarmy.org.au/SALV.1310888:LANDING:511353:pc =PC_60977>.

[12]"Minimum Wage: Facts at a Glance," Economic Policy Institute, April 2007, accessed May 13, 2007, at <www.epi.org/content.cfm/issueguides_minwage_ minwagefacts>.

[13]"CBI Urges Caution on Minimum Wage," BBC—News, September 25, 2006, accessed May 13, 2007, at <http://news.bbc.co.uk/2/hi/business/5371896.stm>.

[14]Daniel B. Woods, "Katrina Casts Light on the *Other* Poor," *Christian Science Monitor*, October 24, 2005, pp. 1, 3.

resegregating America.[15] Unlike other Western countries that fund public education through taxes, American public schools rely on local levies; consequently wealthy school districts often spend twice as much per pupil as poor school districts. This means that the growing numbers of children who attend poorly funded urban public schools have less of a chance of going on to college than their suburban counterparts who attend highly financed schools with cutting-edge technology. As a consequence, some, like their parents, will be stuck in dead-end service jobs that don't pay a living wage. Frankly, this new global economy is going to leave growing numbers of the poor behind in all countries if we don't discover how God might use our mustard seeds individually and collectively to be an expression of God's compassion for the marginalized.

FUTURES OF THE WESTERN POOR REIMAGINED

There has been an ongoing debate between those on the left and right in many countries on how best to help the poor. Those on the left have lobbied strongly for more government assistance. However, a number of the various social welfare programs were conceived in compassion but have created chronic dependency.

Those on the right decry the "nanny state" and lobby to cut back social programs to reduce taxes. Numbers in this camp feel the best way to help the poor is to shrink government so they are forced to help themselves. They see free enterprise, not big government, as the answer. I think it is becoming clear to many in these urban communities as well as those of us outside that we need to use both the creativity of free enterprise and the resources of government. We also need to see a much higher commitment of time and resources from our churches to make domestic poverty history. The question is, will our churches rise to the challenge?

The 2004 American presidential election was largely decided by "values issues." Regrettably, the biblical value of compassion for the poor was not

---

[15]Jonathan Kozol, *The Shame of the Nation: The Restoration of Apartheid Schooling in America* (New York: Crown, 2005).

one of them. But times are changing. Christine and I recently had dinner with Jim Wallis, author of *God's Politics*, who reported that religious conservatives and religious progressives are finally coming together in new ways to help the poor. The more I have opportunity to work with younger conspirators in the mosaic, monastic, missional and emerging streams, the more I discover that they have little patience with the kind of polarized politics that have characterized America's culture wars in recent years. They care about families and the vulnerable, but they also care about social justice and creation care.

Remarkably, the National Association of Evangelicals (NAE) has recently published a report, "For the Health of the Nation," that calls for a broader view of social responsibility; it includes strong advocacy for the poor and the environment. The NAE has also endorsed an even more striking statement setting the bar higher on issues of human rights and torture. Rick Warren has been a leader in influencing American evangelicals to broaden their view of social responsibility. In other words, American evangelicals are expressing views on social responsibility that are less polarized and more similar to those views expressed by Evangelical Alliances in the U.K., Australia and New Zealand.[16]

One of the most encouraging signs that times are changing is the creation in 2007 of a remarkable new coalition called Christian Churches Together. Wesley Granberg-Michaelson, the general secretary of the Reformed Church in America, helped birth this new ecumenical organization that includes evangelical, Pentecostal, mainline Protestant, Catholic, Orthodox, black, Latino and Asian churches plus organizations like World Vision, Bread for the World, Evangelicals for Social Action and Sojourners/ Call to Renewal. According to its website, CCT is a "forum growing out of a deeply felt need to broaden and expand fellowship, unity and witness among the diverse expressions of Christian faith today" and offers "a significant and credible voice in speaking to contemporary culture on issues

---

[16]Tom Sine, *Cease Fire: Searching for Sanity in America's Culture Wars* (Grand Rapids: Eerdmans, 1995).

of life, social justice and peace."[17]

One of the pressing issues that brings this unusual coalition together with a common voice is "the 'scandal' of U.S. domestic poverty and to call upon the candidates from both parties to put poverty near the top of the nation's political agenda."[18] We need to put pressure on not only international political leaders but also economic and church leaders to make a much greater commitment to making poverty history.

If we are serious about this goal, then we need to critically reexamine how we are working for social change with those in poorer communities. Frankly, some governmental and church-based initiatives foster dependency instead of self-reliance. There will always be a place for some "need meeting" programs, with social workers providing services and churches providing food. But since public and church resources for social programs are likely to decline in the future, we need to reprioritize how we use these resources. We will need to shift shrinking resources into programs that seek to empower individuals and families and work for the transformation of our communities.

EMPOWERING INDIVIDUALS

If we are serious about enabling the poor to not only work in this new economy but make a living wage, then increasing educational opportunities is essential. First, we must do much more to increase the quality of public schools in our cities. We also need to find ways to come alongside those schools, like XLP Ministries in London. This school has a double-decker, brightly painted bus that picks up two hundred students from poor communities on seven housing estates in London. The program offers tutoring, computer resources, a study center and a club for the kids on the estates. The Mustard Seed School in Hoboken, New Jersey, has been offering high-quality education to urban kids since 1979. In addition to supporting the

[17]See <www.christianchurchestogether.org>.
[18]Jim Wallis, "Christian Churches Together—Finally," *Sojomail*, February 15, 2007, accessed May 13, 2007, at <http://www.sojo.net/index.cfm?action=sojomail.display&issue=070215>.

important work of public schools, we also need more of these private Christian schools that empower the urban young.

We need to increase the quality of education not only for kids but for parents. We need to provide job training that enables them to make a living wage. For example, Chicago's Project Match tracks women who receive training to become nurses, teachers and social workers. Participants not only see a sharp boost in their pay but also better health insurance and more flexible work hours, and they are able to raise their kids in less dangerous neighborhoods.[19] Years ago when I was working as a social worker in San Jose, California, I helped several women secure funding for education, including one who became a school counselor and never needed public assistance again.

Let me share one single mom's story and the difference one church made in her life. In six months the bottom dropped out of Denise's life in Lancaster, Pennsylvania. She lost her job, her apartment, her car, her boyfriend (he left her when she was three months pregnant) and her family's respect. She cried out to God and met a woman who connected her to Bridge of Hope. Edith Yoder, the director, immediately involved Denise in an innovative program that surrounded her with a trained community of caring friends. Essentially, twelve people from Community Church in Lancaster, Pennsylvania, discovered what God could do with their mustard seeds. They became her mentors, helping her with all aspects of life. The first thing they did was to get Denise off the streets. After her baby daughter was born, they helped her find a place to take computer classes. Now she has a job, a living wage, a new apartment, childcare for her daughter and a car. She is deeply grateful to God and her mentoring community for being supportive in her time of crisis. Imagine what would happen if every church took responsibility to help one single parent achieve a decent way of life for herself and her family.

EMPOWERING COMMUNITIES

We not only need to enable individuals to realize a decent way of life for

---

[19]"Helping the Poor: From Welfare to Workfare," *The Economist*, July 29, 2006, p. 28.

themselves and their families, we also need to help them create cooperative ventures that increase the quality of life in their communities. YouthGROW is such a creative venture in Worcester, Massachusetts. In its first year, a group of fourteen urban teens and staff grew 750 pounds of organic produce on an abandoned half-acre of land. The community markets its fresh produce to local stores and restaurants and supplies the Mustard Seed food pantry, Centro Las Americas and Food Not Bombs, which all serve those on the margins.[20]

Since safety nets for the poor are likely to be shredded even faster than for the middle class, creating local economic cooperatives is essential. They provide jobs, economic income and security for the community, while improving people's quality of life. Couldn't many of our congregations provide leadership to help start economic, agricultural and energy cooperatives that empower marginal communities? Couldn't some urban churches partner with traditional churches and new expressions to create an array of economic cooperatives with the goal of making urban poverty history?

Churches were among the first responders to the Katrina crisis. They were also among the handful of groups that received a positive evaluation for their efforts to resettle and care for refugees in Louisiana and adjacent states. One of the unexpected and under-reported outcomes of Katrina is that a number of churches around the United States are forming disaster preparedness teams. As we move into an increasingly uncertain future with the possible impacts of global warming and other threats, doesn't it make sense for our congregations to create disaster preparedness teams to empower communities and particularly our most vulnerable neighbors? Church World Service offers training resources that could help churches prepare to give aid to communities in times of crisis.[21]

Mike Geertsen, a Seattle resident, has developed a remarkable software product called Simio that enables local communities to draw on the huge amount of data on the Web to do disaster preparedness. This software can

---

[20]Matt Feinstein, "YouthGROW: A Local Food System Grows an Alternative Economy" <www.geo.coop/YouthGrow1104.htm>.

[21]Church World Service Emergency Response Program <www.cwserp.org/training>.

collect information for any community in the world to simulate a weather-related disaster today or five years in the future, and it can stitch that information together into a useable format. The software also secures information on everything from the capacity of local hospitals during a possible earthquake in Los Angeles five years into the future, to community response groups that the church could work with to help the displaced.

As we move into an increasingly uncertain future, we need to join our neighbors in creating new ways to help them achieve their dreams for both their lives and their communities. We also need to discover how we can be a part of God's quiet conspiracy of empowerment in the larger world.

JOIN THE CONVERSATION

- What trends about poverty in your community and country concern you most?

- What are biblical images of God's purposes for those at the margins? How might those images find expression in our cities?

- Imagine one creative way you might help one urban community in your country to help itself.

CHALLENGES FACING
THE GLOBAL POOR

What are some of the challenges that are likely to confront the global poor? What are creative ways we can help them address these challenges?

Since September 11, 2001, the United States has launched a war on terror, but has neglected the deeper causes of global instability," states economist Jeffrey Sachs. He points out that while the nation will spend $450 billion on the military, it only spends $15 billion to address the needs of the world's poor, whose societies have become "havens of unrest, violence and even global terrorism."[1]

WAKING TO THE HORROR OF HURRICANE JEANNE IN HAITI

In Gonaives, Haiti, a village not far from where I worked in earlier days, Jean Pierre Luke, Lillian and their five children were sleeping peacefully in their tiny two-room stick, stone and mud hut when a huge wave of water came crashing through their doorway. Startled, Jean Pierre and Lillian scrambled in the dark to get their children out of their home before it was completely flooded. They had no idea where the water came from, but it was a product of Hurricane Jeanne, which hit Haiti almost exactly a year before Hurricane Katrina hammered the U.S. Gulf Coast.

As they were slowly swimming toward a neighbor's two-story house to find safety on the roof, they started counting heads. They only counted four

---

[1]Jeffrey Sachs, *The End of Poverty: Economic Possibilities for Our Times* (New York: Penguin Press, 2005), p. 1.

BEGINNINGS

The plight of the global poor puts their lives in greater peril, but it also contributes to the growing uncertainty of all of us who travel on this ship of fools together. Let's see how well this new global economy is working for our poorest neighbors. I will also explore some creative ways we might respond that give expression to the compassionate world that is already here.

---

of their five kids. As Lillian helped their four children climb up on their neighbor's roof, Jean Pierre swam back to their home. He dove down and swam around inside their home that was now completely filled and covered with water. He checked both rooms, and Marie Lucy, age nine, was nowhere to be found.

He returned to his family exhausted and deeply grieved by his inability to find Marie Lucy. They spent the night huddled together on the roof, and when they woke early the next morning, they saw their community of Gonaives totally under water. Dozens of human bodies, as well as carcasses of cattle, goats and dogs, floated past. Around noon, they saw a body about a hundred yards away that looked like their missing daughter, but they had no way to retrieve it.

Hurricane Jeanne devastated Haiti and other Caribbean countries, but we read little about it in our newspapers, and it received little coverage on our TV and Web sources. Over 1,514 people were killed and 900 went missing. Two hundred fifty thousand people, like the Lukes, were displaced by this storm.[2]

While the American government response to Katrina was seriously delayed and mismanaged, many poor countries like Haiti have absolutely no governmental agencies in place to respond. The Lukes were entirely on

---

[2]"Haiti Flood Deaths May Top 2,000," BBC—News, September 28, 2004, accessed January 23, 2007, at <http://news.bbc.co.uk/2/hi/americas/3697086.stm>.

their own, just like the other 250,000 displaced people.[3] All over our planet, families like the Lukes are in a chronic struggle to simply survive and try to keep their kids fed each day. This struggling family lost one of its children, its home, the family goat, clothing and cooking utensils.

While the safety net in Western nations is being shredded, most of our neighbors in poorer countries have no safety net at all. As a result of global warming, these weather-related disasters are likely to become more frequent, and families like the Lukes have nowhere to turn.

THE HORROR OF GLOBAL POVERTY

In some ways, poverty conditions have improved since I wrote *The Mustard Seed Conspiracy* in 1981. In the eighties and early nineties, we witnessed regional improvements in the economic conditions of those at the margins in many parts of the planet. Life expectancy has increased from forty-six to sixty-four years, and infant mortality has been reduced from 18 percent to 8 percent over the last fifty years.[4]

In spite of some of the areas of improvement, the future of our poorest neighbors is not promising, in part because the new global economy is leaving many of them behind. As a consequence, their situation is in many ways worsening. Joseph Stiglitz, in *Making Globalization Work*, reports that

outside of China, poverty in the developing world has increased over the past two decades. Some 40 percent of the world's 6.5 billion people live in poverty (a number that is up 36% from 1981). One sixth—877 million—live in extreme poverty (3% more than 1981). The worst crisis is in Africa, where the percentage of the population living in extreme poverty has increased from 41.6% in 1981 to 46.9% in 2001. Given the increasing population, this means that the number of people living in

---

[3]Dan Griffiths, "Agony Piled on Agony in Haiti," BBC—News, September 26, 2004, accessed January 23, 2007, at <http://news.bbc.co.uk/2/hi/americas/3691226.stm>.

[4]Johan Norberg, "How Globalization Conquers Poverty," *Globalization and World Capitalism: A Debate*, Cato Institute, November 6, 2005, accessed January 23, 2007, at <www.cato.org/special/symposium/essays/norberg.html>.

extreme poverty has almost doubled, from 164 million to 316 million.[5]

One of the reasons the situation has worsened for so many of the global poor since 1981, particularly in Africa, is the coming of the HIV/AIDS epidemic in the mid-eighties. Globally, 38.6 million people were living with HIV/AIDS at the end of 2005, according to the UNAIDS 2006 Report. The global poor, particularly in Africa, are running a much higher incidence of infection and loss of life than other regions. This has not only taken a tragic toll on human life, but it has devastated the economy of a number of African countries, like Zimbabwe.

Some are predicting that the epidemic could be even worse in Asia. HIV prevalence jumped almost 50 percent in East Asia between 2002 and 2004 to 1.1 million people. Today, India has the second most infected population on the planet with 5.1 million cases. There is a growing concern that the spread of HIV in India and China could result in an even greater loss of life and economic impact than in countries in Africa.[6] There are other epidemics waiting in the wings that could take even more lives and be even more destabilizing for the global economy than HIV/AIDS.

The most vulnerable in our world are widows, the elderly, the disabled and, of course, children. Nearly one-third of the world's population is under fifteen years of age, most of whom now live in overcrowded cities. In fact 76 million new babies join our global village every year, with most born in poorer regions. The global population is projected to grow from 6.5 to 9.1 billion by 2050.[7] This means that, in the next two decades, we must see a dramatic increase in educational resources, jobs and housing to provide for this burgeoning generation. But first we need to insure that the young and vulnerable survive.

Twenty-five thousand children die every day from hunger and malnutri-

---

[5]Joseph E. Stiglitz, *Making Globalization Work* (New York: W.W. Norton, 2006), p. 11.
[6]Lisa Mastny, "HIV/AIDS Crisis Worsening Worldwide," *Vital Signs 2005: The Trends That Are Shaping Our Future,* The Worldwatch Institute, ed. Lisa Mastny (New York: W. W. Norton, 2005), p. 68.
[7]David E. Bloom and David Canning, "Booms, Busts, and Echoes," *Finance and Development* 43, no. 3 (2006): 9-10.

tion. Ninety-one million children under five years old are severely malnour-ished. Two hundred sixty-five million have never been immunized. Three hundred seventy-six million lack access to clean water. Over fourteen mil-lion children have lost either one or both parents to AIDS.

Heidi, a student at Bethel University, had the opportunity to visit Uganda and do rounds with a doctor who was working with malnourished newborns. Heidi watched their health deteriorate in spite of efforts to save them. She returned to Bethel with a clear sense of calling "to be a voice for the voiceless." She participated in one of the many programs preparing stu-dents to serve God in our globalized society sponsored by the Council for Christian Colleges and Universities, an affiliation of 105 institutions in North America and 24 other countries.

Children are also at serious risk of being sold into servitude in the global sex trade, conscripted into military service or forced to work as bonded ser-vants like many of the children I worked with in Haiti.[8] Education is the key to enabling tomorrow's generation to achieve a sustainable way of life, and educating girls seems to do more to lift an entire village than almost any other strategy.

One of the most imaginative approaches to education is a project at the Massachusetts Institute of Technology that envisions a $100 computer dis-tributed to children in poorer families all over the world.[9] Children who have limited learning opportunities can suddenly be connected to a global class-room with access to high-quality educational resources. Of course it also risks connecting them more directly to the influences of the global mall.

THE GLOBAL POWERS AND THE GLOBAL POOR

How well does this new economy work for the global poor? Not that well. The fact is that it works much better for the global wealthy who have abun-dant assets. The poor have virtually none. In fact, every year the UN Human

---

[8]Paul Stevenson, "Children at Risk," *WHO Review: The Health Need of Children*, Form 5-9.
[9]Christa Case, "A Low-Cost Laptop for Every Child," *Christian Science Monitor*, No-vember 16, 2005, p. 4.

Development Report documents growing inequality between our richest and poorest neighbors. The report states that the richest 516 billionaires now have a combined income of greater than the poorest 416 million people on the planet.[10] This is serious inequality, and it is growing at a concerning rate.

Joseph Stiglitz sees a host of reasons that this new global economy doesn't work nearly as well for the global poor as it does for the rich and for many of the rest of us. First, huge numbers struggle with chronic unemployment because the global lift-off hasn't reached most of the poor in Africa, Latin America and parts of Asia. The volatility of the new economy has resulted in many working poor people seeing their salaries decline, or worse yet, losing their jobs to people willing to work for less.

Economic globalization is also causing huge migrations nationally and internationally. We have just crossed a threshold and become an urban planet with over 50 percent of us living in cities. This number will increase to 60 percent by 2020. Frankly, poorer cities simply don't have the infrastructure—the economic, educational or public health resources—to deal with their swelling urban populations. Bakke Graduate University of Ministry in Seattle is one of the leaders in preparing Christians to engage the mounting urban challenges of the twenty-first century.

Growing numbers of people from poorer countries are being drawn to wealthy countries in hopes of joining the global economy. This causes a serious fracturing of families and makes their communities poorer for their absence. Solana Beach Presbyterian Church in San Diego has responded to this growing trend by working with one community in Mexico called Lomas Chimedia to significantly increase economic opportunities so that men can secure the income they need to support their families in their own community. Clearly churches and mission organizations need to decisively shift their focus to address the swelling cities of the majority world.

Stiglitz further charges that the rules of this new global economy are rigged to benefit rich and powerful nations and corporations, often at the

---

[10]*Human Development Report 2005*, p. 18.

expense of poorer nations, especially in terms of international trade policies. He states, "The United States and Europe have perfected the art of arguing for free trade while simultaneously working for trade agreements
that protect themselves against imports from developing countries."[11]

He is particularly critical of the way the International Monetary Fund
and World Bank required "structural adjustments" in poorer countries to
reduce inflation, a policy that threw thousands of the poor out of work. Following the introduction of structural adjustments, prices often rose three
to four times, making basic goods unaffordable, while at the same time removing the services that have kept poor families afloat. "UNICEF estimates
6 million children under age five have died each year since 1980 as a direct
result of SAPs."[12] Belatedly, the IMF is altering its policies and is finally
making poverty reduction a priority.

Joseph Stiglitz also indicts powerful corporations for working in ways
that increase their wealth at the expense of the poor. For example, major
drug companies successfully persuaded the U.S. government to keep inex-
pensive, generic AIDS drugs off the market in Africa to protect their potential profits. While protecting the profits of the wealthy, this policy has undoubtedly come at a very high cost in the lives of the poor and vulnerable.[13]

In *The Mustard Seed Conspiracy*, I noted that in a historic 1980 decision,
the Supreme Court ruled five-to-four to make it legal to patent life forms.[14]
One of the consequences of that decision was the creation of what is called
biopiracy. Corporations now travel the world and harvest genetic life forms,
which they patent without compensating those in the regions from which
they came. Everything from traditional plant medicines to biological materials from tribal groups has been patented. At the Rio Conference in 1992,
it was formally recognized that there should be fair compensation for those
who live where the genetic material is harvested, but for obvious reasons,

[11]Stiglitz, *Making Globalization Work*, pp. 9-15, 78.
[12]Cynthia D. Moe-Lobeda, *Healing a Broken World: Globalization and God* (Minneapolis: Fortress, 2002), p. 24.
[13]Stiglitz, *Making Globalization Work*, pp. 103-4.
[14]Tom Sine, *The Mustard Seed Conspiracy* (Waco, Tex.: Word, 1981), p. 60.

the U.S. government has never felt inclined to ratify this international agreement.[15]

JOINING THE BATTLE TO MAKE POVERTY HISTORY

There has been a growing awareness among Western leaders that something must be done about the growing inequities in this global economy. One of the first responses was the Jubilee 2000 Campaign, launched in Britain at the beginning of the millennium to persuade powerful nations and financial institutions to forgive Third World debt.

> In July 2005, the world's richest nations agreed to cancel $40 billion of debt that eighteen of the world's poorest countries owed to international lenders like the World Bank and the International Monetary Fund. It was a long-overdue step that would allow countries like Mozambique, Ghana, Nicaragua and Bolivia to spend about $1 billion more per year on schooling and health. Right now, African countries spend four times as much on paying back the debts than they do on health care. They are trapped, making ever-escalating interest payments that never touch the principal. Nigeria, for example, borrowed $5 billion, has paid $16 billion and still owes $32 billion.[16]

Another campaign was launched at the beginning of the new millennium called Make Poverty History. The centerpiece of this effort is the United Nations Millennium Development Goals, which include cutting global poverty in half by 2015. All 191 UN members unanimously agreed to these goals in 2002. They also agreed to end extreme poverty by 2025.[17] Jeffrey Sachs, an economist at the forefront of this important initiative, states,

> The Millennium Development Goals wisely recognize that extreme poverty has many dimensions; not only low income, but also vulnerability to disease, exclusion from education, chronic hunger, under nutrition, lack of access to basic amenities such as clean water and

---

[15]Stiglitz, *Making Globalization Work*, pp. 125-26.
[16]"Drop the Debt," *The New York Times*, September 24, 2005, p. A26.
[17]Sachs, *End of Poverty*, p. 25.

sanitation, and environmental degradation such as deforestation and land erosion that threatens lives and livelihoods.[18]

In other words, this is an integrated effort to not only increase employment opportunities in poorer countries, but also increase educational opportunities, provide immunization and improve public health.

To give you an idea of the difference that concerted activity can make in the poorest parts of the African continent, listen to what happened to the scourge of river blindness. The campaign to fight this disease was launched in 1974. It now spans thirty countries. The campaign has already saved the sight of 600,000 people in West Africa and has opened up 25 million hectares of fertile land for agricultural development.[19] Bill Gates is spearheading an important initiative to develop a vaccine for malaria that will have an even larger impact for those living in the tropics all over the planet.

The way this UN initiative will be funded is through contributions made by wealthy countries. Most developed nations agreed to reach the target of giving .07 percent of their Gross National Income.[20] While virtually all Western countries, including the United States, indicated their support for this approach, it isn't clear that many nations will actually put their money where their mouth is. The United States actually invested 2 percent of its Gross Domestic Product in the historic Marshall Plan that helped rebuild Europe after World War II. But most Americans would be surprised to learn that its government invests less that .02 percent in foreign aid today. British prime minister Gordon Brown, out of his deep concern for the global poor, is challenging Western nations to keep their promises regarding the Millennium Development Goals.

To halve poverty by 2015, we in the church must pressure our governments to support this important venture, insists the Archbishop of Cape

---

[18]Ibid., p. 213.

[19]"The $25 billion question," *The Economist*, July 2, 2005, p. 24.

[20]Note that terminology on this issue is changing. GNP, which the OECD used up to 2000, is now replaced with the similar GNI, Gross National Income, which includes a term of trade adjustment.

Town, Njongonkulu Ndungane. He launched the Micah Challenge campaign at the United Nations in 2004. The Micah Network that initiated this campaign is comprised of the World Evangelical Alliance of 3 million churches in 111 different countries, plus 270 Christian organizations. The Archbishop declared,

> Acting together, Christians can play a vital role in helping global partners meet their commitments. When we work with one another, united across nationalities and races, rich and poor . . . we have an enormously influential voice. We must speak loud and clear. . . . Poverty is evil. In all its ramifications and consequences, it mars the image of God within us, it mars it in the poor as it deprives them of opportunities for abundant life; and it mars it within those of us who have more than enough, but who, through greed, complacency or even ignorance, fail to do justice, embrace loving kindness, that our God asks of us.[21]

FUTURES OF THE GLOBAL POOR REIMAGINED

As we have seen, many of the global poor are likely to be left seriously behind in the new global economy if action is not taken to help them secure enough education and resources to participate. First, we need to join younger leaders in the campaign to make poverty history and urge our governments to support the Millennial Goals to which they committed. But we must also encourage countries, corporations and nongovernmental organizations to make a much greater commitment through our churches and our personal lives to end the "evil" of poverty.

We need to raise our voices with those who are speaking out with the poor. SPEAK is a U.K. lobbying group in which younger Christians speak out in the public arena. They recently held a protest in front of Parliament, based on Ezekiel's call to national repentance, to reduce Third World debt and alter unjust trade laws on behalf of the poor. Organizations like Bread

---

[21]The Most Revd. Njongonkulu Ndungane, "Micah Challenge," *Asian Church Today*, July-October 2004, pp. 5-6.

for the World are important lobbying groups for the U.S. poor.

Various Christian groups also bring faith to bear on a broad range of societal issues, including concern for the poor, social justice, reconciliation and peace making.[22] Ekklesia is rated as one of the top twenty think tanks in the U.K. and is working from a progressive Christian viewpoint. The U.S.-based Ekklesia Project provides progressive faith-based resources and organizes gatherings to raise awareness on a broad range of societal issues.

Empowering individuals. Research shows that educating females not only significantly improves their lives but is also one of the best ways to improve the quality of life of their communities. When my son Clint was sixteen years old, I took him to a community development project in the Plaisance Valley in Haiti that I coordinated. We were there at the request of the local churches to help the ten thousand people in this community lift their community out of grinding poverty. Our team worked with valley leaders to significantly increase their coffee production in order to increase the income and standard of living of the community. We also drilled a series of wells so people could start doing vegetable gardening both for their families and to sell in markets in the region. Finally, we also enabled them to design an innovative but basic health-care system that they could sustain.

During this trip Clint and I met a ten-year-old girl named Marie. Our meeting revealed a side of Haitian culture I had not been aware of. A number of poorer families in Haiti have more children than they can afford to support, so they are often forced to sell one or two of their children into indentured servitude. Many such children never see their families again. Marie was one of thousands of these "servant children." She works from six o'clock in the morning until ten o'clock at night seven days a week. Unlike the biological children in the family, she does not go to school or church and does not celebrate birthdays or Christmas. Often when these "servant

---

[22]See Conversations in Public Theology, the Evangelical Alliance U.K. (www.eauk.org); Zadok Institute for Christianity and Society (www.zadok.org.au); The Veritas Forum (www.veritas.org); the Anabaptist Network in the U.K. (www.anabaptistnetwork.com); Root & Branch (www.rootandbranch.org.uk); and Young Anabaptist Radicals in North America (http://young.anabaptist radicals.org). *The Other Journal* (www.theotherjournal.com) is also a helpful resource.

children" are liberated at age eighteen, they have no education or job skills and the cycle of poverty begins all over again. Many of them will have more children than they can afford.

Clint and I worked with our project coordinator, Chavannes Jeunes, to design a modest education program not only for Marie but for all the servant kids in the community where we were working. Chavannes persuaded the host families to allow their servant children to attend school two hours in the evening five days a week to learn basic literacy and math skills, plus one vocational skill, like dressmaking, so that they could learn to support their families when they are adults. When we returned to Seattle, it wasn't difficult to persuade people to contribute $6 per child per month to support a program that has the potential to break this kind of cycle of poverty.

In Pakistan, a woman named Talut was trapped in an abusive marriage with no resources and little hope. She was very fearful about her future until she met a woman who works with Mennonite Economic Development Associates (MEDA) in Pakistan, who trained her in business and marketing skills and helped her secure a MEDA loan to start a small business. Talut used her own instincts and skills to organize 170 housebound women to make embroidery, which she markets for them. Talut has become a confident businesswoman and is able to make a basic income. She said, "This woman has taken me step-by-step and shown me a world where I can succeed." Clearly this small business venture has provided hope not only to Talut but to the 170 women who work with her.

Empowering communities. Some in poorer countries have discovered the economic advantages of working together in cooperatives, instead of simply trying to make it alone as isolated families. Agros is an unusual ministry based in Seattle that really understands the power of working together cooperatively. Recently Agros has helped thirty families that were living below subsistence level in San Marcos, Nicaragua, to secure land and build homes for a rural agricultural cooperative. Agros is also enabling these families to start a dairy and bee-keeping cooperative that will not only help lift them out of poverty but also make it possible for their kids to go to school.

As Christine and I have had opportunity to travel in Asia, Africa and

Latin America, we see so much of God's quiet conspiracy happening in villages and local communities. One of the concerns that David Korten raises in his book *The Great Turning: From Empire to Earth Community* is that globalization has centralized economic and political power in the hands of a very small elite. Korten argues, "Real change will consist of removing power from a central authority and returning decision making to the local community level."[23] If we can enable people to have a greater voice, like the families in San Marcos, they can fashion their own local solutions to many of the economic challenges they are facing.

Bill McKibben raises the very real specter of global agribusinesses introducing "modern" agriculture on a gigantic scale and displacing local agricultural economies, leaving 600 million rural farmers in India, for example, without a place in the rural economy and driving them into the overcrowded cities.[24]

Some rural farmers in China are discovering creative ways to be a viable part of their rural economies and increase their influence through cooperative efforts. A Chinese philanthropist created a way to empower poor farmers by giving them free rabbits along with a training program. They feed their rabbits on the abundant grass that grows wild on their farms instead of on costly grains so their production costs are minimal. These farmers are raising rabbits both for their own sustenance and as a source of income that may help them keep their farms. To date, 300,000 farmers have received both the training and the rabbits.[25]

We need to encourage corporations to invest their resources to help fund these types of cooperative initiatives. World Vision Australia is offering corporations opportunities to be directly involved in sponsoring community development activities that are "mutually beneficial, measurable and outcome focused." For example, Computershare has invested 236,000

---

[23]Charles Shaw, "The End of 'Business As Usual,'" *Whole Life Times,* November 2006, accessed May 13, 2007, at <http://wholelifetimes.com/2006/11/korten0611.html>.

[24]Bill McKibben, *Deep Economy: The Wealth of Communities and the Durable Future* (New York: Times Books, 2007), pp. 198-99.

[25]Ibid., pp. 207-8.

Australian dollars in a project to help turn around the economy in Chad through working with farmers to create a huge reforestation cooperative venture.

Governments in developing countries also need to play a much more active roll in making poverty history. They need to reduce their debt and corruption and increase their economic growth so they have more resources to empower their poorest citizens. One innovative program in Brazil, for example, has created a new form of "social transfers" called Bolsa Familia. It has been created to help the country's poorest families living in monster cities, like São Paulo, who aren't making enough in their subsistence jobs to even keep their kids fed. The government gives each family 120 reais a month ($52), so they can afford to not only feed their children but also enable them to go to school. However, this monthly check is conditional. Families must have their kids vaccinated and their health regularly monitored.[26] This government program isn't just giving out handouts; it is investing in the future. Philippa Thomas, in a briefing paper on this topic, states, "Social transfers may well be a more cost-effective option than other initiatives that are currently used to address chronic poverty."[27] Thankfully some poorer countries are seeing the value of creating innovative safety nets for their poor at a time when they are being eroded in a number of Western countries.

BECOMING AGENTS OF EMPOWERMENT

The only way that poverty will become history is for those of us whom God has entrusted with God's generous resources to critically evaluate our own lives and priorities. It is estimated that today over 200 million Christians live in dire poverty. Isn't there something terribly wrong, in the international body of Christ, when some of us live palatially and other Christians can't keep their kids fed? Isn't it past time to recognize that we live in an interconnected, interdependent global village in which there is

---

[26]"New Thinking About an Old Problem," *The Economist*, September 17, 2005, p. 36.
[27]Philippa Thomas, "Ending Child Poverty and Securing Child Rights: The Role of Social Protection," briefing paper, October 2005, p. 2.

no longer any such thing as a "private" lifestyle choice?

John and Sylvia Ronsvalle, who direct Empty Tomb, Inc., state that $30 to $50 billion could meet the most essential needs of the global poor. They estimate if all American Christians gave 10 percent of their incomes, it would amount to over $65 billion dollars. With this much income we could cover our usual congregational, institutional and ministry costs and have enough left over to provide the amount needed to lift the global poor out of poverty.[28]

In light of the mounting issues facing us, we must ask, how can we be much more a part of God's compassionate revolution that is committed to not only making poverty history but seeing something of God's new order transform our lives and communities? To answer this question, first we need to answer another question: What are the challenges facing the church in the twenty-first century and will these challenges impede our ability to respond to the growing needs filling our world?

JOIN THE CONVERSATION

- If trends don't change, what do you see as some likely consequences for our poorest neighbors?

- What are our biblical responsibilities to join with the global poor in addressing these challenges?

- Imagine one new way you or your congregation might more fully be a part of God's compassionate conspiracy in addressing one challenge facing the global poor.

[28]John L. Ronsvalle and Sylvia Ronsvalle, *The Poor Have Faces: Loving Your Neighbor in the 21st Century* (Grand Rapids: Baker, 1992), pp. 53-54.

CHALLENGES FACING
AN ENDANGERED CHURCH

Does the future have a church? How can we reimagine and reinvent church to be better prepared to respond to these new challenges in our lives, our communities and God's world?

Scott, a brilliant young dancer in the Australian film *Strictly Ballroom*, gets in serious hot water with those running the national dance competition because he insists on dancing his own steps. Scott informs those in charge, "I am sick of dancing somebody else's steps." During a major confrontational scene Scott blurts out, "What we dance is crap!" Of course the film ends with Scott dancing his own steps to the acclaim of the audience and the dismay of those in charge.

A NEW GENERATION DANCING THEIR OWN STEPS

Growing numbers of the Net generation are making it clear that they are sick of "dancing somebody else's steps." In a consumer-oriented culture they are much happier shopping around for spiritual bits and essentially creating and dancing their own steps. They are exploring everything from online Wiccan chat rooms to psychic festivals. Books like *The Da Vinci Code* and *The Celestine Prophecy* encourage readers to fabricate their own religious expressions beyond traditional institutional offerings. Christian leaders need a wake-up call. While interest in traditional religion is declining, interest in spirituality is experiencing a remarkable revival.

Australian commentator Philip Johnson states,

Put simply, many people are highly suspicious of institutional and organised religions. . . . The Net generations are growing up in a flood of choices, lifestyles and information. Authority figures in religion are less likely to have "street-cred" because religious ideas can be sussed out with the click of a mouse. The outlook is likely to be shaped by whatever trends and fads are ripping through pop culture.[1]

As a consequence of this growing trend, more and more young people, including those raised in our churches, are shopping around. Those in the emerging movement recognize that this shift actually reflects a growing hunger for spirituality. Not surprisingly emerging leaders are the ones who are working the hardest to reach out to the young, hungry and experimental. They often innovatively use resources from pop culture to draw these young people into conversations about Jesus.

However, quite frankly, emerging leaders tell me they don't always feel supported by traditional churches. I am certain that one reason is that leaders in some conventional churches are oblivious to this dual trend. They are convinced that they can persuade the young in their congregations and in their communities to continue dancing the old steps. In fact traditional churches in Britain, Australia, New Zealand, Canada and the United States are hemorrhaging. We are losing those under forty at a rate we have never seen before, and the failure to recognize the changing character of spirituality and religion is one of the reasons.

DOES THE WESTERN CHURCH HAVE A FUTURE?

Virtually all the historic Protestant denominations in Britain, Australia, New Zealand, Canada and the United States are in serious decline. Most of the growth in Western countries is in immigrant, ethnic and multicultural congregations. Some evangelical, charismatic and Pentecostal churches are still experiencing some growth, but it is not off-setting the overall pattern of decline.

Peter Brieley, who heads Christian Research in the U.K., says that reg-

---

[1]Philip Johnson, "DIY Spirituality and Pop Culture," Reflections: Emerging Church.Info, <www.emergingchurch.info/reflection/philipjohnson/index.htm>.

ular church attendance in Britain has declined from 7.5 percent in 1998 to 6.3 percent in 2007, and it is projected to continue declining. In fact, the Methodist church, which was born in England, has become affiliated with the Anglican church again, I suspect in part because of declining numbers. Peter says that while many leaders valued the new forms of emerging church, their numbers weren't statistically significant yet. He estimates the emerging church in the U.K. only includes some seventeen thousand participants.

Churches in Australia and New Zealand have been experiencing a steady decline in weekly attendance patterns as well. In Australia it has declined to 8 percent a week.[2] Reportedly the emerging/missional church planting efforts Down Under haven't had a statistical impact either. The Pew Forum on Religion and Public Life places weekly attendance in Canada at 18 percent and at 35 percent in the United States.[3] The American Church Research Project, however, reports U.S. attendance rates closer to other English-speaking countries; attendance declined in the United States from 20.4 percent in 1990 to 17.5 percent on any given weekend in 2005. Instead of asking people how often they attend church like most pollsters do, The American Church Research Project surveyed how many people actually attend church.[4]

While the church in the West is slowly declining, there is another trend we need to pay attention to. In *Christian Century*, sociologist Mark Chaves highlights the growing concentration of American Christians in megachurches—congregations of over two thousand members. This is happening in not only evangelical but mainline denominations, leaving smaller churches to struggle with graying and declining congregations.[5]

---

[2]Ibid.

[3]Religion News, January 7, 2005, The Pew Forum on Religion in Public Life, <www.pewforum.org>.

[4]David T. Olson, "12 Surprising Facts About the American Church," The American Church Research Project, 2006, accessed May 13, 2007, at <www.theamerican church.org>. (Their survey only included people attending orthodox Christian churches: Catholic, evangelical, mainline or Orthodox.)

[5]Mark Chaves, "Supersized: Analyzing the Trend Toward Larger Churches," *Christian Century*, November 28, 2006, pp. 20-25.

I had the opportunity to work with European megachurch planters in Spain in 2006 and was surprised to learn of the growth of megachurches in Europe too. Growing numbers of people seem to be drawn to large gatherings with more spectacle. While the Western church needs to see more numerical growth, I wonder if megachurches are the answer. I am concerned that this kind of numerical growth could come at the expense of qualitative growth. The reason that I am concerned is that it appears that a number of churches in this movement tend to become very accommodationist to the values of dominant consumer culture in order to ensure high numerical growth and don't invite members into a more serious, whole-life faith.

Overall the U.S. church is still showing a bit of growth, not only in megachurches but in immigrant churches as well. But in relationship to population growth, the American church is actually losing ground. Again the new expressions haven't had a strong numerical impact in North America yet either, but given all the initiatives, hopefully that will change. Part of the reason for the decline is diminishing interest in traditional religion. But it also reflects the seeming inability of institutional churches to find ways to engage the growing interest in spirituality mentioned earlier. Let's look at the implications of these and other changes on the future of church funding, particularly funding for missions.

THE COMING MISSION FUNDING CRISIS

In spite of record giving in some arenas, I am convinced that we are likely to see a serious decline in the amount of money and time that the church in the West will be able to invest in mission locally and globally. While the amount currently being given to churches in Britain, North America and Down Under has indeed increased during the early days of the global economy, this isn't the whole story. Empty Tomb, Inc., paints a more sobering picture for the American church: per capita giving to the church has already been declining for almost four decades. In 1968 members gave 3.11 percent of their income to the church. By 2003 that percentage had declined by 17 percent to 2.59 percent. Empty Tomb also reports that there has been a serious decline in benevolence giving in the major denominations.[6]

At the core of the coming crisis is the aging of the Western church. The "teenagers" in many mainline churches are the fifty-year-olds. In fact, many denominations are aging more rapidly than the cultures in which they are located. For example, the Evangelical Lutheran Church in America (ELCA) reports that the percentage of its members over age seventy-five is twice that of the overall American population. When people retire, their giving usually declines significantly. One of the consequences of these trends is that the American Baptist denomination is contemplating selling its headquarters in Valley Forge, Pennsylvania.

When the huge population of baby boomers retire between 2010 and 2030, it will dramatically increase costs for health care and pensions in Western countries and it could cause an age war, as the young will have to pay more taxes to support us. But it will also result in a major decline in giving to the Western church. However, the retiring of the boomers is also a huge mission opportunity. If we can challenge them to use the second half of their lives for mission before they head for resorts, it could create a huge new volunteer resource to help see us through this tough transition.

Not only are traditional churches losing the under-forties at a rate we have never seen before in Britain, Australia, New Zealand, Canada and the United States. Also remember the under-forties are hitting this global economy at a tough time. They are being hammered by the double whammy of higher school debt and higher housing costs. As a consequence those under age forty who stay involved in either traditional or new church expressions will have much less discretionary income to invest in the work of God's kingdom, particularly if they give their first allegiance to trying to live their parents' lifestyles. It is already clear that their giving patterns are considerably less than the giving of those who are older.

As a consequence of all these trends, I reluctantly predict that in the next ten to fifteen years we will see a sharp decline in giving to the Western

[6]John L. Ronsvalle and Sylvia Ronsvalle, *The State of Church Giving Through 2003* (Champaign, Ill.: Empty Tomb, 2005), p. 7.

church. This decline is likely to result in a major decrease in funding for both local and global mission at a time when we clearly need to do more.

FUTURES OF THE WESTERN CHURCH REIMAGINED

Please understand that these projections are not carved in marble. With sufficient prayer, Spirit-inspired imagination and hard work, these trends can be turned around. However, they should make it clear to everyone why we need to both support and join the new generation of conspirators who are creating missional, mosaic, emerging church plants and monastic communities, because they are the ones who are reaching out to those who are dancing their own steps. For example, last year Moot, an emerging Anglican church plant in the U.K., rented a booth at a fair on spirituality to share their ancient faith alongside booths on Wiccan and New Age spiritualities.

My hope and prayer is that these leaders will not only help us begin to reverse the numerical decline but even more importantly enable us to imagine new forms of discipleship, church and mission that more authentically reflect the biblical faith that we claim and that places God's mission purposes at the center of our lives and congregations.

Turbulent times for our lives and churches are also times of opportunity to reimagine and re-create our communities. They provide an opportunity for traditional suburban and ethnic congregations to partner with multicultural and emerging churches to imagine new ways to grow God's kingdom together.

Since the Western church is likely to face a serious decline in resources, large Christian institutions will soon discover that top-heavy models of corporate organizations will be simply unsustainable. We are going to need to create less expensive networked organizations like emerging leaders are doing. We are also likely to see growing numbers of bivocational pastors and Christian workers who work on the side to support their ministries. Soaring land and construction costs and declining resources will likely mean less new church construction and probably more churches planted in homes, or where people work or gather for recreation.

Those who do choose to build will likely construct new models that are more economically sustainable. For example, a church in Tacoma, Washington, built a two-story building in a light industrial area. The income from renting out the main floor to high-tech businesses makes it possible for the congregation to use the top floor for only the cost of utilities.

Given the trends we have discussed regarding the future of the poor, the middle class and the church, it is time to recognize that a "business as usual" faith will not serve. It is critical that we seek to raise the bar in all our churches on the meaning of discipleship, church and mission. We will all need to more authentically reflect God's new order in which we make our lives and resources more available to the growth of God's quiet conspiracy of compassion in a world of mounting need.

THE GROWING CHURCH IN THE MAJORITY WORLD

While the church in the West is declining, the church in Africa, Latin America and parts of Asia is enjoying remarkable growth. More than half of the world's Christians already live in the majority world. In his classic *The Next Christendom,* Philip Jenkins predicts that by 2025 there will be 2.6 billion Christians in the world—633 million in Africa, 640 million in Latin America and 460 million in Asia.[7] In other words, the axis of the church has shifted. More than half of the world's Christians already live in the majority world. These churches tend to be much more Pentecostal and conservative, as the Anglican Communion is discovering.

Twenty-two Mennonite college students spent three months living with Africans in Paris and then living and going to church with African Christian families in Benin, West Africa. One participant, Jeremy Webster, reported, "Never in my home church back in the States did the whole congregation stand up and form long lines to praise, sing and dance through the sanctuary!"[8]

---

[7]Philip Jenkins, *The Next Christendom: The Coming of Global Christianity* (Oxford: Oxford University Press, 2002), p. 3.

[8]Jeremy Webster, "Shouting and Dancing Our Way to Worship," in "What I Learned from the African Church: Twenty-Two Students Reflect on a Life-Changing Experience," ed. James R. Krabill, *Missio Dei* 11.

Something new is happening. These churches are doing reverse missions back to Europe and North America. I have seen Brazilian church plants in Spain, Ugandan churches in Britain and Kenyan churches in the United States. In fact, the largest church in Europe is the Embassy of the Kingdom of God in Kiev, Ukraine, with 25,000 members. Planted by a Nigerian pastor named Sunday Adelaja, it ministers to the poor and the addicted, as well as to government leaders, and has planted over five hundred churches in a number of other Western nations.

FUTURES OF THE MAJORITY CHURCH REIMAGINED

It is past time for those of us in the Western church to work collaboratively with our sisters and brothers in Africa, Asia and Latin America to steer the church in this new millennium. When we from the Western church go into other people's countries, we need to go as learners and servants, under their leadership. We also need to generously support their mission activities without insisting on controlling the purse strings. And, if we are to hear the full counsel of God, we also need to start reading what God is saying to the global church in the twenty-first century through leaders in Africa, Asia and Latin America.

The Overseas Ministry Studies Center (www.omsc.org) is collaborating on a project with churches and universities all over the African continent to capture the stories and biographies of Christian leaders. The *Dictionary of African Christian Biography* is being done to inspire and educate the global church and preserve the memory of a uniquely African Christian faith. A must-read book to prepare yourself to live in a new majority world and relate to the new majority church is *Whose Religion Is Christianity? The Gospel Beyond the West* by scholar Lamin Sanneh. We also have the opportunity to collaborate with immigrant churches that are being planted in Western countries and learn from their new expressions of faith.

We need to join in partnership with our sisters and brothers in Africa, Asia and Latin America in rediscovering a more vital, Spirit-filled faith and deeper commitment to the advance of God's kingdom in the transformations of our lives, communities and God's world.

In the next section, we'll explore how we join followers of Jesus all over the planet in imagining into that world that is already here innovative new forms of whole-life faith, community and mission to engage these new challenges in ways that reflect something of God's loving future for a people and a world.

JOIN THE CONVERSATION

- What are likely to be the consequences of the Western church's ongoing decline in participation, particularly among those under age forty?

- What biblical questions do these trends raise for us and how should we respond?

- Imagine one innovative new way your church might partner either with an immigrant church or new expressions of the church to reach out to a new generation.

TAKING OUR IMAGINATIONS SERIOUSLY

REIMAGINING THAT WORLD THAT IS ALREADY HERE

Are you ready to join the new conspirators in imagining and creating new approaches to whole-life faith, community and mission that engage the new challenges and give creative expression to that world that is already here?

What could you do with an unexpected $20,000? You could purchase one sable scarf or two Louis Vuitton handbags. Or you could spend three days on a fifty-foot yacht with five of your closest friends, cruising off the coast of the Yucatán. Or you could purchase two matching luxury Kawasaki jet skis and spend a lot more time in the water.

For around $20,000, you could create a luxury home entertainment center with a Panasonic Plasma TV and Bose surround-sound speakers. I found a website in Florida through which you can purchase fifteen twenty-eight-foot artificial palm trees for your yard, shipping included. Imagine your neighbor's reaction. EBay has a 1966 Mustang convertible in mint condition for just a bit more, with registration and taxes.

For $20,000 you could purchase 600 cases, or 14,400 cans, of Spam, which could keep you and yours eating Spam burgers for at least the next ten years. I wouldn't be surprised if one of the official Spammobiles (www.spam.com/mobile) would be willing to deliver the Spam directly to your door.

UNLEASHING OUR IMAGINATIONS
Seriously, if you unexpectedly received $20,000, what would you do with it?

Would you pay off school loans or credit card debt? Have a long holiday in a distant land or purchase a Mini Minor? Maybe you would use some of it to help your family, pay for repairs at church or remodel your kitchen.

The Simple Way Community in inner-city Philadelphia actually received an unexpected $20,000. Shane Claiborne and the others in this monastic community live frugally to be something of God's shalom in their neighborhood. With much dreaming, brainstorming and laughing, they decided to use the money to celebrate the coming of God's Jubilee and the New Jerusalem.

First, they sent $100 to one hundred different organizations that they felt incarnated the spirit of Jubilee. Along with the $100, they enclosed an invitation to join them on Wall Street to participate in the in-breaking of God's new order in one of the nerve centers of the global economy.

At 8:15 a.m. on a chilly winter morning, the young people from Simple Way and about a hundred of their friends gathered in the public square in front of the New York Stock Exchange. At 8:20 a.m., one of Simple Way's friends, Sister Margaret, blew a ram's horn to announce the Jubilee, which got everyone's attention in the square. Shane Claiborne shouted, in his loudest voice, the words quoted at the beginning of this book:

> Some of us have worked on Wall Street, and some of us have slept on Wall Street. We are a community of struggle. Some of us are rich people trying to escape our loneliness. Some of us are poor folks trying to escape the cold. Some of us are addicted to drugs and others are addicted to money. We are a broken people who need each other and God, for we have come to recognize the mess that we have created of our world and how deeply we suffer from the mess. Now we are working to give birth to a new society within the shell of the old. Another world is possible. Another world is necessary. Another world is already here.[1]

Just as Shane announced this impromptu Celebration of the Jubilee,

---

[1] Shane Claiborne, *The Irresistible Revolution: Living as an Ordinary Radical* (Grand Rapids: Zondervan, 2006), p. 188.

thousands of dollars in bills were thrown from the balconies by his collab-
orators and silver bounced in the streets. Shane said, "Joy was contagious.
Some bought bagels and began giving them out. People started sharing
their winter clothes. . . . Another guy hugged someone and said, 'Now I can
get my prescription filled.'"[2]

I can almost hear some readers saying to themselves, *What a waste of
money!* But stop and reflect on the remarkably imaginative way that this
event, for a brief moment in time, arrested the attention of a huge number
of people. It momentarily challenged the view of reality presented by the
new global marketplace. More than that, it gave those present a brief
glimpse of another reality: "that another world is already here."

BEGINNINGS

**In this final conversation, I want to invite you to join those on the
imaginative edge all over the planet who are creating new ways to
more fully live into that world that is already here. This is an invitation to allow the Spirit of God to blow through your imagination to create new forms of whole-life faith, whole-life community and whole-life mission, engaging the challenges of our
turbulent world today and tomorrow. If you accept this invitation you will more fully discover the good life of God by joining
those who are creating the future one mustard seed at a time.**

BACK TO THE FUTURE: TAKING THE NEW
CHALLENGES SERIOUSLY

First, it is essential to recognize that we find ourselves living in a very uncertain new neighborhood overnight, a new one-world economic order.
Many are aware of the benefits, but few seem to be aware of the ways storytellers of this new imperial economy are seeking to shape the aspirations
and values of people everywhere. As we have seen, this new economy works

---

[2]Ibid., p. 189.

exceedingly well for the rich, and particularly well for the new super-rich. Many in the middle class have seen their incomes increase too. However, many others, particularly young adults, are struggling to keep their noses above water. And most of our poorest neighbors globally, and even many in our Western countries, are being left behind.

My deep concern is that people of faith may not rise up in significant enough numbers to address these new challenges. In fact, as we have seen, unless we raise the bar in our lives and churches, our capacity to respond is likely to decisively decline.

BACK TO THE PAST: TAKING OUR FUTURE HOPE SERIOUSLY

In spite of these daunting challenges, God is powerfully at work in our world today in and through the lives of ordinary followers of Jesus, "like grass coming up through cement" and coins coming down on Wall Street. What all of these conspirators seem to share is a commitment not only to Jesus but also to God's loving purposes for a people and a world. Shane Claiborne states that this mustard seed revolution "is not a frontal attack on the empires of this world. It is a subtle contagion, spreading one . . . life . . . at a time."[3]

Reflecting on five months spent in Rome, Henri Nouwen said it wasn't the pomp and circumstance of Rome that arrested his attention.

> I met a few students of the San Egidio community "wasting" their time with grade-school dropouts and the elderly. . . . I met young men and women picking up the drunks from the streets during the night and giving them a bed and some food. . . . I met holy men and women offering their lives to others with disarming generosity. And slowly, I started to realize in the great circus of Rome, full of lion tamers and trapeze artists whose dazzling feats claim our attention, the real and true story was told by the clowns.[4]

---

[3]Ibid., pp. 335-36.
[4]Henri J. M. Nouwen, *Clowning in Rome: Reflections on Solitude, Celibacy, Prayer, and Contemplation* (Garden City, N.Y.: Image Books, 1979), pp. 1-2.

Of course Nouwen is right. It is not primarily the "high wire acts" of the wealthy and powerful in our large global village who are destined to write the final chapter of the story. The clowns are dancing with the homeless; it is the "ordinary radicals" and the mustard seeds in your community and mine who will be most likely to tell the "real story." We need a new level of imagination, innovation and creativity like we witnessed in The Simple Way's impromptu celebration on Wall Street. This is a movement of poets, artists, clowns and tricksters, all applications accepted!

REIMAGINING WITH CREATIVITY AND COURAGE

In this final conversation, I invite you to let God ignite your imagination and enable you to create new possibilities for your life, family and community of faith. I urge you to keep a notebook, sketch pad or palm pilot handy to write down your creative ideas and share them with family and friends. Then consider joining the new conspirators and actually give life and breath to the new possibilities God is stirring up within you. I suspect you will be surprised at how God might use your mustard seed to give expression to that world that is already here.

If you wander onto the campus of the University of Toronto, you are likely to see a poster that announces, "Wine Before Breakfast? What do you expect from a drunkard and a glutton?" Every week, university students, members of mainline and emerging churches, and friends of Catholic Workers meet at 7:30 a.m. on Tuesday mornings in Wycliffe College Chapel, where student pastor Brian Walsh leads them. They spend the first hour in a Eucharistic celebration with scriptural reflection, in which a student band plays a variety of music—Rich Mullins, Taize, Blind Willie Johnson and U2. Then they fellowship over a breakfast of homemade bread provided by the Catholic Workers, jam, muffins, fruit, juice and fair-trade organic coffee. Over breakfast, the group brainstorms ways to make the Scripture come alive for its community during the coming week. Clearly, this group has gotten in touch with its collective imagination.

One of the gifts of globalization is that we are increasingly being introduced to music, film and art from cultures all over our small planet, and we are richer for it. Globalization has also enriched our lives with food and flavors from a broad spectrum of different cultures. We live in a world swept up in great waves of imagination, innovation and creativity. Increasingly, however, the new imperial economic order has become the chief employer of many of our artists and designers. As a consequence, art and design are increasingly employed to fashion symbols and myths to draw us into the fables and fictions of the global marketplace.

Brian Walsh and Sylvia Keesmaat remind us in *Colossians Remixed*, "Everything in this monolithic culture of McWorld globalization is allied against you, and will keep your imagination captive, stripping you of the courage to dream of alternative ways to live." They challenge us to join many others who are discovering God's "subversive imagination"—that is, giving creative expression to God's vision for the global future, "the coming of the shalom of God to our terribly broken world."[5]

THE ADVENTURE OF FAITHFUL IMPROVISATION

The source of this "subversive imagination" is God's own creative extravagance. Out of nothing, God created everything. God's inventiveness and imagination are astonishing. "God thinking up a giraffe, a cucumber, the overtone series, sexual reproduction, gravity, dolphins and strawberries. He is none of these and there were none of these for him to copy."[6] The first creation is indeed remarkable. The new creation is going to be breathtaking. But we don't have to wait!

Incredibly, God invites us to be cocreators in giving imaginative expression to God's new creation in the here and now. In the life, death and resurrection of Jesus, God's new creation has broken into our world. The Creator invites us to imagine how God can use our mustard seeds to express God's new creation in partial ways now, in anticipation of the day when Christ returns and all things are made new.

5Brian J. Walsh and Sylvia C. Keesmaat, *Colossians Remixed: Subverting the Empire* (Downers Grove, Ill.: InterVarsity Press, 2004), p. 40.
6Harold Best, "God's Creation and Human Creativity," unpublished paper, Wheaton College, 1983, p. 8.

On a Canadian radio broadcast called *The Vinyl Café,* I recently heard about a middle-aged homeless man, whom we will call Alex. He lives in a small town in Manitoba. Though a bit disoriented, Alex saved the money that his neighbors gave him over a couple weeks and bought a universal TV remote control. His neighbors chalked up the unusual purchase to his eccentric inclinations, but learned it was really a product of his creativity. Now, every afternoon, Alex sits in his old lawn chair in front of the town's only TV store. He uses his new remote control to change channels on the TV in the window and increase the volume so he can hear the evening news outside the store. Clearly we all have the gift of imagination, and we need to use it.

Every time Christine and I conduct a creativity workshop, participants are surprised by their own creativity as they imagine innovative possibilities for their lives, families and congregations. Erwin McManus, the leader of the multicultural emerging church Mosaic, reminds us that "the future depends on creativity. . . . 'Creativity is the natural result of spirituality.' Spirituality and creativity are not the captives of an elite few, but the birthright of all."[7]

N. T. Wright reminds us that followers of Jesus are called to the imaginative task of "faithful improvisation." God has given us all—not just the artists and poets in our midst—the gift of imagination. We want you to discover, like so many leaders of the conspiratorial streams, how to become more imaginatively involved in the faithful improvisation of the good news in a world that certainly needs a bit of good news. Many of the young leaders in the emerging church take the work of faithful improvisation very seriously. Johnny Baker and Doug Gay from the U.K. describe emerging church worship innovation as "'faithful improvisation' that will be judged by its faithfulness to the story and the author."[8]

---

[7]Erwin McManus, "Is the Church Still Relevant?" in *The Relevant Church: A New Vision for Communities of Faith,* ed. Mike Howerton et al. (Lake Mary, Fla.: Relevant, 2004), p. 15.
[8]Johnny Baker and Doug Gay, *Alternative Worship: Resources from and for the Emerging Church* (London: SPCK, 2004), pp. 139-43.

Baker and Gay are right. Much of the innovation in established churches, particularly megachurches, tends to be pragmatic without a clear connection to either the story or the author. I feel it is essential that we remain faithful not only to the author and the story, but also to the imagery of God's new world that is breaking into this one. Faithful improvisation is really about joining God in the imaginative task of cocreation in our lives, communities and God's world.

Herbert Anderson and Edward Foley argue that "because of God's graciousness . . . human beings are called, through community, to coauthor their stories in light of the divine narrative."[9] God invites us to be cocreators, fully aware that even on our best days, we are a broken people who chronically fall short of God's best. Scott Bader-Saye, in discussing the emerging church, helpfully offers an encouraging word about our struggling efforts and even our failures:

> To improvise church is to release control of the outcome precisely because we trust that the outcome has been assured through the life, death and resurrection of Christ. The church can risk being creative in its faithfulness because we trust that in God's providence even our broken stories and our failures will be gathered up and made to contribute to the final act of the drama.[10]

GUIDELINES FOR FAITHFUL IMPROVISATION

If we want to move beyond the kind of pragmatic innovation that is normal for many churches, I offer some guidelines to focus our creativity:

1. We need to keep the author and the story in mind, but we also need to remember how the story ends. We need to create new possibilities for our lives, communities and mission that express both the images and values of God's new order. Stanley Grenz and John Franke remind us

---

[9]Herbert Anderson and Edward Foley, *Mighty Stories and Dangerous Rituals: Weaving Together the Human and the Divine* (San Francisco: Jossey-Bass, 1998), p. 43.

[10]Scott Bader-Saye, "Improvising Church: An Introduction to the Emerging Church Conversation," *International Journal for the Study of the Christian Church* 6, no. 1 (2006): 12-23.

how important it is for followers of Jesus to take God's eschatological vision for a better future seriously: "As God's image bearers, we have a divinely given mandate to participate in God's work of constructing a world in the present that reflects God's own eschatological will for creation."[11]

2. We also need to create new expressions that not only address today's needs but also tomorrow's challenges. Remember, the extent to which we can anticipate even a few of the new challenges and opportunities facing the world and the church is the extent to which we have lead time to imagine and create new responses.

Ready to unleash your imagination? Let's start by imagining new possibilities of a more serious approach to whole-life faith.

REIMAGINING WHOLE-LIFE FAITH

Efrem Smith, in *The Hip-Hop Church*, calls "the need to find authentic people . . . a cry we all share, no matter what or where you have been in your life."[12] Efrem and others in the four streams of renewal we've been discussing are hungry to discover a more authentic faith that impacts every part of their lives.

Christine and I recently had John Hayes, the founder of the monastic movement InnerCHANGE, over for dinner. He explained that those of their order, regardless of whether they live in Caracas or San Francisco, live incarnationally with the poor at the same economic level—a kind of new Franciscan perspective that really challenges my middle-class lifestyle, and raises questions regarding what authentic discipleship looks like. As I look at the lives of these monastics and hear other younger Christians call for greater authenticity, I find myself asking, is it possible we got discipleship wrong?

Really tough question: Have we settled for a dualistic discipleship in

---

[11]Stanley J. Grenz and John R. Franke, *Beyond Foundationalism: Shaping Theology in a Postmodern Context* (Louisville: Westminster John Knox, 2000), p. 272.
[12]Efrem Smith and Phil Jackson, *The Hip-Hop Church: Connecting with the Movement Shaping Our Culture* (Downers Grove, Ill.: IVP Books, 2005), p. 87.

which our faith has very little influence on how we live our daily lives? Have we settled for a compartmentalized piety that has little impact on the direction or major decisions of our lives?

Stuart Murray, in his book *Post-Christendom,* indicts much of the Western church for largely abandoning the countercultural, prophetic role in society that often characterized premodern Christian communities. He argues that established churches out of the Christendom model have become little more than a chaplain to the modern culture.[13] For many of us, the dominant culture is more influential in defining the focus and character of our lives than we realize.

Young leaders in the emerging church have no patience with a division of the sacred and the secular. But too often, as we seek to achieve integration, the dominant culture still seems to gain the upper hand. In spite of our best attempts, we wind up with a dualistic form of discipleship and rarely seem to notice.

I suspect the reason that many of us wind up with a dualistic discipleship is that we attempt to live into two different stories: one from our ancient faith and one from our modern culture. On one hand, many of us allow modern culture, as expressed through the global mall, to define our notions of the good life. Our efforts to get ahead in our jobs and in our comfortable lifestyles often define both the focus and the character of our lives.

On the other hand, many of us have been nurtured in a faith that looks forward to a disembodied homecoming in the clouds. Which of these two competing visions—getting a piece of the rock or waiting for soul rescue—is more motivational as we start our week? For many it is getting ahead economically. Thus many of us wind up with not only a dualistic discipleship but a way of life that is more influenced by the impulses of the global mall than by the inspiration of an ancient faith. Of course the extent to which we are drawn into the seductions of living a more self-interested life is the extent to which we also have less time and money to invest into the work of God's kingdom.

---

[13]Stuart Murray, *Post-Christendom: Church and Mission in a Strange New World* (Milton Keynes, U.K.: Paternoster Press, 2004), pp. 84-85.

I love something John Alexander wrote when he was the editor of *The Other Side:* "Christians spend a lot of time and energy explaining why Jesus couldn't have possibly meant what he said. This is understandable. Jesus is an extremist, and we are all moderates. What is worse, he was an extremist in his whole life—not just some narrowly 'spiritual' areas . . . but in everything."[14] Jesus really was an extremist in his whole life, and those of us who have decided to follow him need to consider becoming "extremists" in our whole lives too.

REIMAGINING AN "EMBODIED" FAITH

A number of books have been written by leaders in the emerging church, the missional church and the monastic movements calling us to "an incarnational faith." The words imply that our faith should shape our entire lives, not just fill a spiritual compartment. The only problem is there don't seem to be many practical examples of what an "embodied," "incarnational," whole-life faith looks like.

Ron Sider's classic *Rich Christians in an Age of Hunger* challenged many Christians in Britain, North America, Australia and New Zealand "to live more simply that others might simply live." His readers responded, freeing up more of their money and time to empower those at the margins. However, the message clearly lost momentum as we raced into our global economy of affluence and over-choice.

In the last few years, books like *Affluenza* and groups like the New American Dream have been calling social progressives to become "downshifters"—to live more simply not only out of concern for the poor but also for the environment. This growing movement, however, seems to be taking place largely outside the church.

As important as simplifying our lifestyles is, I believe it misses the central issue. I am convinced that we don't need a simplified version of the American or Western Dream; we need to reinvent it! We need to discover that God calls us to an image of the good life and better future that isn't

---

[14]John Alexander, "Why We Must Ignore Jesus," *The Other Side,* October 1977, p. 8.

only simpler but also much more festive than anything the consumer mall can offer. What would our lives look like if we intentionally lived into the imagery of the new world breaking into this one?

REIMAGINING CHRISTIANS AS A "THIRD CULTURE"

Rob Bell, pastor of Mars Hill Church in Grandville, Michigan, reminds us that the early church was "partnering with God to create a new kind of culture, right under the noses of the Caesars. . . . The resurrection for them was not an abstract spiritual concept; it was a concrete social and economic reality."[15] The early disciples in the first century no longer accepted the empire's view of reality. They became a dangerous, incarnational model of a different reality—that new resurrected world that was breaking into this one.

Church historian Wayne Meeks suggests that the first church had a very different view of what it meant to be a disciple of Christ than we do today. "Becoming a Christian meant something like the experience of an immigrant who leaves his or her native land and then assimilates the culture of a new, adopted homeland."[16] In other words, becoming a disciple wasn't simply heart change and changing moral behavior, it involved the transformation of cultural values as well. Becoming a Christian in the early church was as radical as an American assimilating to Vietnamese culture.

The first community of the followers of Jesus were "an island of one culture in the middle of another, a place where the values of home were reiterated and passed to the young, a place where the distinctive language and lifestyle of resident aliens are lovingly nurtured."[17]

Many in our four streams, particularly the monastic stream, are involved in the process of discovering what it means to be a "countercultural society." Andy Crouch, author of the forthcoming *Culture Making*, calls Chris-

---

[15]Rob Bell, *Velvet Elvis: Repainting the Christian Faith* (Grand Rapids: Zondervan, 2005), pp. 163-64.
[16]Wayne Meeks, *The Origins of Christian Morality* (New Haven, Conn.: Yale University Press, 1993), p. 12.
[17]Stanley Hauerwas and William H. Willimon, *Resident Aliens: Life in the Christian Colony* (Nashville: Abingdon, 1989), p. 12.

tians to become cultural creatives. "We seek the transformation of every culture, but how we do it is by actually making culture."[18]

However, before we can hope to change our culture, we need to be more deeply changed ourselves. Bruce Bradshaw, in his important book *Change Across Cultures*, states, "We renew our minds when we transform the narratives that govern our lives; only then can they empower us to live into a different story."[19] Bradshaw is suggesting that Scripture calls us to a much deeper conversion—much more than the forgiveness of our sins and receiving God into our lives. It also involves the very radical step of inviting the Spirit of God to "transform the narratives that govern our lives," so that we are empowered to "live into a very different story." I really believe that, in spite of our brokenness, we can all be much more a part of that story that is quietly changing our troubled world.

One of the major reasons we don't invite God to transform the cultural narratives to which we give our lives is that many of us tend to view God as primarily interested in our personal spiritual and moral transformation. As a consequence, many Western Christians uncritically embrace the aspirations and values of the global mall as though that's what God had in mind for us. But it simply isn't possible for us to authentically work for the transformation of culture if we already embrace many of the same values.

Tito Paredes, a Peruvian anthropologist, said something at a missions conference that I found very helpful on this subject: "God is in all cultures both affirming and judging." The journey toward a whole-life faith begins by discerning which stories and cultural values we have given our lives to, and then candidly reflecting on which of these values genuinely reflect something of the values of God's new order and which seem to be in conflict with it.

When I was a social worker working with poor Hispanic families in east

---

[18]"Being Culture-Makers: An Interview with Andy Crouch," StudentSoul.org, January 19, 2007, accessed January 28, 2007, at <www.intervarsity.org/studentsoul/item/andy-crouch>.

[19]Bruce Bradshaw, *Change Across Cultures: A Narrative Approach to Social Transformation* (Grand Rapids: Baker Academic, 2002), p. 21.

San Jose, California, I discovered how individualistic my values were. These families taught me about a way of life, reflective of that in the book of Acts, that valued community and mutual care within extended families. The Hawaiian families I got to know when I lived in Maui freely shared their lives and resources with everyone; their generosity was different than anything I had seen in middle-class churches on the mainland. It reminded me of the incredible generosity of the Jerusalem church.

Listen to Paul calling us to a more radical whole-life faith that is counter to the values of our culture:

> With eyes wide open to the mercies of God, I beg you, my brothers [and sisters], as an act of intelligent worship, to give him your bodies, as a living sacrifice, consecrated to him and acceptable by him. Don't let the world around you squeeze you into its own mould, but let God re-mould your minds from within, so that you may prove in practice that the plan of God for you is good, meets all his demands and moves towards the goal of true maturity. (Rom 12:1-2 Phillips)

Let's explore how we might do Bible studies for cultural transformation.

DOING DANGEROUS CULTURAL BIBLE STUDIES

There is really no reason that we, as followers of Jesus, should allow the global mall, our class or income to define for us what constitutes the good life and better future. Remember the imagery of the better future that Jesus, "who for the sake of the joy that was set before him endured the cross" (Heb 12:2), looked forward to. What was the "joy set before him"? It was to see "God's kingdom come and God's will be done on earth as it is in heaven." It meant looking forward to that homecoming day when he returns to a world in which healing comes to the broken, justice to the poor and shalom to the nations—all made possible because he endured the cross and because he rose as the first member of a new humanity.

We might ask, what is the joy set before us? Giving our lives as Jesus did, to see something of God's kingdom come instead of allowing the global mall to define our notions of what is important and what is of value. I suggest readers do cultural Bible studies in three different generational groups: starters, settlers and second-halfers. Let's look at how each of these groups might engage the writings of Luke in his Gospel and the book of Acts to address the question: What is the good life of God, and how can we move it to the center of our lives?

Consider doing a "cultural" Bible study in Luke/Acts, in which you seek to find some of the imagery of the good life of God in the life and teachings of Jesus and those who were a part of the first countercultural community. I am suggesting the bizarre proposition that these biblical images should define the direction of our lives and the values on which our lives are based, instead of those of the dominant culture.

Starters seeking first the good life of God. This first study is for young people in college or at the beginning of their adult lives. Begin your study by taking pictures with your cell phones and cameras from life or by clipping pictures from magazines of celebrities you enjoy, peers who are cool, elegant weddings, cars with class or other prized possessions, delicious places to holiday and dream houses where you would like to live. Share your photos with each other and ask: "What message do these images communicate about the good life? Why do we seem to be so drawn to these images?" Finally ask: "Do these images seem in any way to be in tension with your faith values?"

Next invite your group to do a study over several weeks through Luke/Acts asking: (1) What are some images of the good life reflected in the life and teachings of Jesus and his disciples? (2) How would our lives be different if we gave ourselves to seeking first these images of the better future?

Now, I encourage you to actually visit people your age who already seek to give creative expression to alternative images of the good life, such as monastic communities, those working with the poor, or those living in intentional communities or in ways that reduce their ecological footprint. After your visit, discuss what seemed to be notions of the good life implicit in these groups and your responses to these models.

Next, I encourage everyone in your group to create composite images on their iPods, draw pictures or write poems of what life might look like if you started by more intentionally seeking first the good life of God. Discuss how your life direction and your life choices might change if you lived into these images.

Now help one another draft a beginning statement of calling for your lives that comes from your Luke/Acts study and your images and poems on the good life of God. Use both Scripture and images to develop criteria for making life decisions about (1) how God might use your mustard seed to make a difference, (2) how to develop your spiritual disciplines, (3) what kind of work to pursue, (4) what is important regarding singleness and marriage, (5) where to live and what kind of housing to secure, (6) how to steward your time and money, and (7) ways to celebrate life and relationships that reflect something of the good life of God.

Finally, plan to get together monthly to help one another actually put wheels under your calling statements. Reimagine how to more intentionally seek first the good life of God and party every step forward as you learn to more fully live into that world that is already here.

We at Mustard Seed Associates (www.msainfo.org) have developed a curriculum called *Living on Purpose* for college students to help them draft a beginning calling statement and a one-year life plan that helps graduates put first things first as they begin adult life. It is designed to be used by student services staff or those involved in campus ministries for weekend student retreats. Contact us if you are interested in more information.

Settlers seeking first the good life of God. This study is for singles or couples, many with kids, who are pretty settled into their lives, careers and congregations. I recommend that you begin by walking around your neighborhoods and making two lists: one identifying the images of the good life implicit in the homes, cars, churches, shops and artifacts of your community; and the second listing responses from parents you meet about their aspirations for their children as they grow up. Then regroup and discuss your lists candidly, paying particular attention to where there may be tension between these images and aspirations, and the values of your faith.

Next I encourage your group to visit "settlers" you know who have consciously changed their lifestyles and parenting styles to more authentically reflect something of God's new order, such as returned missionary families, monastic communities or families pursuing more sustainable lifestyles. Discuss the images of the good life that seem to be a part of their lives and how they are similar to, or different from, the images in your community.

Spend several weeks doing a study through Luke/Acts identifying the images of the good life reflected in the life and words of Jesus and the earliest disciples. Discuss where these images are similar to and different from the ones you found in your community and those you talked with. After this discussion, ask everyone to prayerfully discern a sense of God's call on your family. Draw pictures or write descriptions of specific ways you might make the kingdom call of God a central feature of your life and family. Parents, also describe how you may alter your expectations for your children's future. Come back together and discuss your words and images for living more intentionally into the good life of God. Identify beginning steps to living more fully into the good life of God. You might start by working with kids in your group to plan a kingdom party.

Then use these words and images of the good life of God to help one another develop criteria to guide your important ongoing decisions of life regarding your sense of calling, your spiritual life, your relationships with family and friends, your employment, your housing, shopping, hospitality, parenting, the stewardship of both time and money, and how you celebrate life.

Have each person write a letter outlining small steps they plan to take to begin refocusing their life and guiding their decisions. Share your letters with everyone in the group and solicit prayers and support. Finally, set times to gather regularly. Celebrate every accomplishment and help each one overcome setbacks. Plan ways to party the good life of God together throughout the year.

Second-halfers seeking first the good life of God. This group is comprised of those trying to decide what to do with the second half of their lives. I suggest you begin with participants bringing brochures and advertisements on luxury retirement and travel options to the first gathering. Have people gather stories of second-halfers they know who opted for luxury retirement and travel, describing what impact it has had on their lives and relationships. Encourage people to identify and discuss what seem to be the messages about the good life implicit in both the brochures and the stories. Discuss the costs of these options and other ways that seniors could have used that time and money in terms of the needs that fill our communities and our world.

Next have participants collect stories, pictures and reports from people who chose to invest the second half of their lives in service to others and identify the differences this choice made in the lives of those they served and in their own lives. Ask members to discuss what seem to be images of the better future in these models and how they are similar to or different from those in the stories and brochures you discussed.

Now do a Bible study through Luke/Acts and identify the images of the good life in the teachings and life of Jesus and in the lives of his disciples. Explore how these images are similar to or different from the others you examined. Ask people to prayerfully discern how God may be calling them to put God's purposes first as they plan how to steward the second half of life. Have them write down what they discern and share it with the rest of your group.

Then ask everyone to draft a statement of the kind of legacy they want to leave behind. Use your biblical reflection, your calling and legacy statements to draft criteria that help you make informed decisions about how God might use your seasoned gifts, your time and your resources in the second half of life to more fully express something of the good life of God. Develop a process to regularly support each other as you pursue your dreams and possibilities for the best years of your life. Celebrate every step forward and be there for each other when setbacks come. Once a year gather your friends and any family you have in the area and create a party celebrating "the joy that is before us."

REIMAGINING A MORE FESTIVE FAITH

Rob Bell observes in *Velvet Elvis*, "The church has nothing to say to the

world until it throws better parties."[20] I encourage people of all generations to begin a journey of cultural transformation by adding a little festivity to life.

As impressed as I am by the faithful improvisation of leaders in the
emerging church, almost all the creativity seems to happen within the box
called "worship." I propose that we blow the walls and doors out of the worship box and bring the celebration into our entire lives 24/7, joining with
family and friends in an array of ways to party into God's kingdom.

The Jews participated in celebrations of remembrance of the acts of God
in their past. As followers of Jesus, we can not only participate in the Jewish
celebrations of remembrance, but we can also create celebrations that anticipate our great homecoming jubilation. "By playfully entering into celebration, we rehearse for the future," reflects Sara Wenger Shenk in *Why Not Celebrate!* "It is as though we play an 'eschatological game,' believing that the
grand fulfillment that will come can be envisioned and rehearsed now."[21]

Every year, Christine and I and a group of friends "rehearse" for the
great homecoming with a party called Advent II—Homecoming. One year,
we prepared food from all over the world and sought to enter in to the joy
of coming home to a multicultural future with all those who have gone before us.

This year we called our Advent celebration "Feasting into the World That
Is Already Here." Mark and Ana Mayhle hosted eighteen of us, including
two couples involved in an emerging church plant, in their historic Tudor
mansion in Seattle.

Over hot punch and dips people viewed the classic film *Babette's Feast*,
about a French refugee who becomes a cook for two sisters who are part of
a very austere Protestant sect in Denmark. Unexpectedly Babette wins
10,000 francs in the lottery. She decides to use the entire amount to prepare
a sumptuous French feast to show her appreciation to the sisters for taking
her in years earlier. We discover Babette was once a premier chef in Paris.

---

[20]Bell, *Velvet Elvis*, p. 170.
[21]Sara Wenger Shenk, *Why Not Celebrate!* (Intercourse, Penn.: Good Books, 1987), p.
13.

The sisters had never seen such a lavish spread before and clearly suspected it might be demonic, but as the film ends, not only does the austere group of believers begin to slowly enjoy the gracious feast, but the celebration is a catalyst for the restoration of damaged relationships.

We asked our friends to identify imagery in the film that connects to the advent of Christ and God's new order. Tim and Kerry Dearborn were deeply moved by the "extravagant abundance of God's love and grace." Someone else observed that as people let down their guard to eat unusual new food, they also seemed to open themselves to the reconciling love of God in their relationships. It was clear to all of us that this film captured imagery of that future day when we will all feast together at God's homecoming banquet and experience the full realization of God's loving purposes for a people and a world. Before we dined, Christine led us in a brief liturgy of the banquet feast of God, using the passage on the homecoming banquet in Isaiah 25:6-9 (NIV):

On this mountain the LORD Almighty will prepare
    a feast of rich food for all peoples,
    a banquet of aged wine—
    the best of meats and the finest of wines.

On this mountain he will destroy
    the shroud that enfolds all peoples,
    the sheet that covers all nations;

he will swallow up death forever.
    The Sovereign LORD will wipe away the tears
    from all faces;
    he will remove the disgrace of his people
    from all the earth.
    The LORD has spoken.

In that day they will say,
    "Surely this is our God;
    we trusted in him, and he saved us.
    This is the LORD, we trusted in him;
    let us rejoice and be glad in his salvation."

One thing I love about worshiping with emerging churches is the emphasis on participating not only intellectually but also experientially. So we invited our friends to continue the conversation at the lavish feast that followed. I spent most of that Friday with help from Christine and some of our MSA staff preparing a four-course French meal. Our friends were patient with my struggling effort, and no one wound up in the hospital.

We started with a salad of mixed lettuce, beet root, green onions and goat cheese, then had wild mushroom soup, and finally stuffed pheasant. We also enjoyed French wines and chocolates, imported cheeses, fruit and fair-trade coffee. Through our friendship, conversation, feasting and reflection, we all experienced a little bit of that world that is already in our midst.

I have a number of friends who are also learning to celebrate into that world that is already here. During Advent, one couple, Dave and Nancy, shared key stories from the Old Testament with their preschoolers. The children drew a picture of each story that slowly covered all the walls of the living room and dining room. On Christmas Eve, they held a birthday party for Jesus. Christmas morning, their two children helped prepare Christmas for a family in their church that was struggling with serious health issues.

When Jeff and Patty planned their wedding, they didn't send us the usual list of wedding registries. Instead, we received a list of food items to bring to the church the morning of the wedding, including hams, potatoes, canned corn, bread and lots of salad makings. Early in the morning of their wedding day, friends helped Jeff and Patty prepare a feast for nearly three hundred people, even though they only expected about a hundred guests to come to their wedding.

Immediately after the ceremony and the exchange of vows, everyone streamed downstairs into the social hall below the sanctuary for the feast. The wedding guests only filled about a third of the chairs around the tables. Then Patty and Jeff opened the outside doors to the streets and two hundred street people slowly streamed in, obviously stunned by the feast that awaited them.

Patty went to the mic and announced, "Jeff and I just got married and we wanted all our friends to participate in the celebration with us. Since we have gotten to know you over the past year, we arranged our dinner reception so it would replace the soup and bread we normally would share together with you on Friday nights. Welcome to our friends, old and new!"

Doesn't that have something of the flavor of God's marriage feast about it?[22] Instead of allowing the culture to call the tune, why not take back our celebration of life? It doesn't mean we don't continue to enjoy the rich forms of celebration offered in all our cultures and communities. But it means we increasingly create celebrations that "rehearse" with great festivity that world that is already here.

The journey toward a whole-life faith begins not only by learning to party into God's new future, but also by learning to live into God-loving purposes for a people and a world. Instead of simply allowing our careers, class and culture to define our life direction, we choose to more intentionally connect our lives to the purposes of God.

REIMAGINING LIVING ON PURPOSE

Leading a seminar at the 2006 Urbana Student Missions Convention, I told college students that life decision number one for followers of Jesus is not where to work or where to live; it is not even whom to marry. Life decision number one is discovering how God wants to use our lives to be a part of God's loving conspiracy. Then we make all the other important life decisions—where to work, where to live and even whom to marry—in light of that first decision.

I am convinced the Bible clearly teaches us that not just pastors and missionaries are called to be a part of God's loving conspiracy. If we believe this, then one of the most important responsibilities for God's community is to actually help us discern our calling, write it down and begin to orchestrate our entire lives around our sense of God's call, just like Jesus did.

---

[22]For those who are interested in creative marriage celebrations that make a difference, there is actually a new charitable wedding registry called the I Do Foundation that informs friends of couples' unorthodox requests to give to selected charities in their names. Brad Foss, "Couples Choose Charity on Wedding Day," *Christian Science Monitor*, June 15, 2006, p. 16.

Christine and I actually wrote a book to help Christians more clearly hear God's call on their lives: *Living on Purpose: Finding God's Best for Your Life.*[23] In that book we argued that regardless of whether we're in college, in the work force or working at home, most of us really do want to find God's best for our lives. At the center of God's call is the discovery that the good of God is found in making a difference in the lives of others, not in the endless pursuit of more for ourselves. In the midst of this call, God intends us to live a less driven and more festive life than anything the global mall offers.

We are concerned that fewer than 10 percent of the believers we work with in North America have any time outside of home and church to work in ministry with others. Clearly this level of involvement will not begin to engage the mounting challenges in our world today and tomorrow. Remember, when Jesus stood up in his hometown at the beginning of his ministry, he read the following passage out of Isaiah 61:

> God's spirit is on me; he's chosen me to preach the Message of good news to the poor, sent me to announce pardon to prisoners and recovery of sight to the blind, To set the burdened and battered free, to announce, "This is God's year to act!" (*The Message*)

For Jesus to be the Messiah meant he committed himself not only to God but to God's loving purposes. As Jesus healed the sick, hugged children and brought good news to the poor, he gave compelling expression to God's new future that he announced had already arrived.

To follow Jesus meant exactly the same thing. Those first disciples not only committed their lives to God, but also to the mission purposes of God. In fact, most of the disciples left their jobs and orchestrated their entire lives around their new sense of calling. I am not suggesting that everyone go into full-time ministry, but I am suggesting we find how we are called to intentionally work for God's purposes in our own situations.

---

[23]Christine and Tom Sine, *Living on Purpose: Finding God's Best for Your Life* (Grand Rapids: Baker, 2002). Our book came out three months before *The Purpose Driven Life*, but we haven't been troubled with 22 million in sales . . . yet!

Therefore this journey to a more serious whole-life faith begins by helping one another discern God's call on our lives and families. Then we write
it down and actually begin the creative venture of organizing our entire
lives around our sense of calling, discovering innovative ways God might
use our small mustard seeds for God's kingdom. In *Living on Purpose*, we encouraged people to go on retreat with their spouse or a friend and participate in what we call an "active listening process" to listen for God's call on
their lives. In this process, we listen for God's call through Scripture,
prayer, the needs of others that tear at our heart, our own gifts and even our
areas of brokenness.

Then we show people how to use their calling statements to create time-
styles and lifestyles that are less stressed and more festive. They often find
ways to free up more time and resources to invest in the advance of God's
new order in their communities and the larger world. Invariably people are
surprised and gratified at the ways God uses their mustard seeds to touch
the lives of others. In the process they invariably discover the good life of
God is found in giving, not seeking.

ONE LIFE AT A TIME

People who have discovered something of God's call on their lives enjoy the
satisfaction of living into that sense of calling. Some pursue it during their
work time, some pursue it through their discretionary time, and some support themselves on twenty to thirty hours of paid employment to free up a
generous portion of time to follow it. For a few, following their calling
means beginning their lives over again.

Ian was a student in electrical engineering at Sydney University. He
planned to enter the IT field, buy a home in an upscale neighborhood and
enjoy the "goods life." During a meeting of the Tertiary Student Fellowship,
Ian learned that God could use his training in engineering to design site-
specific energy resources in poorer parts of the world. He did some research and discovered an opportunity to design hydropower and solar energy systems to help provide energy for rural health clinics in Uganda. The
more he prayed about this possibility, the more he realized how God could

use his life in unique ways. It became a clear call on his life.

Jonathan and Irma had heard us speak about *Living on Purpose* at Spring Harvest in the U.K . They decided to take time to discern God's call on their lives, write it down and, most importantly, act on it. Their calling statement read quite simply, "To be the hospitality of Christ in our community." Each week, a different member of their family invited a neighbor over. As the weeks passed, both their community and their family changed. They told us they were gratified by the opportunities God gave them to reach out to neighbors experiencing tough times. They were particularly grateful that their kids also discovered that God could use their lives to share God's hospitality with others.

Judy, Wilson and their two children live in San Jose, California, eleven months of the year. Come vacation time, they do short-term mission trips everywhere from Puerto Rico to Thailand. In the last few years, Judy and Wilson worked with their two teens to teach English as a second language in communities in Southeast Asia. Jonathan, age thirteen, writes,

> We returned to Chonga, Thailand. It was hot, and there was no air conditioning. Despite these challenges, the kids were ready to learn. We taught children words and phrases, played games and sang songs. God taught me to be content with what I had, and not to take my own education for granted.

In Chichester, U.K., twenty-five young men in the Warehouse emerging church plant covenanted together to organize their entire lives around their call to work with at-risk kids in their neighborhood. These young men pledged to work no more than thirty hours a week for income in order to free up an additional twenty hours a week. As a consequence of their decision, they reduced their lifestyle costs so they had more time for the kids they care about.

In his book *Joy at Work*, Dennis Bakke describes the role of calling in his business career. Some years ago he felt a strong sense of calling to express his faith in innovative ways in the world of commerce. He created an energy business called AES that decentralized decision making to empower all the company's employees. Chuck Colson commented on Dennis's inspired in-

novation, saying, "The idea of creating a workplace in which everyone max-
imizes his or her God-given potential and serves the community is a strong
biblical principle."[24] Since leaving AES, Dennis and his wife, Eileen, have
started a venture called Imagine Schools, lifting the quality of education for
the next generation through charter schools. The Bakkes also generously
funded a large number of ministry start-ups all over the world through their
Mustard Seed Foundation.

What might happen if a small group in your church worked through an
active listening process to enable you and your friends to more fully discover
God's call on your lives? What might happen if you wrote your calling statement down and even began to reinvent your life to more intentionally become part of God's quiet conspiracy? I think you might be surprised at the
difference it could make in your life and church, and in the lives of others.

ONE PRAYER AT A TIME

On his radio program *A Prairie Home Companion*, Garrison Keillor interviewed a client named Sue Scott, afflicted by "cyber-space." Sue shared
her crisis, "I just can't stop myself. Yesterday I was online for twelve hours
straight. I didn't have time to eat. . . . I am powerless to resist. I need the
help of a higher power." Garrison prescribed a retreat to a monastic center called St. Xavier of the Screen. In the background, we hear monks
chanting, "Log off. Step away from the keyboard. . . . Open a new window
in your mind."[25]

Really not bad advice for the cyber-addicted. Many of us could benefit
from taking a fast from being online, on screen and on iPod all the time.
A book titled *Blessings for the Fast-Paced and Cyberspaced*[26] recommends
that busy people develop prayers for all those transitional moments of the

[24]Dennis W. Bakke, *Joy at Work: A Revolutionary Approach to Fun on the Job* (Seattle,
Wash.: Pearson Venture Group, 2005).
[25]"Net Script," *A Prairie Home Companion with Garrison Keiller*, National Public Radio,
January 27, 2007, accessed January 31, 2007, at <http://prairiehome.publicradio
.org/programs/2007/01/27/scripts/net.shtml>.
[26]William John Fitzgerald, *Blessings for the Fast-Paced and Cyberspaced* (Leavenworth,
Kans.: Forest of Peace, 2000).

day, like before going online, dropping off kids at school or getting stuck in traffic.

Not only the cyber-addicted but many followers of Jesus struggle to find regular time for prayer. In fact, you would be surprised at how many leaders in flourishing congregations we've surveyed confess that the only time they pray during the week is during the Sunday morning service when the pastor prays aloud. A busy emerging church leader confessed to me that he "prays on the bounce"—when he can work it in.

We have no hope of becoming whole-life disciples or of engaging the mounting challenges of our world by praying "on the bounce." My first spiritual director, Richard Foster, told me that "spending more time in prayer doesn't make us more spiritual but it does put us in a place where God can speak to us."

Serious musicians, artists and athletes cannot hope to be at their best without serious and regular discipline. "Being conformed to the image of Christ" requires we free up regular time, like the monastics, for spiritual practices as a part of a rhythm of life that permeates our waking moments. Of course that rhythm is centered in regular times of worship of the living God with our community of faith.

Even though Christine and I weren't raised in a liturgical tradition, we find tremendous value in the liturgical calendar—living through the life, death and resurrection of Christ each year through Scripture, prayer and celebration. As a Eucharistic Christian, my prayer life really centers on encountering the living God in the mystery of the bread and wine. As I participate in this ancient ritual, I suddenly find myself not only in the presence of the Triune God, but also sitting down at table with all those who have gone before—a foretaste of the homecoming feast.

We have found it essential for us to carve out generous time for Scripture, prayer and meditation each day using the Book of Common Prayer. We encourage others to develop a liturgy of life that includes joining with others in following the liturgical calendar.

An important part of the liturgy of our lives is taking two-day prayer retreats three to four times each year (with our golden retriever Bonnie) to rediscover afresh God's call on our lives individually and as a couple. The first day involves rereading our journals for the last three months and asking for God's forgiveness and help where we aren't moving forward. Day two is always a day to be present with God and listen for a fresh sense of call through Scripture and prayer. We then use our new sense of vocation to draft goals for every area of life, and fashion a new time schedule. We have discovered that this process not only changes our priorities, but also our cultural values. We recommend that every Christian retreat at least once a year to discover, with growing clarity, how God is calling them to be more a part of the quiet conspiracy with their entire lives.

Imagine the difference it might make in your church, regardless of whether it is a conventional or experimental congregation, if everyone in your small group took time to discern God's call on their lives, created one way God could use their mustard seed to care for others, developed a regular rhythm of prayer and learned to party the good life of God 24/7. If we are really serious about living a more authentic whole-life faith, then one of the first steps toward whole-life discipleship is in radically reimagining how we steward our time and money.

JOIN THE CONVERSATION

- What would be involved in discovering God's call on your life and taking steps to implement that call?

- What do you believe is the biblical basis for a whole-life faith? What is its impact on our cultural values? How might it change your life if you invited God to transform not only your spiritual and moral values but cultural values too?

- Imagine one concrete way that living into the good life of God might change the focus and character of your life.

REIMAGINING WHOLE-LIFE STEWARDSHIP

Did we get stewardship wrong? Do the radical teachings of Jesus call us to more than simply tithing? Is it possible our assumptions about stewardship reflect our cultural values more than our biblical values?

Religion exists to make our lives more comfortable and to help us grow on a spiritual level. Reading the old Bible isn't much fun," explains Time to Turn, a group of younger Christians in the Netherlands (www.timeto turn.nl/new/english.php). They explain that Jesus was a carpenter, not an economist, and some of his "cranky" teachings about money and materialism simply don't make any sense in our modern free-market global economy. Clearly Christianity needs to be a "modern" religion that recognizes that the new global economy needs us all to increase our appetite to consume more to keep the global economy healthy and growing. "It is time to take steps. . . . It is time for a new bible translation." *The Western Bible: Director's Cut for the 21st Century Consumer* cuts out all the naive and unrealistic teachings of Jesus on money to make the Bible more user-friendly to those of us who live and shop in our modern global consumer culture.

Of course our friends in the Netherlands are having a little fun. But you would be surprised at the number of Christians I meet whose "Christian" worldview is built not on Scripture, but on the foundational assumptions of free-market liberalism born of the Enlightenment. They tend to baptize the pursuit of economic growth as the greatest societal good, and consumerism and the pursuit of economic self-interest as what God had in mind, which, of course, also largely defines their notion of the good life. They then seek to work Scripture about a largely personal faith in around the edges of these neo-liberal assumptions. There are even a few evangelical theologians who baptize the pursuit of self-interest as the way God intends the human order to work.

BEGINNINGS

If we are serious about becoming whole-life disciples, it will require that we become whole-life stewards too. This means going back to Scripture to not only reimagine our notions of the good life but also to reexamine our fundamental assumptions about the stewardship of our lives and resources. I will share both a biblical basis of a more whole-life approach to stewardship as well as some creative examples of what it might look like. I will also discuss the remarkable ways in which the Spirit of God could use our time and resources to give much fuller expression of God's conspiracy of compassion in our broken world.

I find that many younger Christians in the monasticism network and emerging and mosaic church movements are often very generous with both their money and their time. Many live more simply and give to those in need in their communities instead of giving to meet needs inside the congregation. I've talked to a number of younger Christians who also voice strong concern about how little of the Western church's total giving is directed outward to those at the margins. Ryan Bolger and Eddie Gibbs point out that since a number of these emerging leaders spend little on buildings, programs or salaries, they have much more to share with those in need. Emerging church leader Joel McClure says that "money should go for people who can't provide for themselves or for throwing parties." He adds, "Instead of placing emphasis on the tithe, we teach being generous. When we see a need, we give to that, for people who are truly in need."[1]

---

[1]Eddie Gibbs and Ryan K. Bolger, *Emerging Churches: Creating Christian Community in Postmodern Cultures* (Grand Rapids: Baker Academic, 2005), pp. 150-51.

Shane Claiborne and others with limited incomes in the new monasticism movement developed what they call a "relational tithe" that they give directly to those in need through their network of relationships instead of giving to a Christian institution to distribute for them. Shane writes that a new reformation of stewardship is long overdue. He quotes Ignatius, saying that "if we are not caring for the poor, the oppressed and the hungry, then we are guilty of heresy." He urges that we reimagine stewardship as part of God's redistributive economy that characterized the first-century church. Essentially, all those in this network pool their relational tithe and use it to help the poor in their respective communities and around the world. Reportedly, 100 percent of what they collect goes to help others. They even used their pooled resources to send supplies to victims of the Asian tsunami and for volunteers to help the victims of Katrina.[2]

As mentioned earlier, many in the monastic stream live at the economic level of their poor neighbors. Others in emerging and mosaic churches live frugally to help those around them, which leads me to question standard models of stewardship.

Really tough questions: Did we get stewardship wrong? Do the radical teachings of Jesus on stewardship call us to more than tithe stewardship? Is it possible we are working from assumptions about stewardship that reflect our cultural values more than our biblical values?

Christians of all generations are concerned about stewardship issues. Institutional churches have published huge amounts of materials on how to be better stewards of the resources God has entrusted to us. Most of these materials, however, focus on being more responsible "managers" of our money. Few of these stewardship materials question the basic cultural values underlying how money ought to be managed.

I am convinced that our lifestyles in the West are much more defined by our income level, our class and the values of the global mall than by anything that comes out of Scripture. As a consequence, simply focusing on

---

[2]Shane Claiborne, *The Irresistible Revolution: Living as an Ordinary Radical* (Grand Rapids: Zondervan, 2006), pp. 333-34.

being better "managers" really misses the point. I suspect our uncritical acceptance of tithe stewardship as normative for New Testament believers may be part of the problem. As soon as believers give a tithe (or some portion of the tithe), they tend to feel they are off the hook; what they do with the rest is up to them. This compartmentalized approach to stewardship is very much at home with a compartmentalized piety and the dualistic approach to discipleship we discussed earlier.

While it would be wonderful if most Christians gave a tithe, I don't think the tithe was normative in Jesus' teachings. As we watch Jesus interact with Zacchaeus and the wealthy young ruler, there was no discussion of faithfulness being equivalent to sharing 10 percent of their income. A growing number of New Testament theologians, like Craig Blomberg, feel (as I do) that Jesus raised the bar beyond tithe stewardship. One can't read the Gospels or the book of Acts without realizing that Jesus expected his followers to radically reexamine how we use all of our resources.

A BIBLICAL BASIS FOR WHOLE-LIFE STEWARDSHIP

Redina Kolaneci, in a survey of giving among British Christians, advocates calling followers of Christ to a "stewardship lifestyle . . . rooted in understanding stewardship as a 24 hours a day, 7 days a week mentality."[3] The "stewardship lifestyle" begins with the hard work of finding a biblical basis for more of a whole-life approach to stewardship that reflects something of God's purposes.

I believe that Christ's approach to whole-life stewardship begins with the reminder of the psalmist: "The earth is the LORD's, and everything in it, / the world, and all who live in it; / for he founded it upon the seas / and established it upon the waters" (Psalm 24:1-2 NIV).

A biblical approach to stewardship should be based on the assumption that all we have is God's. If that is true, then it is no longer a question of "How much of mine do I have to give up?" but rather "How much of God's

---

[3]Redina Kolaneci, *Who Gives to What and Why? Getting to Know Evangelical Donors: A Survey of Individual Giving to Churches and Charities Amongst Evangelical Christians in Britain* (Oxford: Whitefield Institute, 1997), p. 16.

should I keep, in both a church and a world where needs are so great?" Can you imagine the difference it might make if we in the Western church decided to steward all our resources in ways that intentionally seek to advance God's purposes first instead of prioritizing our own needs and wants?

Jesus insists that how we steward our lives and resources must begin with the important cultural question of what we truly value. He reminds us,

> Don't store up treasures on earth! Moths and rust can destroy them, and thieves can break in and steal them. Instead, store up your treasures in heaven, where moths and rust cannot destroy them, and thieves cannot break in and steal them. Your heart will always be where your treasure is. (Matthew 6:19-21 CEV)

Glen Stassen and David Gushee, in their book *Kingdom Ethics,* quote Robert Guelich, who insists, "'Heaven,' for Matthew, is 'the sphere of God's rule where his will is done. . . . To have your treasures in heaven means to submit oneself totally to that which is in heaven—God's sovereign rule.'" Stassen and Gushee continue, "The transforming initiative is to invest one's treasures in God's reign of justice and love through practices of economic generosity and justice-making."[4] Clearly, this teaching of Jesus is a call to reexamine the stewardship of all that God has entrusted to us.

In other words, if our view of the good life is focused on accumulating consumer goods and experiences for ourselves, instead of looking for opportunities to make a difference in the lives of others, we could totally miss what this journey is really all about. We are indeed called to live under God's rule, practicing "economic generosity and justice-making" with all that God has entrusted to us.

We are invited to join so many who have gone before in discovering that the good life of God is to be found not in seeking life but in losing our lives in service to God and others. Jim Elliot, who lost his life in mission to the Auca Indians, wrote shortly before his death, "A man is no fool to give up what he cannot keep to save what he cannot lose." Numbers of followers of

---

[4]Glen H. Stassen and David P. Gushee, *Kingdom Ethics: Following Jesus in Contemporary Context* (Downers Grove, Ill.: InterVarsity Press, 2003), pp. 410-11.

Christ in Sudan, China and other parts of the world know better than we do that this journey can end with a cross, as it did for the one we follow. But as we know, the cross is never the last word.

In *Good News to the Poor*, his definitive study of Christ's view of steward-ship and its impact on the early church in Luke and Acts, Walter Pilgrim demonstrates convincingly how Jesus connected the coming of God's new order and the just use of resources. Pilgrim explains,

> The ultimate hope of the poor is the coming eschatological reversal. In the future kingdom of God, Jesus promises a complete reversal of the conditions between the rich and poor, the mighty and the power-less. The motive for this reversal is not some kind of eschatological revenge, but ultimate justice.[5]

Pilgrim links the issue of biblical stewardship to the in-breaking of God's new order of justice. Jesus Christ calls his disciples to incarnate a radical form of whole-life discipleship and stewardship that reflects God's inten-tions to create a more just society, in which "Zacchaeus is offered as an ex-ample for individual believers and Jerusalem as the pattern for communi-ties of believers."[6]

Once we decide to follow Jesus by participating in the great reversal, the first question we need to ask is: How much is enough? How much floor space do we really need in our homes? How much wardrobe? How many ve-hicles? How much do we really need to spend on weddings, entertainment and vacations?[7] Clearly if we find ways to reduce our needs and wants, we will free up more time and resources to invest in God's call to be increas-ingly a part of God's quiet conspiracy.

In an interview with *Relevant* magazine, Shane Claiborne provides advice as to where to begin this journey. "We can begin by surrounding ourselves

---

[5]Walter E. Pilgrim, *Good News to the Poor: Wealth and Poverty in Luke-Acts* (Minneapolis: Augsburg, 1981), p. 161.
[6]Ibid., p. 165.
[7]Jim Merkel's *Radical Simplicity: Small Footprints on a Finite Earth* (Gabriola Island, B.C.: New Society, 2003), offers practical tools on how to evaluate "enoughness" and ways to live more on less (p. 125).

with the other people who are asking the same questions—who are suspicious of the emptiness of consumption and who dare us to risk just a little bit more and to love just a little bit deeper."[8]

ONE LIFE AT A TIME

Let me share some examples of people who have dared "to risk just a little bit more." They may give you some ideas for your own journey into whole-life stewardship.

Reimagining Lenten stewardship. Ben Clowney works for Tearfund U.K. He found an unusual way to discover "how much is enough." Concerned about poverty in Britain and having the British have-a-go spirit, Ben tried a new discipline for Lent. He lived on minimum wage for the entire forty days to experience something of the life of the working poor. The minimum wage in Britain is currently £4.25 per hour (over $8 in the United States). Ben reported that the first week was kind of a honeymoon. Then he found himself faced by a constant stream of tradeoffs. He wanted to go to a soccer game on Saturday, which meant a baked potato was all he could afford each night for his evening meal. He gave up his regular Friday night visit to the neighborhood pub in order to have money for train fare to visit his parents on Sunday. Ben states,

> Going back—albeit with a better handle on my spending—to my former life of takeaway coffees and music downloads was different. I had a whole new perspective on the reality of life and a better awareness of what I actually need compared to what I really want. Best of all, I saved 200 pounds (almost $400 US) that I was able to give away. That alone made it all worthwhile.[9]

Consider taking this Lenten challenge this year. If you don't have the grit that Ben did for the full forty days, consider just a week and decide ahead

---

[8]Interview with Shane Claiborne, "How Do You Break the Addiction to Money?" *Relevant*, May 2007.

[9]"Lent Challenge: Live on the Minimum Wage," *Uncovered Extra*, e-mail newsletter of Tearfund, <http://youth.tearfund.org/>.

of time where you want to invest the money you free up to grow God's mustard seeds among the poor and vulnerable.

Alternatively you might like to consider what we did at the Mustard Seed House here in Seattle for part of our Lenten discipline. Because half our world's population lives on $2/person/day/year, we restricted our food budget to $2/person/day and gave the excess money to the Mutunga Partnership in Australia, the group that first thought of this concept.[10]

Reimagining community stewardship. Jonathan and Leah are the founders of Rutba House, a part of the new monasticism network, in Durham, North Carolina. The Rutba Community has two houses in a low-income neighborhood that provide accommodation for twelve people. Shared housing reduces their living costs for accommodations, utilities and food to $500 per person per month. This is remarkably inexpensive given living costs in the United States these days. Because of their reduced living costs, Leah can stay home and run an after-school program for neighborhood kids.

Leah got to know Caley and Taley, ages twelve and fourteen, in the after-school program. One day, Caley and Taley invited Leah home to help them fix up their room. When Leah visited, she found the girls' room needed a lot of help and asked the girls if they would like other kids in the after-school program to join them in repairing and repainting their room. Caley and Taley were delighted and loved the results.

Reimagining personal stewardship. Ron Sider, author of *The Scandal of the Evangelical Conscience*, has proposed an approach to whole-life stewardship called "the graduated tithe." Those just starting out in life should decide how much they need for a decent way of life. That serves as a cap; as their income increases, people increase the amount they give, instead of how much they spend. Craig Blomberg, a New Testament theologian teaching at Denver Seminary, said that he and his wife have worked from the graduated tithe concept for over twenty years and now invest over 40 percent of

---

[10]Christine produced a Lenten guide, *A Journey into Wholeness,* which provided other practical suggestions for Lenten disciplines. You can check it out at <www.msainfo.org/clopcont.asp?id=614&subject=46>.

their gross income in the work of God's kingdom.[11] Numbers of us in the Western church could double or triple our tithe without sacrificing our lifestyles one bit. Another couple donating a graduated tithe used the generous funds that were freed up to start a family foundation. Imagine the difference the resources God has entrusted to you might make if you used them to implement the new ways God is prompting you to use your mustard seed to have an impact for God's new order. The place many of us need to begin is in getting creative in how we house ourselves.

Reimagining housing stewardship. Sandy and Dale were trapped in a cycle that afflicts many boomers in North America. Each time they sold a house they bought a bigger house to avoid paying capital-gains tax. Dale said, "I realized I was working to support the house." So seven years ago they took their lives back, selling their expensive house in California and using $100,000 of the proceeds to buy a rural acreage in Cottage Grove, Oregon, plus building materials to construct a more modest home. The home is heated by solar energy and a wood stove. Sandy and Dale grow most of their own food and no longer spend money on expensive vacations. As a consequence, their living costs are only $720 per month, of which the largest share goes to insurance. They support themselves by investing the remaining $170,000 from the sale of their house in San Diego in certificates of deposit, which pay about $10,000 to $12,000 per year—more than enough to sustain their scaled-down lifestyle. In addition to having more time to enjoy hospitality and hiking, they spend a generous amount of their time volunteering with groups working for environmental care and sustainable agriculture in their community.[12]

When Brent and Sharie told people they had bought a new house in Grand Rapids, "they all asked if were buying a Super-Sized house. They were all surprised when we said no. We explain that we sold our large four-bedroom house in an upscale community for $207,000 to buy a smaller three-bedroom for $126,000."

---

[11]Craig L. Blomberg, *Preaching the Parables: From Responsible Interpretation to Powerful Proclamation* (Grand Rapids: Baker, 2004), pp. 51-52.

[12]"The Good Life on $8,000 a Year?" *Kiplinger's Personal Finance Magazine* 55, no. 8 (2001): 68.

"When we married right out of college, Brent and I joked that we would keep our lives so simple that we could always move our belongings in our Toyota Tercel. Since we have had two kids, that hasn't been possible. We believe God's call on our lives is an invitation to live out our faith in our entire lives. We believe this call also includes an invitation to live below our means so we have more to share with those in need in a community in Peru that we are connected with."

Brent adds, "We realized that we really didn't need all the space the other house provided or the huge mortgage payments that went with it. So we decided to scale back to increase our missions giving. Plus, we wanted to prepare our kids to get ready to live in a richly multi-cultural future, and our new neighborhood wonderfully makes that possible."

Tim, their high-energy ten-year-old, chirps, "Now we will also be able to go on a short term mission trip to Peru next August. Our whole family will spend two weeks helping Uncle Andy build a school for kids in his village and I am going to learn to speak Spanish."

Imagine how your life might change if you joined in community with those who are discovering the possibilities of creative improvisation in the stewardship of their entire lives! Imagine the amount of time and resources your congregation could make available to the work of the kingdom if people were nurtured in whole-life stewardship. The only way any of us can begin to do the hard work of imagining and creating new forms of whole-life stewardship is in supportive communities with other sisters and brothers who are on the same journey.

JOIN THE CONVERSATION

- What is your response to the possibility that Jesus may be calling you to whole-life stewardship instead of tithe stewardship?
- What difference might it make in your church if everyone became creative whole-life stewards?
- Imagine one creative way that you and those you go to church with could start growing into becoming whole-life stewards.

REIMAGINING
WHOLE-LIFE COMMUNITY

*Is it possible we have gotten what it means to be the church
wrong? Is church simply a place to go once a week to get our
needs met or is it something else?*

It was a chilly gray day in London as we waited to enter St. Paul's Cathedral to celebrate the bicentennial of the British Bible Society. It was an impressive gathering. We sat near the rear and watched the elegant sanctuary rapidly fill with two thousand heads, almost exclusively gray, largely of Anglican persuasion. The celebration began with a brilliant dramatic dance scene based on the dispersal of the nations at Babel. As two dramatists read the narrative, the dance company reenacted its interpretation of the scattering of the nations, which concluded with the dancers scattering in all directions into the audience.

Archbishop Rowan Williams then addressed us, reflecting on how the Word of God was translated into the many cultures in our world, creating a global family of God. Immediately after his remarks, the two narrators reappeared and read the drama of the coming of the Holy Spirit on the infant church at Pentecost. As they read, the dispersed dancers slowly danced back into the center of the sanctuary, reenacting the gathering and everyone hearing the good news in their own languages. It was a compelling and powerful presentation celebrating the two hundredth anniversary of one of the oldest Christian organizations in Great Britain.

Two days later, Christine and I celebrated the bicentennial of the Round Chapel in inner city Hackney, East London. The Round Chapel was an engineering masterpiece when it was constructed at the beginning of the nineteenth century, seating nearly two thousand people before anyone had coined the term *megachurch*. This celebration included very few gray heads, but a lot of children and parents who had emigrated from Jamaica and other Caribbean countries. There were also a few young adults who were planting a small emerging church called Host, plus a few visitors, like us. A total of fifty of us met in a small social hall, not in the grand sanctuary. Instead of professional dancers and dramatists, three Jamaican kids read Scripture. A brief history of the Round Chapel was read, we sang, offered prayers and shared a generous buffet of luscious tastes from the Caribbean.

Not only were these two bicentennial celebrations starkly different remembrances of our Christian past, they also raised many questions for me regarding our Christian future. Does the inherited church that was deeply invested in Christendom have a future? Do multicultural congregations and small emerging experiments like Host have a prayer? In the future, will the church be more scattered or gathered, and what new forms will emerge?

BEGINNINGS

I am not the only one asking questions about the future of the Western church. In fact, I hear more uncertainty expressed about the future of the church in the West today than at any other time during the last thirty years. In Britain I hear a growing discussion about a post-Christendom, post-institutional, post-Western, post-congregational future. But neither leaders in traditional churches nor those in the four streams seem to know what these new expressions will look like. Here we will revisit the biblical basis for communities of faith and suggest a spectrum of new possibilities that may even be a stretch for our innovative church planters.

In his book *Revolution*, George Barna predicts that the local church will increasingly be replaced by a spectrum of other ways for Christians in the United States to meet their spiritual needs, ranging from "alternative faith-based communities"—including homeschooling groups, house churches, worldview groups, various marketplace ministries, Christian creative arts guilds and others—and "media, arts and culture," including, I suspect, a number of burgeoning online spiritual chat groups as well. He calls these "spiritual mini-movements."

Barna predicts that by 2025 the majority of U.S. Christians will gravitate out of the local church entirely, and two-thirds will find their spiritual nurture equally in the other options. "Ultimately, we expect to see believers choosing from a proliferation of options, weaving together a set of favored alternatives into a unique tapestry that constitutes the 'personal church' of the individual."[1] Barna says he welcomes the change if it makes personal "faith come alive."[2] If church is simply a place we go once a week to get our needs met, then why couldn't a homeschooling group or an online chat room be our church?

Really tough questions: Is it possible we have gotten what it means to be the church wrong? Is church simply a place to go once a week to get our needs met or is it something else? Is church simply our own personal creation—weaving together from a range of options what works best to meet our needs? Is it possible that we may be unwittingly working from seriously flawed assumptions about what it means to be the community of God?

In *Missional Church*, the authors reflect on misperceptions of what it means to be the church: "Popular grammar captures it well: you 'go to church' much the same way you might go to the store. You 'attend' a church, the way you attend a school or theater. You 'belong' to a church as you would a service club with its programs and activities."[3] If the church isn't simply something we "belong" to or "attend," then what is it?

The authors of *StormFront* similarly insist that "longing for a God who only meets our needs . . . skews our vision of the church."[4] They argue that

---

[1]George Barna, *Revolution* (Carol Stream, Ill.: Tyndale House, 2005), p. 66.
[2]Ibid., pp. 48-55.
[3]Darrell Guder, ed., *Missional Church: A Vision for the Sending of the Church in North America* (Grand Rapids: Eerdmans, 1998), p. 80.
[4]James V. Brownson et al., *StormFront: The Good News of God* (Grand Rapids: Eerdmans, 2003), pp. 32-34.

Christians have been conditioned by the global consumer culture "to see [themselves] first and foremost as consumers with needs to meet." This invariably leads to a self-absorbed approach to life that I believe undermines a biblical spirituality and our ability to focus outward on the needs of others. Is it possible that many of us unwittingly accepted this popular cultural notion that we are first and foremost consumers and the church and all the other options primarily exist to meet our needs?

First, I think it would help to glimpse what the pre-Christendom church looked like. The early church operated from a very different view of reality than the empire in which it grew. In his thoughtful book *Church After Christendom* Stuart Murray characterizes pre-Christendom churches as subversive, countercultural communities working from the underside of society and critiquing the dominant culture. He urges churches to shift from being largely maintenance-minded institutions for those inside the building to outward focused missional communities, creating "mustard seed" and "yeast-in-the-dough strategies" of witness and influence.[5]

The authors of *StormFront* similarly assert that "to receive salvation is to be called into something larger and greater than we are, to be invited to participate in God's saving purpose and plan for the world."[6] Amen! Let's try to find a biblical beginning point to rediscover what it means to be the community of God in mission to our world.

REIMAGINING CHURCH AS A NEW "FIRST" FAMILY

Rodney Clapp's intriguing book *Families at the Crossroads* is a study of the biblical view of family. But it is also an important book on ecclesiology, presenting an alternative biblical view of the nature of the church. The New Testament, Clapp observes, says little about family, and what it does say is pretty radical. Jesus, working out of the spirit of covenant, "turned away his mother and brothers and declared instead, 'Whoever does the will of God is my brother and sister and mother.'. . . Jesus' primary family is not com-

---

[5]Stuart Murray, *Church After Christendom* (Milton Keynes, U.K.: Paternoster, 2004), p. 149.
[6]Brownson et al., *StormFront*, p. 34.

posed of those who share his genetic makeup, but those who share his obe-
dient spirit." Clapp continues,

> With the coming of the kingdom—a kingdom that manifests itself
> physically as well as spiritually, socially as well as individually, and in
> the present as well as the future—Jesus creates a new family. It is the
> new first family, a family of his followers that now demands primary
> allegiance. In fact, it demands allegiance even over the old first fam-
> ily, the biological family. Those who do the will of the Father (who, in
> other words, live under the reign of God) are now brothers and sisters
> of Jesus and one another.[7]

As the early church spilled out into the world, it was perceived to be a
"new family" composed of Jews and Greeks, slaves and free, that cut across
race, class and cultural boundaries. Clapp calls it a "third race."[8] The first
community of the followers of the risen Jesus was not simply a group of people that went to a building once a week to worship and get their needs met.
They were a living, breathing expression of a new resurrected reality that had
broken into this world—twenty-four hours a day, seven days a week. They
were indeed a new family who embodied a whole new way of being that was
clearly counter to every culture in which they found themselves.

Stanley Hauerwas and William Willimon suggest that we reimagine
church in our post-Christendom world as an exile community, where the
values of a new home, which are part of that larger narrative, are nurtured.
We are encouraged to revision the contemporary church as an exile community, like the Jews in Diaspora. They remind us of how important it was for
those first Jewish Christians, as a community of "resident aliens," "to
gather to name the name, to tell the story, to sing Zion's songs in a land
that didn't know Zion's God."[9]

One of the most compelling characteristics of this unusual new "first"

---

[7]Rodney Clapp, *Families at the Crossroads: Beyond Tradition and Modern Options* (Downers Grove, Ill.: InterVarsity Press, 1993), pp. 73-77.
[8]Ibid., pp. 83-84.
[9]Stanley Hauerwas and William H. Willimon, *Resident Aliens: Life in the Christian Colony* (Nashville: Abingdon, 1989), p. 12.

family, as it emerged in the early church, was the remarkable ways these first followers of the Way loved each other and their neighbors. Communities like the Jerusalem church sold their possessions and shared resources like one large family. Christians rescued infants from garbage dumps and brought them home. They cared for those in their neighborhoods who were ill, sometimes with highly contagious diseases. While they didn't all live under the same roof, they operated more like a large, organic, extended family. They often lived in proximity and were involved in one another's daily lives, "breaking bread from house to house."

Christine Pohl, in her important book *Making Room: Recovering Hospitality as a Christian Tradition*, stated that one of the defining characteristics of the early church was the way individuals opened their homes and lives not just to their friends, but to total strangers and outcasts. "The practice of hospitality almost always included eating meals together. Sustained hospitality requires a light hold on material possessions and a commitment to a simplified lifestyle." Pohl noted that when early disciples shared meals with others, "the presence of God's kingdom was prefigured, revealed, and reflected."[10]

Ian Bradley in *Colonies of Heaven* states that for seven centuries the church in the British Isles was community-based rather than individualistic, due to the influence of Celtic Christianity. Men and women, ordained and lay lived together in communities that had a strongly monastic character, offered hospitality to strangers and reached out to those in need. They sought to embody their faith.[11] What would our churches look like if we reinvented them as relational, missional families of which we are a part more than institutions we maintain? Eddie Gibbs and Ryan Bolger state that the emerging church has already moved away from an ecclesiology of church as institution. Some emerging church leaders already embrace this more relational view of church as a family to whom we give our allegiance.[12] They em-

[10]Christine D. Pohl, *Making Room: Recovering Hospitality as a Christian Tradition* (Grand Rapids: Eerdmans, 1999), pp. 11-12, 30.
[11]Ian Bradley, *Colonies of Heaven: Celtic Christian Communities: Live the Tradition* (Kelowna, B.C.: Northstone, 2000), pp. 4-7.
[12]Eddie Gibbs and Ryan K. Bolger, *Emerging Churches: Creating Christian Community in Postmodern Cultures* (Grand Rapids: Baker Academic, 2005), pp. 96-97.

phasize that as those in the emerging church seek to follow Jesus as part of this new first family in mission, they often "live highly communal lives."[13] Certainly, all those in the monastic stream experience church more as family in mission because they live together, share life, practice ancient liturgies and even work with the poor together.

One of the most astonishing characteristics of that first community is that, unlike most churches today, it was comprised of believers from across the spectrum of race and class. What would it look like today if church became family that cut across lines of race and class, like we saw in the imagery of God's great homecoming?

Spirit and Truth Fellowship in Philadelphia is one of a growing number of multiethnic congregations in major cities that are a part of our mosaic future. In an article profiling the church, Harvey Conn wrote, "Into the world where class, power and ancestry divide rich from poor, slave from free, men from women, came a society that welcomed all that bore the name of Jesus (I Cor 1:26-29) . . . [yet today] Black, White, Hispanic and Asian Christians still watch each other pour out of their church buildings. . . . But there is another model for church. . . . They open the treasure chest of multi-ethnicity and rejoice."

The Spirit and Truth community is a community that celebrates the rich gifts of its African American, Hispanic, Asian and European cultures; believers have become family to each other in a real way. The pastor, Manny Ortiz, artfully draws on the gifts and insights of the different cultures in this mosaic family. He reflects that all its members are discovering how much they really need and value each other. This community reflects the imagery of all the nations sharing their contributions when we come home to the New Jerusalem.[14] As we move into an increasingly multicultural future, wouldn't it be encouraging if the church led the way by modeling the cre-

---

[13]Ibid., p. 45.

[14]Larry Sibley, "Church Profile: You Want Salsa or Kimchi with That? Spirit and Truth Fellowship, Philadelphia, Pennsylvania," *Reformed Worship Magazine* no. 71, accessed January 30, 2007, at <www.reformedworship.org/magazine/article .cfm?article _id=1297>.

ation of a spectrum of new multicultural families in which we share our gifts with one another and the larger world?

TIME AND PLACE MATTER

Recently I visited Hot House, a monthly gathering of emerging church planters representing churches in Seattle. These young leaders are involved in different church plants. One pastor observed that for many busy Christians, regular church attendance is now down to once a month. As I reflected on this reality, I remembered that more Christians are turning to occasional informal gatherings and online resources for their spiritual nurture. I asked myself if it's possible, by using online resources, showing up at casual gatherings, going to a local church once a month (or even once a week), to achieve anything like the family that was normative for the earliest followers of Jesus. Is it really possible for any real Christian formation to take place in our lives with such limited contact?

As we discussed earlier, there is a reason people have less time for religious gatherings and spiritual practices: the new global economy places increasing pressure on us to work harder and longer and give more of our time to the exploding array of onscreen and online entertainment options. Not surprisingly, we have much less time left over for church, prayer, family and others. As a consequence, growing numbers are opting for less-demanding online and occasional gatherings as Barna suggested.

David Caddell and David Diekema, exploring how formation takes place in Christian higher education, argue that Christian education is not just about imparting information; it's also about shaping values. They concluded that online education (i.e., distance learning) is not able to achieve the same kind of formation in the lives of students because students don't meet in face-to-face classroom settings and don't have the informal encounters of a residential learning community. Caddell and Diekema based their conclusions in part on the writings of social theorist Pierre Bourdieu,[15] who

---

[15]David Diekema and David Caddell, "The Significance of Place: Sociological Reflections on Distance Learning and Christian Higher Education," *Christian Scholar's Review* 31, no. 2 (2001).

urges educators to create "habitus," a learning community in which there is not just face-to-face contact, but people living and learning together 24/7.[16]

Is it possible that the church was not intended to be a building we go to once a week or once a month to have our needs met? Is it possible that the church was not intended to simply be an ever-expanding array of online resources and various informal gatherings that we weave together to nurture our personal faith?

I am persuaded that a biblical view of the church is really a call to become part of a new family that transcends race, class and even biology. It is a family where we corporately worship the triune God and sit down to table with that great community. It is a family deeply rooted in an ancient story and a future hope where we nurture our life and faith together. It is a family where we take time to be known, loved and challenged to follow Christ into a more radical whole-life faith. It is also a family where we generously share our lives and resources with one another and with those in need. It is a family who is called to place God's mission purposes at the very center of our lives and communities of faith, focusing outward and giving primacy to addressing the needs of others.

Clearly, it isn't possible for any of us to be known in any real way if we only find two hours a week to attend church. There simply isn't enough time after worship to really get to know those we just worshiped with. Neither do I have any enthusiasm for simply encouraging religious consumers to shop around for whatever works best to meet their needs. Instead I encourage some risk takers to consider raising the bar and creating new forms of church as countercultural families giving creative expression to an ancient faith and future hope in a myriad of different ways that are clearly focused outward. The first challenge is finding ways, in our time-stressed world, to actually carve out time and space to be truly known, deeply loved and radically challenged to follow Christ with our entire lives.

---

[16]Pierre Bourdieu, *Outline of a Theory of Practice* (London: Cambridge University Press, 1977), as cited by Diekema and Caddell, "Significance of Place," p. 11.

REIMAGINING SMALL GROUPS WITH A DIFFERENCE

Popular in Britain, Australia and New Zealand, cell groups offer a modest version of being family together. The Order of Mission in the U.K. has small groups called "huddles" in which members work together like families, nurturing one another in a more serious whole-life faith. And one of the most effective models of small groups, Mission Groups at the New Community Church in Washington, D.C., seems to foster a real sense of community while focusing outward on mission. The life of the church's core comes out of these groups.

A new mission group might start with one person standing up in worship and announcing that God has given him or her a growing concern for at-risk kids in the immediate neighborhood. The person asks if there is anyone else who senses God stirring a similar concern in their hearts. Four or five other hands go up and these people become a mission group. They meet one evening a week to not only become family and nurture one another, but to create an innovative way to reach out. In other words, instead of leaders planning programs to plug people in, these followers take initiative to create their own mustard seed ministries and carve out time every week to get the ministries going.

New Community, planted by the innovative Church of the Saviour—an organic, relational church that bears some similarity to the emerging churches—describes the call to be family together in the invitation to be part of a home mission group:

> In the book of Acts, the first Christians met in small groups in each others homes for worship, mutual support, instruction, sharing meals and material possessions, and ministry. In the bible, there are no individual Christians who function outside of belonging to some form of Christian community.[17]

Reimagining church as proximity communities. Over the years, I have met a number of Christians who have bought or rented residences in proximity

---

[17]"Handbook on Mission Groups," New Community Church, Washington, D.C., 2005-2006, p. 2.

to one another as another expression of community. What is new is that some of the new expressions of church are discovering that time and space matter. They are inviting members to relocate in one neighborhood where they have greater proximity in order to have both more community and more impact on the lives of others.

Recently Christine and I met with Zoe Livable Church in Tacoma, Washington. Community leaders invited this emerging congregation to move into a twenty-square-block area in downtown Tacoma. Zoe leaders reported that as their members have moved into the same neighborhood, they are not only more involved in each other's lives, but they are also finding more time to reach out to the homeless and vulnerable in their community.

Seven, a worshiping community in the Mission District of San Francisco that symbolizes the seven days of creation, is comprised of thirty-five people living within a ten-block radius of each other. Mark Scandrette, leader of ReIMAGINE (a ministry that sponsors learning labs in creative approaches to faith, culture and engagement), describes the people in this community as largely young—twenty-five- to thirty-five-year-olds—and post-congregational. The rhythm of their life together includes helping in a community feeding program on Monday night, worshiping together on Wednesday night and playing with neighborhood kids at Garfield Park on Thursdays. Their rhythm also includes daily reading of Scripture and prayer.

Reimagining church as residential communities. If we are serious about embodying a whole-life faith and experiencing church as family, then living in shared residence obviously makes a great deal of sense. Furthermore, given the rising costs of housing, the residential option could also reduce costs, particularly for the younger generation. Those living in monastic communities also report that shared residential models not only reduce living costs, but they also reduce the time spent on household chores by operating like a large extended family. Groups like the Jesus Army in the U.K., Cornerstone Community in Australia and the Sojourners Community in the United States also offer examples of intentional residential Christian communities. They seek in different ways to embody something of God's new order.

Christine and I struggle to give modest expression to this reality in a small community experiment here in Seattle called The Mustard Seed House (www.mustardseedhouse.wordpress.com). Some years ago, I bought a large house with three separate apartments. Eliacin and Ricci Rosario and their two kids, who work with us at Mustard Seed Associates, live in our top-floor flat. Christine and I live in the middle. Peter and Anneke Geel live downstairs. We meet Sunday nights for a meal, share our lives and do a liturgy together. We garden together and create celebrations of that world that is already here throughout the year. A central part of the vocation of The Mustard Seed House is offering hospitality to friends from all over the world. We follow a monastic rule of life and enjoy Celtic liturgies. We all attend different local churches, but The Mustard Seed House is where we find our community.

Over thirty years ago, innovators in Denmark who weren't even religious created a new model of shared living called cohousing communities. These communities were designed to reflect both community-based and environmentally sensitive values. It is now one of the most rapidly growing social movements in North America. There are some five thousand people living in eighty-five cohousing communities across the United States and Canada, with more new communities on the drawing board.[18] CoFlats Stroud was one of the first cohousing communities in the U.K. It provides smaller flats in the town center of Stroud for £79,000 to £185,000 each.[19]

In this alternative, every resident has his or her own private flat, but instead of backyard and front yard, they typically share a common green, an area for the kids to play in and a place to garden together. They also share a common room with kitchen and dining room. Typically, they eat together one or two nights a week. Even though these are usually intergenerational communities, many seniors love this alternative because it operates like a huge extended family, and members help seniors with shopping and chores if they become disabled.

---

[18]Camille Sweeney, "The 21st-Century Commune," *The New York Times,* September 10, 2006.
[19]Karen Dugdale, "Communal Living Comes Back into Fashion in New Flats," *Observer,* August 20, 2006.

Two different Christian cohousing communities in the United States have adapted this model in order to more fully live out the values of God's new order. In March 2000, twenty-three people, including nine children, moved into the Temescal Cohousing Community in a poorer neighborhood of Oakland, California. They seek to give expression to their Christian values, including creation care values, in both the physical design of their community and in their common life.

For instance, they installed high-efficiency appliances and on-demand water heaters. Most importantly, they installed solar panels on the roofs of their homes to generate most of their own electricity. In fact, they collect so much energy during the summer that the state utility buys it back from them. Their total electrical bill every month, including appliances, heat and water, is only $5 per family. Temescal Cohousing is a regular stop for those touring sites of innovative environmental design in the San Francisco Bay area.

This community also designed a living space that facilitated being family together instead of enshrining the individualistic values that characterize most suburban communities. Community members eat together at least one night a week in their common building. They share their joy, struggles and faith during these meals.

By living in community, these folks can free up time to be more involved in their neighborhood. They host block parties, exhibit art and take an interest in neighborhood kids who struggle with school. In fact, this summer the Temescal family hosted a neighborhood film festival one night a week in its courtyard, inviting neighbors to join them on warm summer evenings.

The Bartimaeus Community is the first Christian cohousing community constructed in the Seattle area. It was particularly satisfying to see the twenty-five homes and spacious community center on its seven-acre site in Silverdale, since we have been involved with this daring group since its founders first conceived the project. The Bartimaeus Community is also concerned for creation care and values community and care for others. Their homes are clustered together to preserve a large area of wetlands on the property. They designed a separate area to park their vehicles, and created walkways and gathering areas between their homes to facilitate relationships with one another.

Even though members come from a broad range of religious traditions, the Bartimaeus Community already operates as a large extended family, and members share meals and life together at least once a week in a common building. The community wanted to reach out to those in need, so members jointly funded one of the units to be a home for families in transition.[20]

If we can design these new forms of Christian residential communities that seek to more authentically embody something of God's new order and are less expensive, then we can free up more generous amounts of our time or money to invest in the growth of God's quiet conspiracy. We can become the family of God with a central commitment to advancing God's loving purposes in our turbulent world.

JOIN THE CONVERSATION

- What are some possible consequences of redefining church not as a place we go but as a new family where we are known, loved and held accountable?

- What is your response to biblically redefining church as a more relational family that is focused outwardly in mission to others?

- Imagine one creative way you might create a community that cares for one another, your neighbors and God's good creation.

---

[20]If you are interested in a practical secular source for creating new forms of residential community, check out Diane Leafe Christian, *Creating a Life Together: Practical Tools to Grow Ecovillages and Intentional Communities* (Gabriola Island, B.C.: New Society, 2003).

REIMAGINING
WHOLE-LIFE MISSION

Is it possible we have gotten missions wrong—directing our efforts primarily toward those inside the church and relegating global mission to an annual conference and occasional readings from prayer newsletters? Should we consider joining many of the new conspirators who put mission at the center of their gathered life?

When Christine and I arrived at Heathrow Airport in London on a chilly, wet, September morning, it seemed totally abandoned. In fact, we claimed our baggage and cleared customs in a record fifteen minutes. We arrived on the first United Airlines flight to Britain from the United States after the terrorist attack in New York on September 11, 2001.

Christine and I were speaking on globalization and the future of mission at the first meeting of the Micah Network on Integral Mission. Essentially, World Evangelical Alliance sponsored this new network to start a conversation on how to define a more biblical integration of word and deed mission.[1]

Delegates from all over the planet settled into a large auditorium at Oxford University. During his welcome, Steve Bradbury, the Australian moderator, said, "We want all the Americans present to know that we are praying with them for the tragic loss of life as a result of the recent terrorist attack on the Twin Towers in New York City. But I also want to remind all

---

[1]More recently the Micah Network has also launched the Micah Challenge, which organizes churches all over the world to support the Make Poverty History campaign.

delegates, as we gather for this conference on integral mission, that 25,000 innocent lives are lost every single day as a result of global poverty." I will never forget that reminder. Nor will I forget the deep commitment of those who attended that first session to address the urgent challenges facing our poorest neighbors.

MOVING BEYOND MISSION AS USUAL

As I will demonstrate, God is doing something new in missions all over the world: using the lives of ordinary people and small congregations to make a difference in ways they never expected.

Mission: The heartbeat of the church? Many of us are inspired by the way God's cause is flourishing in Africa, Asia and Latin America. Thousands of Chinese Christians are taking menial jobs as domestic servants along the old silk route, putting their lives at risk to share their faith. Christians in Brazil are reaching out to the street children on the dangerous streets of São Paulo and Rio de Janeiro. Church plants are spreading across a number of African nations like wildfire.

Michael Frost and Allen Hirsch, in *The Shaping of Things to Come*, remind us, "Mission is not merely an activity of the church. It is the very heartbeat and work of God. It is in the very being of God that the basis for the missionary enterprise is found. God is a sending God, with a desire to see humankind and creation reconciled, redeemed, and healed."[2]

If mission is indeed the "heartbeat of God," why don't we see more congregations getting more directly involved in it locally and globally? It should be clear by now because of the turbulent times in which we live that "business as usual" will no longer serve. We need new models where the new buzzwords of "missional," "God's sent people" and "mission-driven churches" become a reality.

Really tough question: Is it possible we have gotten missions wrong? Is it possible that we have settled for a de facto view of mission as primarily

---

[2]Michael Frost and Alan Hirsch, *The Shaping of Things to Come: Innovation and Mission for the 21st-Century Church* (Peabody, Mass.: Hendrickson, 2004), p. 18.

mission to those inside the church? Have we relegated mission to the world to an annual missions conference and occasional reading of a missionary prayer newsletter?

BEGINNINGS

In this section, I will revisit what it means to do mission and be a missional people, but I will also share creative ways that followers of Jesus are responding to the growing challenges in their own communities and our world. God invites us to join followers of Jesus all over the planet who are discovering how God can use our ordinary lives and congregations to be a part of God's quiet conspiracy.

MISSION CENTRAL

Many traditional churches with whom I work, particularly in North America, don't sponsor a single ministry in their own communities. But it would be unusual to find a church in Britain, Australia and New Zealand that didn't sponsor several ministries in their own communities. However, many churches in the United States and in these other countries do support mission work abroad. But churches in English-speaking countries that I have worked with often invest less than 10-to-15 percent of their income in local or global mission. Clearly based on my anecdotal observation, mission appears to be at the margins, not at the center of congregational life. Check how much of your church's resources are invested in local and global mission.

How did churches wind up making missions such a marginal concern? Swiss theologian Walbert Buhlmann explained a serious change in the way the church viewed itself: "Having Christianized the Roman Empire from within, having become a state religion, having received privileges and lands, the Jesus-movement . . . became an institution."[3] The maintenance

---

[3]Walbert Buhlmann, as quoted by David Smith, *Mission After Christendom* (London: Darton, Longman and Todd, 2003), p. 3.

of the institution and serving the needs of those who were a part of the institutional church became our de facto view of "mission."

In the last section, I suggested that many churches have settled for a consumer model that is focused primarily on meeting our needs. In other words, designing programs to meet the needs of those inside the building seems to have become our central mission. In contrast, the four streams all share a common concern for the needs of those beyond their doors. The central focus of the monastic stream is addressing the needs of their neighbors in poor communities. The majority of emerging churches I have visited have mission at the center of their DNA. In my research, I found a number of mosaic and missional congregations that are also "walking the talk." How can all of our congregations follow the lead of these new expressions and become more outwardly focused in mission to others?

David Bosch reminds us that Jesus announced the in-breaking of God's future through his life and ministry. "We today can hardly grasp the truly revolutionary dimension in Jesus' announcement that the reign of God has drawn near and is, in fact 'upon' his listeners, 'in their very midst' (Luke 17:21 NEB). . . . The future has invaded the present."[4]

As a consequence the primary focus for the earliest Christian community was expressing God's new resurrected future by reaching out to neighbors, tending the sick, rescuing infants, caring for the poor and the stranger, and sharing the good news of God's love for all. Clearly mission was at the center, not at the margins of their common life.

Some of the most impacting movements of the church through the ages—from the Celtic church reevangelizing Europe in the sixth century to the Wesleyan Renewal during the industrial revolution in Britain—have always placed God's mission purposes at the center of community life.

I urge the leadership of local congregations, traditional and experimental, to begin the deliberate journey toward placing mission at the center of

[4]David J. Bosch, *Transforming Mission: Paradigm Shifts in Theology of Mission* (Maryknoll, N.Y.: Orbis Books, 1991), p. 32.

the church's gathered life by rediscovering the biblical vision of God's "future invading the present." To be part of this story means discovering creative new ways that we can collectively express this good news in our own communities and God's world.

Some missional church plants are scrapping a programmatic approach that is focused on the needs of insiders for a small group approach, equipping members to discover their calling and reach out to their neighbors.

Churches in the U.K. are becoming more missional by participating in a program sponsored by the Evangelical Alliance, called A Square Mile. The program challenges churches all over Britain to reach out to their neighbors within one square mile of where they meet for worship. Churches all over the U.K. are taking up the challenge, such as a multicultural congregation in East London, which has set up tutoring and food cooperatives for those in its immediate neighborhood.

If we are serious about becoming more missional, it is essential we find concrete ways, like British congregations, of addressing the needs of people in our own communities as well as in the larger world. It is also essential that we embrace a more integral view of God's mission out of the imagery of God's coming kingdom.

MISSION INTEGRAL

When I was speaking on missions in a local church in the Northwest, I found that those in my class, like many evangelicals, view mission as almost exclusively about evangelism and church planting in the so-called 10/40 Window. I found that many of these students were so immersed in this narrow view of mission, they had difficulty accepting that helping the poor is "real" mission, not simply a strategic prelude to evangelism.

A number of these students seemed to be working from a spiritualized eschatology in which they saw God's redemptive initiative as singularly focused on "saving souls." Such a limited view of God's purposes doesn't include, of course, the idea of God redeeming us as whole persons, or the church working for justice, reconciliation and creation care. As a consequence, mission is understood narrowly as spiritual transformation reaching people and nurturing them in a faith that is often somewhat private and disconnected from the needs of our neighbors.

Theologian Obery M. Hendricks Jr. states, "The primary lesson of the biblical judges is that fighting for the liberation of those who are oppressed is as important a responsibility of our faith as developing sound personal piety."[5] African American churches have long taught that the mission of the church includes working for justice and reconciliation.

Catholic and mainline churches have had less difficulty in finding integration than those from evangelical backgrounds. At the Lausanne 1974 conference, evangelicals first articulated that mission must include social responsibility. At the 1982 International Consultation on the Relationship Between Evangelism and Social Responsibility (CRESR) they took another step toward integration, as John Stott defined word and deed mission as "two oars in a boat or two halves of a pair of scissors."

World Evangelical Fellowship (WEF) hosted a conference to continue the conversation at a gathering called Wheaton 1983. I had the responsibility of coordinating Track III for WEF: "The Church's Response to Human Need." Since we were defining a biblical response to global poverty, we wanted to ensure that the gathering was as inclusive as possible, therefore over half the participants came from the majority world, and one-third of the participants were women. The editorial committee was also broadly international and included those who have written extensively on mission, like René Padilla, Vinay Samuel, David Bosch and Ron Sider. They produced an important document on a more integral view of mission called "A Statement on Social Transformation." David Bosch wrote in *Transforming Mission*,

> For the first time in an official statement emanating from an international evangelical conference, the perennial dichotomy was overcome. 'Evil is not only in the heart but is also in social structures . . .' The mission of the church includes both the proclamation of the Gos-

---

[5]Obery M. Hendricks Jr., *The Politics of Jesus: Rediscovering the True Revolutionary Nature of the Teachings of Jesus and How They Have Been Corrupted* (New York: Random House, 2006), pp. 50-52.

pel and its demonstration. We must evangelize, respond to immediate human needs, and press for social transformation.[6]

René Padilla observes that after the statement was published, a more holistic approach to mission became more evident among evangelicals.[7] The Micah Network is continuing the important conversation regarding a more integrated view of the mission of the church. Frankly, almost all those with whom I work in the mosaic, missional, emerging and monastic streams hold a major commitment to social transformation that includes working for social justice, reconciliation and creation care.

It is essential we not only get our theology of mission right but always keep before us the "end game." It is easy to get focused on activities and forget the larger biblical vision of what God is seeking to give birth to. It is not enough to simply do good word-and-deed mission projects in the "hood" in Chicago or a village in Kenya. I urge those working with the poor to study Scripture together to begin to imagine how their neighborhood in Chicago will be transformed or how their village in Kenya will be changed when that new world breaks into this one. We need to encourage people to paint pictures of hope, write songs and tell stories about how lives and communities will be transformed when God's kingdom fully comes. This kind of awakening of biblical imagination can give people a much larger vision to work for.

REIMAGINING MISSION CENTRAL ONE CHURCH AT A TIME

I will share three models of missional, mosaic and emerging churches that are moving mission to the center of their common life that might inspire and challenge all of our congregations. As you will see, they are working from a clearly integral view of mission. They are also discovering how God can use their mustard seeds collectively to have an impact on the lives of

---

[6]Bosch, *Transforming Mission*, p. 407.
[7]C. René Padilla, "Holistic Mission," Occasional Paper No. 33, Lausanne Committee for World Evangelization, Pattaya, Thailand, September 29 to October 5, 2004. He attributes the change more to a rise in Christian conscience than to the impact of the statement, however.

others locally and globally. Also, you will see how their strong outward focus is altering the way they steward their time and resources individually and congregationally.

Mission central in SoCal. Life Covenant is a missional church plant in Torrance, California. Tim Morey, the pastor, worked with his team to create innovative ways to move mission to the center of their life together. Instead of offering programs to meet the needs of those inside the building, Life Covenant offers a small group program with a difference. The small groups focus on equipping the church's 125 members for mission in their local neighborhoods. There is also a strong emphasis on carving out daily time for spiritual disciplines and weekly time for witness and service with accountability in small groups.

Even though it is only three years old, Life Covenant is planting two churches targeting twenty- and thirty-year-olds—Restoration Covenant and the predominately younger Asian/African congregation, Catalyst. In addition to these projects, their members are highly involved in Habitat for Humanity, a battered women's shelter and remodeling for poor families. Globally, they have gotten involved in funding a microenterprise development project in Mozambique, one of the poorest nations in Africa.

The congregation rents a worship space from an established church so it can limit the amount of income spent on their own needs. Remarkably in 2006, 30 percent of this new church's income was invested in local and global mission.

Mission central in Minneapolis. Efrem Smith is the creative young pastor of Sanctuary, a mosaic church in Minneapolis that exists for the sake of the inner-city community in which it is located. He is also coauthor of *The Hip-Hop Church*. In addition to providing a weekly worship service for the multiracial congregation, the church has a small group program and the Sanctuary Community Development Corporation (CDC). It is a separate not-for-profit organization. CDC sponsors a hip-hop academy, a mentoring program for young women and a tutoring program at local schools. The corporation also sponsors a program called Momentum Workforce Development that helps those at the margins develop job skills to support their families.

Ashaki, a mother of eight who has endured long periods of unemployment, completed job training at the Momentum Program and landed a job as an office specialist—the first job she had ever had. It pays $30,000 a year. As a result of her increase in income, she was able to relocate her kids into a neighborhood with less drugs and violence.

Smith calculates the amount of Sanctuary's resources invested outside the church to be at 50 percent, used either in direct service to the community or to pay the salaries of those who serve them. They also rent office space in a drug and alcohol rehab center, and they worship in a middle school—which, Smith points out, is another way to give back to the community.

Mission central in Raynes Park, U.K. Several years ago, Phil and Wendy Wall planted an emerging church with a founding vision that included making a difference for God's kingdom both locally and globally. They intentionally planted their church in Raynes Park, outside London, near the Carter Estates, which houses poor families. A number of the single people in the church started getting married. Four couples chose to rent run-down flats in the Carter Estates to start reaching out to families and kids who lived there. All four couples said, "Don't bother giving us any wedding presents; we are OK. Give the money to our church fund to help the people in Carter Estates."

Phil relates the story of one family these young couples touched. "Several years ago, a single mom named Marilyn and her three kids were living in an apartment that was slowly coming down around them, and they had no funds to repair it." Working with others from their church, the four couples gave Marilyn and her three kids a three-day holiday and totally repaired and remodeled the apartment. Marilyn and her kids were overwhelmed by the care of their neighbors.

Wendy and Phil became deeply concerned about the plight of AIDS orphans in Africa. They tried unsuccessfully to adopt Zodwa, a two-year-old girl whose mother was dying of AIDS. "Even though the adoption didn't go through, God didn't lift the burden from our hearts." They took their small family savings out of the bank and persuaded several of their other friends in the church to do the same. Then, they held a banquet for AIDS orphans in Liverpool. The creative twist was that they didn't ask for money. Instead, they gave each of the 1,600 people who attended £10 (almost $20 U.S.) out of their savings. Phil recalled what he said at that first banquet,

> If you need this money more than AIDS orphans, feel free to spend it on yourself. But if you want to test out the parable of the talents, here is a brochure that outlines some ways you can invest this ten pounds and get back to us.

Since then, they received back over £500,000. They used the funds to start HopeHIV to help orphans in Africa and to raise up a new generation of African leaders.

Come with me to Zimbabwe and meet Samuel, a young man who lost his parents and fourteen other members of his family to AIDS. Listen to his experience with HopeHIV.

> When my parents died I was left to look after my four younger brothers and sisters and it was a very bad time for us. I didn't know what to do and I was very depressed. . . . Then I met Martha from Hope-HIV. She helped me work through this very hard time. With her encouragement, I dug out my father's sewing machine, which had been buried under our house. They helped train me and I started a tailoring business with it. Now I am able to not only support my brothers and sisters but to pay their tuition so that they are able to go to school. In appreciation for the help we received, I volunteer regularly at HopeHIV helping other young kids who have lost their families to start over.

Can you imagine the impact our churches could have if we made the commitment to become churches for others, investing a greater share of our time and resources in making a difference locally and globally?

REIMAGINING MISSION CENTRAL IN YOUR LIFE AND CHURCH

As you have seen we are racing into an uncertain future in which our world

and our churches face daunting new challenges. To respond to these challenges we must resolve, by the power of God, to become whole-life disciples
and whole-life communities committed to placing God's mission purposes
at the center of our lives and churches, giving compassionate, creative and
celebrative expression to that world that is already here.

Where to start? Begin really, really small. Consider starting a mustard
seed group in your college, neighborhood or church and prayerfully imagine one idea of how God might use your mustard seeds to make a difference
tutoring kids in your neighborhood, shooting hoops with teens or spending time with seniors who are alone. Let God surprise you.

For those seeking to join the conspiracy in a local church, I have some
candid advice. If your church is content with status quo faith, then don't try
to change them—even if you are the pastor. Instead I encourage you to
prayerfully find a couple of other people who are inspired by the Holy Spirit
to put God's purposes first and start a small mustard seed group. Pray together to help each other discern something of God's call on your lives individually and as a group. Then create one way God might use your mustard
seeds to make a difference in the lives of others where you live. Perhaps
when others in the church discover what a good time you are having, they
might be inspired to join the conspiracy too.

For churches that are more serious about moving mission to the center
of congregational life, I have no silver bullets or canned programs to offer.
However, I think we all need to pay more attention to what God is doing
through the new conspirators in the missional, mosaic, emerging and monastic experiments and be open to learn from them. Quite honestly sometimes these leaders fall on their face, but sometimes God uses them in surprising ways to touch the lives of people who would never come to many
of our churches. They might be able to teach us how to engage those who
are "dancing their own steps." They often take huge risks with virtually no
resources and it is wonderful to see what happens when their gardens
flourish. We could learn from their often inspired creativity and their
dogged initiative.

Many in our more traditional churches could also learn from these new models of church that are often more outward focused in mission and use far less resources on building and bureaucracy costs. We can learn from both their successes and failures. But we can also learn from some of their new images and understandings of God's kingdom, their hunger for authentic discipleship, their celebration of church as family and their determination, by the power of the Holy Spirit, to make a little difference in the world around them.

I know many of these younger leaders are looking for mentors and would welcome the opportunity to learn with those of us who are older what it means to follow Jesus in these turbulent times. You might even find ways to collaborate for the sake of God's kingdom with some of these new conspirators.

If your congregation is willing to begin the journey to become more mission-centered, like some of the more experimental expressions, it could change everything. After taking time to learn from those on the creative edge, I would encourage you to go back to the Bible and rediscover afresh God's loving purposes for a people and a world. Create ways to enter into the images of what God "is on about" through creating celebrations that bring God's coming creation to life. Then prayerfully ask God to enable you to discover afresh how your congregation is called to advance God's compassionate purposes both in your community and in the larger world.

Next do some research on urgent needs in your own community today and tomorrow and on those facing our poorest neighbors around the world. Brainstorm one creative new way God might use your mustard seeds locally and globally. Then prayerfully start one ministry to engage one need in your community. You might consider partnering with an urban church to start an agricultural or economic cooperative to help empower those on the margins in your community. Start small and build well with much prayer and team work, celebrating every milestone.

Also consider creating a small group program that enables participants to discover God's mission call on their lives. Then enable them to follow that call into a more mission-focused whole-life faith. Be sure to provide resources that help participants deal with the mounting pressures on their time and resources. In other words, create small groups to equip your members to look beyond their own needs and discover how God can use their mustard seeds to be a part of God's compassionate response to the needs of others in your community.

Explore a more relational way for your congregation to do mission locally and globally. See if you can find a way to link your new local mission with a new global mission. One Presbyterian church in Oregon has already begun this journey. They are exploring starting a three-way partnership model with a Hispanic church nearby and a church in Juarez, Mexico, in which all three churches minister reciprocally to each other. This approach reflects a more relational, networked approach to mission that is likely to be more sustainable in the future than cost-intensive models. As congregations in North America develop these partnering relationships, and as they see the needs of others firsthand, many start becoming more generous in sharing their resources with their new family and in shared mission.

I would also urge all congregations to do an annual audit of how much of their time and money is directed outward in mission and set the goal to increase that amount 5 percent to 10 percent a year. To increase mission giving in many traditional churches will likely require the painful step of slimming down bureaucracy and taking a hard look at the amount of resources you are spending for programs for people inside the building.

The congregations I see that are flourishing are both traditional and new expressions who are committed to placing God's mission purposes at the center of their lives and congregations. They are becoming communities for others and are creating ways to give compassionate and concrete expression to that other world that is already here. They are people who are learning to party the kingdom 24/7 and they are discovering that the good life of God is indeed the life given away.

In our final section we will visit the entrepreneurial edge. We will ask you to invite the Spirit to ignite your imagination to discover how you and your community might become much more a part of God's creative conspiracy that is quietly changing our world.

JOIN THE CONVERSATION

- Where have you seen experimental or traditional churches that have become more outwardly focused in mission, and what difference is it making?

- What is your response to the biblical discussion that integral mission needs to be much more of a central focus of our churches?

- Imagine one creative way your church could become more outwardly focused in mission and address one concerning need in your community.

JOINING THE ENTREPRENEURIAL EDGE

Should we consider joining the new conspirators and inviting
God's Spirit to ignite our imaginations to create new ways to
give expression to that world that is already here?

As you have seen, God is stirring up the imagination of ordinary radicals all over the planet to create new expressions of that new world that is already here. God is igniting the imaginations of artists, poets, architects, street performers, clowns, worship curators, activists, designers and social entrepreneurs to participate in this quiet but creative conspiracy. In fact one of the defining characteristics of the emerging, missional, mosaic and monastic streams is the way in which they have allowed God to ignite their creativity to imagine new forms of life, community, church, celebration, advocacy and mission.

But as you have also seen, God's creative Spirit is stirring up many of us in more traditional churches to join this conspiracy of creativity to reflect something of the imagery of God's new order in response to the challenges of tomorrow's world as well.

JOINING THE ARTISTS, CLOWNS AND ENTREPRENEURS

Instead of simply allowing the architects of the global mall to design the symbols, living arrangements and celebrations of our lives—where following Jesus is trivialized to little more than a devotional afterthought—this is an invitation to be cocreators with our God in all areas of life, community and mission. We have the remarkable opportunity to give creative expression to new possibilities that offer a small glimpse of that new creation.

BEGINNINGS

In this final jaunt, I will argue that our participation in God's conspiracy begins by not only putting God's mission purposes first in our lives and congregations but also inviting the Spirit of the living God to help us imagine and create new ways that we can more fully live, advocate, demonstrate and celebrate into that world that is already here.

Reimagining from the underside. Harvey Cox writes that in medieval Europe, a popular festival called the Feast of Fools welcomed each new year:

Ordinarily pious priests and serious townsfolk donned bawdy masks, sang outrageous ditties, and generally kept the whole world awake with revelry and satire. Minor clerics painted their faces, strutted about in the robes of their superiors and mocked the stately rituals of church and court. . . . During the Feast of Fools, no custom or convention was immune to ridicule and even the highest personages of the realm could expect to be lampooned.[1]

The Feast of Fools demonstrated that a culture could periodically make sport of its most sacred royal and religious practices. It could imagine, at least once in a while, a wholly different kind of world—"one where the last were first, accepted values were inverted, fools became kings and the choir boys were prelates."[2]

God is indeed at work, as the images in Isaiah affirm, in turning our world inside out and upside down. God has always worked from the underside through ordinary people, fools and clowns, to unmask the pretentious and powerful and give birth to something new and surprising. As an exile community living in an imperial global reality, we have the opportu-

---

[1]Harvey Cox, *The Feast of Fools: A Theological Essay on Festivity and Fantasy* (New York: Harper and Row, 1969), p. 3.
[2]Ibid.

nity to imagine and create mustard seed alternatives to those offered us by the empire.

Cox sketches his vision of a new way home to the future God has planned for us:

> Christian hope suggests that man is destined for a City. It is not just any city, however. If we take the gospel images as well as the symbols of the book of Revelation into consideration, it is not only a City where injustice is abolished and there is no more crying. It is a city in which the delightful wedding feast is in progress, where the laughter rings out, the dance has just begun, and the best wine is still to be served.[3]

Sound familiar? Let's join the new conspirators who are creating from the underside and try to imagine compelling new ways to more fully give expression to this imagery as we pray and work to see God's kingdom come "on earth as it is in heaven." We will look at a spectrum of imaginings, some of which have taken wings and soared, and some of which are still incubating. Keep notes of new possibilities that God may stir within your imagination.

REIMAGINING NEW EXPRESSIONS IN WORSHIP

If we are serious about moving mission to the center of our congregational life, we need musicians, poets and artists to create new forms of worship, in which we celebrate coming home as a great resurrected community to a world where the broken are made whole, justice comes for the poor and shalom to the nations. One such group is the Psalters, who write music to remind us of the world beyond our lives in the global mall:

> we are the cry of exodus.
> there is no home for us here.
> we are a nomadic tribe of psalters,
> walking in the footsteps of the ancients past
> to the far corners of the present,
> united as one voice against the

---

[3]Ibid., p. 162.

oppression within and without.
one more echo in the eternal song of our
First Love, our Hope, and our Pillar of Fire.[4]

Mustard Seed Associates ran a contest for our last conference in which songwriters created word images of God's resurrected homecoming. The lyrics that won the day came from Nigel Mann in Australia. Let me share one verse and the chorus:

Lord let us feel the dawn break over those who mourn.
The poor will be set free and their oppressors flee,
in days to come in days to come.

Jesus, you're making a new heaven and creating a new earth.
You rose in resurrection power.
The days to come have already begun.

In addition to new music, we need to create worship experiences that draw us powerfully into God's love for a world, that remind us Jesus didn't just die for the comfortable, but for the marginalized and the impoverished. Grace, one of the first emerging churches in the U.K., meets on Sunday nights at St. Mary's Anglican Church near Heathrow. One night the congregaton focused its entire worship service on Jubilee 2000, the campaign to cancel Third World debt. Participants brought their concern for the poor into the worship service in a way I have never seen before or since. In the front of this elegant sanctuary was an enormous block and tackle—the kind that would hold a truck motor. But instead of a truck motor, a huge block of ice was supported by chains. The block of ice represented the cold hearts of Europeans and North Americans, an image of unwillingness to cancel Third World debt.

The entire focus of the service was about worshiping a God who cares for the poor. Can you guess what the final liturgy was? That's right—the sanctuary full of young Christians brought candles forward to place under the block of ice, praying for God's Jubilee to come to earth as it is in heaven.

---

[4]The Psalters, "Psalters Mission," <www.psalters.com>.

I am confident that if we started worshiping a God who is passionate to see a new world transform this one, bringing hope for the poor and forgotten, many more of us would be motivated to join God in this missionary venture.[5]

NEW COMMUNITY DESIGN

As followers of Jesus I invite you to view not only worship but all of life as a "design opportunity." All of life offers us the opportunity to become co-creators with God—to imaginatively express the hope within us in urban design, monastic community design and even urban residential church design that reflect something of God's new order. Let's start with urban design.

In *Sidewalks in the Kingdom: New Urbanism and the Christian Faith*, Eric Jacobsen explores how biblical values can be part of creative urban design. Architect Kathryn Schuth reviewed the book on the Institute for Sacred Architecture website.

The false gods of individualism, independence, and freedom . . . 'consistently fail to deliver what they promise.' . . . The city is a place of redemption, a place of restoration from our sinful human-ity, and a place that God is using for good. The city is important to us, because it is a place that is important to God.[6]

God instructed the Jewish captives in the Babylonian Empire to work for the good of the city in which they found themselves exiled. We could, with a little imagination, work for the good of our cities and design new urban villages that both reflect some of the images and values of the New Jerusalem and welcome those whose lives are involved in other stories.

NEW MONASTIC COMMUNITIES

Steve Taylor, an emerging church leader in New Zealand, envisions a post-

---

[5]Wild Goose Resource Group (www.iona.org.uk/wgrg/wild.htm) has some very moving liturgies that focus on God's concern for justice and care of creation.
[6]Kathryn Schuth, "The City as a Place of Redemption," *The Institute for Sacred Architecture Journal* 8 (2003), accessed January 30, 2007, at <www.sacredarchitecture.org/pubs/saj/books/sidewalks.php>.

modern community of monks becoming centers of "Web design, filmmaking and graphic design. . . . Together, these monks can develop a few commercial projects to fund their lifestyle, such as authentic, low-budget, group creative projects—video downloads for the world. They can invite teenagers from their neighborhood to use the high-tech gear as a way of building relationships, sharing skills and developing their spirituality."[7]

In Seattle, Karen Ward is redesigning a Lutheran church building as the Fremont Abbey, a living, breathing monastic village. She plans to make the Abbey an urban third space for people living in the area.

We at Mustard Seed Associates are designing a rural, Celtic monastic community on forty acres on an island north of Seattle. Instead of simply constructing functional camp buildings, we intend to design something that reflects the spirit of a seventh-century Irish monastery. We will also design this village to provide for a highly sustainable lifestyle. We have three goals:

1. We will host thirty-to-forty students at a time. They would come for three months to explore a broad spectrum of Christian prayer traditions in order to develop their own spiritual practices, while experiencing life together in this Celtic community.

2. The students will also help lead directed prayer retreats on the weekends for those from all generations.

3. Finally, the community will also become a birthing center for the creative and entrepreneurial. We will invite artists, entrepreneurs and those on the innovative edge to come together to imagine and create new sustainable approaches to life and community, giving fresh expression to God's new creation.

NEW COMMUNITIES WITH A DIFFERENCE

In *The Institute for Sacred Architecture Journal*, Michael Enright identifies a concern that I share: that the huge decision about where we choose to live

---

[7]Steve Taylor, *The Out of Bounds Church? Learning to Create a Community of Faith in a Culture of Change* (Grand Rapids: Zondervan, 2005), p. 128.

and how we house ourselves is seldom informed by our Christian faith. "After the decision about who you will spend the rest of your life with, the next most important question has to be where you will live. . . . Until now, we have not found a way to inform that decision with the values of the Gospel."[8] The single-family, detached model of housing has become a cultural icon in Western countries. What I think has happened is that we have not only allowed modern culture to largely define our notions of what constitutes the good life, but we have also allowed those same values to often influence the decision about how we house ourselves. Doesn't this iconic model place individualism above community and privacy above mutual care? Don't many of the newer trophy houses also celebrate the values of status, prestige and luxury?

I am concerned about not only the kind of values reflected in this model but also the costs for us and the environment. Clearly the single-family detached model is one of the most land-, energy- and capital-intensive ways to house ourselves. As we have seen, growing numbers of people under age forty can't afford this model. Those who can often wind up spending over half of their income over thirty years working for a mortgage company, which significantly limits their availability to reach out to others.

I would love to bring a group of architects together with monastic leaders, emerging church planters and a few of us from more traditional congregations to imagine and design some new possibilities for residential design that seek to more authentically embody the values of God's new order while reducing costs and environmental impacts.

I imagine the residential community we design would be similar in some ways to cohousing communities with a mix of private and community spaces. To reduce costs it will likely be necessary to build with greater density and more creative design of private spaces. It would likely also require moving from private yards to shared areas for gardens, for kids to play, for people to socialize as well as have quiet places for retreat. It seems

[8]Fr. Michael Enright, "The Second Most Important Question," *The Institute for Sacred Architecture*, <www.sacredarchitecture.org/pubs/saj/articles/2nd.php>.

to me it would be essential to design to reduce our carbon footprint and create highly sustainable dwellings with edible vegetation.

I am also a strong advocate of designing no-interest loan options for the under-forties who are willing to devote five years to working in urban mission or social advocacy. Many would likely be able to pay off the actual cost of their unit in seven years instead of three times the price over thirty years. And that would mean these younger residents would have more of their lives available for family, community and ministry with others. In fact, I am confident that with innovative community design we could all free up either more time or money to invest in the work of God's kingdom—perhaps providing housing for the poor.

We would also encourage this group to intentionally design ways to more authentically embody something of the values, rhythms and celebration of that new world that is already here. Those values would likely shift from the modern values of individualism, privacy and status to include nurturing community, mutual care, community care and care for the creation. Imagine how we might bring the celebration of the great homecoming into the interior design and the rhythm of life of those who live in this community. Imagine how we might incorporate sacred space into both the living environments and the natural environments of this community.

I don't expect for a moment that most readers would consider designing or living in this kind of alternative residential community. But it would be a tremendous gift to the kingdom if innovative and daring entrepreneurs would design and construct at least three dozen alternative residential communities that seek a range of imaginative ways to express some of the values of the kingdom, while providing more affordable dwellings.

REIMAGINING RESIDENTIAL CHURCH PLANTS

What might it look like if we created an alternative model of church as a residential community in which we seek to embody the values of the kingdom 24/7 where we also happen to worship?

Several years ago, Jeff, a young leader who was a part of an aging Mennonite church in Southern California, came up with an imaginative concept for a residential church plant. Housing costs in Southern California are as high as anywhere in the nation. Jeff discovered that the per-square-foot cost of space in apartments in his neighborhood was less than half the cost of space in a modest suburban house in the same neighborhood. A rapidly growing Indonesian church plant that had been renting the church building offered to buy it, and Jeff determined that the income from the sale of the church building would be enough to purchase a fourteen-unit apartment building in the community.

Jeff's idea was to open up the first floor by taking out the two ground-floor apartments. This space would be used for worship, a tutoring program for neighborhood kids and a place for the entire community to gather for food and celebration. The remaining twelve apartments would be sold as condos to younger people involved in this new church plant for less than half what a house would cost in the same community. The income from their payments provided an ongoing income stream to fund ministry to the poor in their community. The old paradigms of single-family isolation and church as a place you go once a week would be replaced by creating church as a family you are a part of seven days a week, where you also happen to worship and care for those in the neighborhood.

This is an invitation to give creative expression to God's new creation by considering designing new forms of urbanism, housing and even residential church plants that reflect something of God's new order. But it is also an invitation to give expression to God's hope-filled future in street theater, art and advocacy.

REIMAGINING HOPE-FILLED ART

The Jubilee Jester: Joining the "Buy Nothing Day Party." On a chilly Friday in November, a group of street performers organized by members of The Simple Way monastic community, including Pogo the Avenger, a ten-foot-tall Jubilee Jester and a host of other antiheroes, invaded the Gallery Mall in Philadelphia. As they handed out free hot cocoa and flyers to weary shoppers, they used humor and parody to challenge the corporate messages of "shop till you drop," inviting shoppers to participate in a "Buy Nothing Day

Party" on the Saturday after Thanksgiving, the busiest shopping day before Christmas in North America. What ways could you imagine doing street theater to provide a glimpse of other possibilities?

Coming home to the Nu Jeruz. Soaring above the restored Norris Square Park in inner-city Philadelphia is a huge three-story butterfly on the side of an apartment house made entirely of ceramic tiles. A group of Christians from different cultures and different faith traditions had built new housing, provided a center for drug rehab, started a new café and restored the Norris Square Park. A Cuban artist, Salvador Gonzales, worked with the community's children to paint the tiles for the mural that is, of course, a Christian symbol of resurrection. "The Badlands have become green lands for the people of Norris Square, the NU JERUZ is come, and it looks every bit like heaven."[9]

A mountain of hope in Soweto. Welcome to the Soweto Mountain of Hope located in Johannesburg, South Africa. This creation is a forty-five-acre site with a mountain and a water tower that was transformed from a dangerous garbage dump into a symbol of hope. Mandla Mentoor "prayed day in and day out so that God could give the power and lead this process"[10] as he organized young people to not only clean up the mountain, but to create a process that is transforming the entire community. Volunteers not only cleaned up the garbage from decades past but also planted vegetable gardens and fruit trees on the hillsides. Residents created makeshift theaters, cooking huts and dialogue circles for community gatherings and performances. Initially, Mandla sold his art to help fund this venture, but in recent years the venture has received funding from a number of environmental groups.

The inspiration that created the Mountain of Hope has spread like a green contagion through the townships. Small bits of land have been

---

[9]J. Nathan Corbitt and Vivian Nix-Early, *Taking It to the Streets: Using the Arts to Transform Your Community* (Grand Rapids: Baker, 2003), p. 179.
[10]"Interview with Mandla Mentoor: The Soweto Mountain of Hope: Making People Free," *In Motion Magazine,* June 8, 2003, accessed January 30, 2007, at <www .inmotionmagazine.com/global/mm1.html>.

turned into community gardens. One community planted olive trees down a long middle divider between two roads, which has become a lucrative source of income for the community. If you visit the Mountain of Hope, you will find it surrounded with bakeries and sewing shops, as well as film and recording studios that have all grown from a small seed planted on a garbage dump in Soweto with much prayer and many willing hands.[11]

Creating guitars of hope in Colombia. In Colombia over 100,000 people have been killed over the last forty years between leftist guerillas and right-wing paramilitary forces fighting each other and the government. Of course, there is also violence connected to drug trafficking. It is estimated that there are between two and three million illegal weapons floating around Colombia. Musician Cesar Lopez found a very unusual way to respond to the ongoing violence. He created an artistic "rapid response battalion," mobilizing a group of artists to put on concerts for victims of violence at the scene of recent attacks in Bogotá. After one attack, Cesar asked the mayor of Bogotá for some of the guns they were collecting from the streets. The mayor gave him five confiscated shotguns. Five weeks and $800 later, during a concert, Cesar thrust into the air a new guitar made from those shotguns and announced, "This is about transformation. . . . It's about turning something bad into good. . . . It's about possibilities." Since he held up that first strange new instrument, demand for the *escopetarra* (*escopeta* = shotgun/rifle; *guitarra* = guitar) has grown; other musicians in Latin America are using them in performances, and the Museum of Modern Art is negotiating the purchase of one. It is very much "like grass coming up through concrete."[12]

REIMAGINING ENTREPRENEURSHIP WITH A MISSION

Something new is stirring that has tremendous possibility to bring good news to those at the margins. The kind of innovative savvy of leaders in the

---

[11]Megan Lindow, "From Rubble to Revival," *Christian Science Monitor*, February 26, 2004, pp. 14, 16.
[12]Dana Harman, "Beating Guns into Guitars," *Christian Science Monitor*, June 13, 2006, p. 6.

business and IT world is being harnessed in remarkable ways to impact our society. Social entrepreneurship is essentially a practical, innovative, sustainable way to change the lives of individuals and communities as one of the creative components of the quiet conspiracy.

Social entrepreneurship is a huge and growing wave that people of faith need to take seriously. Oxford University hosts the Skoll Centre for Social Entrepreneurship in the Saïd Business School. The University also sponsors The Skoll World Forum on Social Entrepreneurship. In both the school and the annual forum, their goal is to raise up a new generation of change makers. New challenges are profiled and then participants are invited to create innovative ways to address these challenges. American public television also sponsors an annual contest called Project Enterprise in which people are encouraged to nominate social entrepreneurs in their own community as a way to encourage this kind of social change.

Several Christian groups also help people give expression to the new and entrepreneurial. The Servant Leadership School in Washington, D.C., is, among other things, a place where people have the opportunity to create and implement new social ventures to have an impact in their communities. Groundwork, with both U.S. and U.K. branches, is devoted to enabling students to create new possibilities such as creating sustainable communities in areas of need.

We in Mustard Seed Associates want to provide an opportunity for all, but especially the young, to create new forms of social entrepreneurship as well as imagine new ways to employ art, design and theater to give fresh expression to God's new order. This year we are launching an online site called "Imagine That," where we invite people to actually give birth to new possibilities and discover how they can become change makers.

We also encourage people to identify new challenges and underutilized resources that can be transformed into tools for the kingdom.

BECOMING CREATIVE CHRISTIAN SCROUNGERS

Some thirty years ago, in *The Mustard Seed Conspiracy*, I urged followers of Jesus to become creative Christian scroungers—learning to do more with less. That message is even more important today, as many churches and mission organizations are likely to face declining resources in the coming decade. We need to use our entrepreneurial imagination to transform vacant lots, empty buildings and throw-away resources into new resources for God's new order.

For example, seminaries could help students identify church buildings likely to be vacated in the coming decade, then reimagine those buildings as places to engage new challenges and opportunities facing residents in the neighborhoods where they are located. The buildings could be redesigned to serve as a center for new urban ministries, monastic communities, church plants or cooperative businesses, to name a few possibilities. Students and faculty could seek funding for the most creative projects.

An African American Episcopal Methodist church identified the underutilized resources of parking strips and backyards in their inner-city neighborhood in Chicago. Their creative idea was to partner with a white Methodist church in the rural outskirts of Chicago that would grow and graft large numbers of fruit tree seedlings for them to plant in their inner-city neighborhood to significantly increase fruit production in that community.

Building housing hope in Boston. One of the greatest underutilized resources in Western societies is housing stock. A group in Boston called Build Together discovered that older people were having difficulty maintaining large homes with their small retirement incomes and were at risk of turning their homes into ATM machines. They came up with a stellar entrepreneurial idea to make this underutilized housing stock more readily available. Essentially they helped older residents secure loans to rehab and redesign their homes to create a private unit for themselves, plus generous low-cost rental space for single moms and others who are struggling. As a consequence of this creative scheme, older folks get their homes upgraded and typically make an extra $1,000 a month (part of which goes to pay for the remodel), and affordable housing is provided for people in need.[13]

---

[13]Stacy A. Teicher, "Initiative Turns Seniors into Landlords," *Christian Science Monitor*, May 17, 2004, p. 15.

Getting entrepreneurial with coffee beans in Seattle. Arminda made the longest trip of her life to meet with new friends involved in Pura Vida Coffee in Seattle, which purchases coffee from her home in Nicaragua. Pura Vida buys exclusively fairly traded, organic, shade-grown coffee from all over the world and sells it to consumers in North America that want to make a global difference in the products they buy. Arminda toured Pura Vida headquarters, located in an old warehouse that looks a bit like a shantytown with corrugated metal dividers between each office space. Ironically, Pura Vida's headquarters are directly across the street from the headquarters of global giant Starbucks.

Arminda hesitantly stood to her feet.

My husband and I and our six children want to express our sincere gratitude for purchasing our coffee at a fair traded price. Before you purchased our beans, the entire family worked very long days to pick enough beans to provide a bare subsistence income. Now since we are getting a much better price for our beans, our six children are able to go to school. Who knows? One day one of them might go on to college. Something we never dared to dream of.

John Sage started Pura Vida (www.puravida.com) with an intriguing, twofold vision: first, to harvest the power of free enterprise to enable the poor to actually participate in the new global economy by being fairly compensated for their labor. Second, to plow a generous portion of their corporate profits back into community development in poorer parts of the world where the company purchases its coffee. John has achieved both goals: Pura Vida is a money-making company that sponsors a range of literacy programs, health education and computer courses in the same communities where they purchase their coffee.

Kick-starting entrepreneurship with hope in Africa. KickStart is an organization that creates innovative technological solutions to enable the poor in Africa to improve their lives. For example, KickStart designed a rolling twenty-gallon water drum that even a child can pull by a cord to transport water long distances in remote areas. The group has also designed human-powered water pumps and other appropriate technology to help lift people out of poverty. To date, fifty thousand Africans have received technological support so that they can start new businesses.

REIMAGINING WITH OUR ENTREPRENEURIAL YOUNG

We live in a remarkable age of innovation. One of the most remarkable characteristics of the four streams is their brilliant use of imagination in creating everything from worship experiences that artfully blend together images from iconic art with film clips from popular culture to the kind of street theater we just visited to promote a no-shopping day. But I find it hasn't occurred to many of us in traditional churches to tap into the imagination of our youth.

Of course we have heard that youth as young as thirteen are creating imaginative online businesses. Too many of our youth ministry, campus ministry and educational models tend to be focused on "doing for the young," where they are constantly passive recipients of our care and instruction. I suspect many of us unconsciously assume that youth can't possibly come up with any worthwhile ideas until they graduate from college, or gain some life experience. As a consequence I have come across very few youth ministries, campus ministries, Christian schools or colleges that invite the young to imagine and create new ventures to impact the lives of others.

I find that the churches that are retaining the highest percentage of youth at the highest levels of participation are those placing teens and twenty-somethings in significant leadership roles and sincerely inviting their ideas and creativity. I encourage you to take the daring step of sitting down with your teens and young adults, openly asking them for creative ideas on how your church can more effectively engage a younger generation and better serve those in need in your community. I suspect you will be surprised by their response.

What might it look like if our youth groups started challenging teens to create new ways to make a difference? A youth group might enlist their teens to actually design video games that use humor to enable young children to decode the bogus messages that they are being bombarded with from the merchants of cool. Or they might be challenged to create innovative ways to design art for the blogosphere that raises awareness regarding global warming. Let me share one model that we saw some teens create.

Getting entrepreneurial with the urban young. Christine and I had the opportunity to do a creativity workshop with a large group of teens and twenty-somethings at a recent Christian Community Development Association conference. We invited these young people to create an innovative way to bring together an urban African American youth group and suburban white youth group. Their idea was to give young people in both groups digital video cameras and have them document their family lives, their lives at school and their peer experiences in their respective church youth groups, editing it into a forty-minute video that fairly represents their lives. The two youth groups would then share their videos and stories on a weekend retreat together in an effort to create bridges and mutual understanding across racial and cultural divides.

This type of entrepreneurial innovation is lying latent in many young people. Can you imagine the God-inspired creativity that could be unleashed if students were encouraged to devise ways to have an impact for God's new order? Colleges and campus ministries might create an opportunity for students to actually become social entrepreneurs while they are still in school. Let me share the story of one student who did it on his own initiative.

Getting entrepreneurial in Fresno. Jeremy, a computer science student at California State University, Fresno, told me, "I was raised in a very upscale, suburban, Anglo community and never had encounters with the poor before." When he was a sophomore, he started attending InterVarsity Christian Fellowship on campus. InterVarsity put Jeremy to work tutoring poorer Hispanic kids. "At first, this situation sent me reeling, but I really liked the kids and stuck with it."

Jeremy not only stayed with the tutoring program but developed a business plan with his friend, a business major. While they were still students, they started a nonprofit ministry to offer computer education to Hispanic kids in Fresno and their families. Part of the innovative strategy includes giving every family who successfully completes the program a home computer. Can you imagine the God-inspired creativity that could be unleashed if college students were regularly encouraged to create entrepreneurial ways to have an impact for God's new order?

Getting entrepreneurial in Africa. The most impressive entrepreneurial birthing center for the young that I have discovered anywhere, Launch, was created by Carl Nash for Youth Unlimited (Toronto Youth for Christ). I would love to see youth groups and campus ministries create opportunities like Launch all over the planet.

Carl and his team invite fifteen- to twenty-five-year-olds to bring an entrepreneurial idea for a new kingdom ministry that God is stirring up within them. A mentor is assigned to work with each student to help them fashion their beginning dream into a bold initiative and helping them get it launched just like a new business start-up.

Ted Webb was a nineteen-year-old "bike-aholic." He brought a dream to Launch that traced back to his trip to Malawi during the summer of 2004. Ted met pastors there who had to walk two-to-three hours to visit church members because they didn't have access to any other form of transportation. This was the beginning of Africycle.

Ted returned to Toronto and got Canadians to donate 180 bicycles, which he repaired, restored and took back to the pastors in Malawi. He returned recently to Malawi with another four hundred refurbished bikes. The containers used to ship the bikes have also been designed to function as small bike-repair shops. He brought spare parts with him and showed locals how to maintain the bikes, so that now the income from the bicycle repair shops provides support for disabled and orphaned children. Their mission statement reads:

> Africycle will mobilize Canadians to exploit the potential of the bicycle as a catalyst to create economic development to empower Africans to improve their quality of life.

God is doing something new through the imaginations and initiative of a new generation who are involved in the emerging, missional, mosaic and monastic streams. I am convinced God could do much through the creativity of our teens and twenty-somethings if we help them give birth, like Ted and Jeremy, to what God is stirring up in their imaginations, if we invite their ideas and innovation. Imagine what God might do with our mustard seeds and those of your young people if we choose to join this creative conspiracy by inviting God to ignite our imaginations to give expression to something of that new creation.

JOIN THE CONVERSATION

- What might be the consequences of inviting God to ignite our imaginations and those of the young to create new expressions of God's new creation?

- What is the biblical basis for seeking to create new ways to give expression to God's new order in every area of our lives and God's world?

- Imagine one creative and innovative way God might use your mustard seed to be much more a part of his creative conspiracy. Share your idea with your small group or close friends and ask them to join you on the journey with their regular prayers and support. We pray that your life and witness will flourish in ways you never expected and that you will discover that the good life of God is indeed the life given away.

AFTERWORD

Something Really, Really Small

As we race into the second decade of the twenty-first century, we are traveling into a turbulent global future in which the world, the church and particularly our poorest neighbors are facing some daunting challenges. But the creator God has not lost control. We know at the very core of our beings that the Author of this story will write the final chapter and the kingdoms of this world will indeed become "the kingdoms of our God and of his Christ." That's a celebration I certainly want to be a part of.

But the very good news is we don't have to wait. Remarkably, God invites us, in spite of our brokenness and failures, to join with others and become much more a part of this quiet conspiracy that is changing our world.

Andrea, a member of Camden House Community in Camden, New Jersey, is a part of this quiet conspiracy. Camden House, part of the new monasticism movement in North America, is located in one of the most polluted neighborhoods in America.[1] New Jersey has more Superfund toxic waste sites than any U.S. state, and Andrea tells us that her neighborhood "has the most toxic waste sites of any community in the state."

> We have three Superfund sites, 15 brown fields, the major waste incinerator and a sewage treatment plant two blocks from where we live that processes 50,000,000 gallons of sewage a day. Add to that 250,000 trucks that go through our neighborhood a year spewing their diesel smoke. Over 250,000 people live in our toxic neighbor-

---

[1]Members of Camden House have joined with other community organizations in lobbying to change truck routes to reduce pollution in communities where kids live.

hood. Over 61 percent of the kids develop serious respiratory diseases before their fifth birthday.

Andrea teaches urban farming to students at the primary school operated by Sacred Heart Church, where she worships. The school recently constructed two fifty-by-twenty-two-foot greenhouses where forty-five fifth graders carefully plant trays of vegetable seedlings to grow in a large urban garden for their families and neighbors in their community.

One day, while Andrea and the kids were walking past a brown field next to their school, they got a creative idea. They put balls of compost filled with clover seed in old refrigerators. Then, one evening at dusk, they bombarded the brown field with hundreds of their compost balls. Clover seed leeches toxins from the soil, so after several good spring rains, the children were delighted to see the brown, toxic field awash with a sea of white clover blossoms.

CREATING THE FUTURE ONE MUSTARD SEED AT A TIME

We are all invited to join Andrea and her kids and followers of Jesus all over the planet to discover the small, surprising ways God might use our lives and communities of faith to give festive expression to that world that is already here. God is indeed doing something really, really small and the good news is we can all be much more a part of it. It all begins with a handful of seeds.

If you start a mustard seed group on a college campus, at a church or at a home group, we would like to invite you to join this creative conspiracy. Write us at Mustard Seed Associates and let us know what you are doing (mail@msainfo.org). Mustard Seed Associates is a community of Christians all over the world who are trying to be a difference and make a difference and help other followers of Jesus create the future one mustard seed at a time. We would love to hear how your mustard seed is growing. We would also love to hear from churches that are experimenting with new ways to impact your own community and your world.

Be sure to visit our website (www.msainfo.org) and check out the resources there; they may be of help on your journey. Also be sure to sign up for our free ezine, *The Seed Sampler.* We share stories from all over the world of ways people are finding to be a difference and make a difference. Regardless of whether you are from a traditional or an experimental church (or no church at all) we would like to hear from you and possibly use some of your stories to share with other conspirators.

We work with all generations, but we are particularly committed to enabling a new generation who want to discover creative ways God can use their mustard seeds to get started. We want to enable individuals and communities of faith to discover how they can much more fully live, celebrate and do mission that expresses something of that new world that is already here.

Looking forward to hearing from you,
Tom Sine
Mustard Seed Associates
Christine Sine, director
www.msainfo.org
e-mail: mail@msainfo.org
phone: 206-524-2112
P.O. Box 45867
Seattle, WA 98145

INDEX OF ORGANIZATIONS

Africycle (www.africycle.com)

Agros (www.agros.org)

ALOVE (www1.salvationarmy.org.uk/alove)

Alternatives for Simple Living (www.simpleliving.org)

Anabaptist Network in the U.K. (www.anabaptistnetwork.com)

Anglican Church Planting Initiatives (www.acpi.org.uk)

Anglimergent (http://anglimergent.groups.vox.com)

A Rocha U.K. (www.arocha.org)

Book of Acts Project (www.bookofacts.info)

Bread for the World (www.bread.org)

Bridge of Hope (www.bridgeofhopeinc.org)

Built Green (www.builtgreen.net)

Christian Churches Together in the U.S.A.
(www.christianchurchestogether.org)

Christian Community Development Association (www.ccda.org)

Christian Ecology Link (www.christian-ecology.org.uk)

Churches for Middle East Peace (www.cmep.org)

The Community of Aidan and Hilda (www.aidantrust.org)

Creation Care Study Program (www.creationcsp.org)

Ekklesia (www.ekklesia.co.uk)

The Ekklesia Project (www.ekklesiaproject.org)

Emergent Village (www.emergentvillage.org)

Evangelicals for Middle East Understanding (www.emeu.net)

Global Urban Trek (www.intervarsity.org/trek)

Greenbelt Arts Festival (www.greenbelt.org.uk)

Grist (www.grist.org)

Groundwork (www.groundwork.org.uk)

Harvest Time (www.harvesttime.cc)

Hope HIV (www.hopehiv.org)

Imagine Schools (www.imagineschools.com)

InnerCHANGE (www.innerchange.org)

Iona Community, Scotland (www.iona.org.uk)

KickStart (www.kickstart.org)

Launch (www.321launch.org)

The Lifeline Expedition (www.lifelineexpedition.co.uk)

Mennonite Economic Development Associates (www.meda.org)

Micah Network (en.micahnetwork.org)

Michigan Interfaith Power & Light (http://www.miipl.org)

Mission Year (www.missionyear.org)

Mustard Seed Associates (www.msainfo.org)

Mustard Seed Foundation (www.msfdn.org)

The Mutunga Partnership (www.mutunga.com)

New Tithing Group (www.newtithing.org)

Northumbria Community (www.northumbriacommunity.org)

The Order of Mission (www.missionorder.org)

The Order of the Mustard Seed (www.mustardseedorder.com)

Presbymergent (http://presbymergent.org)

Radical Christian Vision Network (www.rootandbranch.org.uk)

La Red del Camino (www.lareddelcamino.net)

ReIMAGINE (www.reimagine.org)

Restoring Eden (www.restoringeden.org)

Schools for Conversion (www.newmonasticism.org/sfc/index.html)

Servant Leadership School (www.slschool.org)

Servant Partners (www.servantpartners.org)

Servants to Asia's Urban Poor (www.servantsasia.org)

SPEAK (www.speak.org.uk)

TheOOZE (www.theooze.com)

Transformational Business Network (www.tbnetwork.org)

Urban Neighbors of Hope (www.unoh.org)

Urbana Student Missions Conventions (www.urbana.org)

Veritas Forum (www.veritas.org)

Word Made Flesh (www.wordmadeflesh.com)

World Vision (www.worldvision.org)

Zadok Institute for Christianity and Society (www.zadok.org.au)